AIRBRUSHING
FOR
RAILWAY MODELLERS

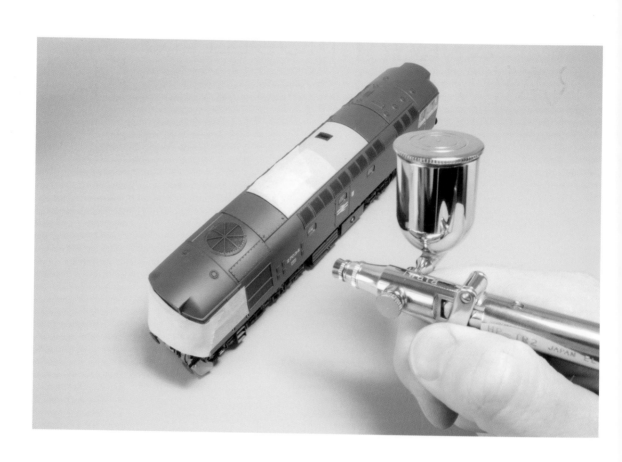

AIRBRUSHING
FOR
RAILWAY MODELLERS

George Dent

THE CROWOOD PRESS

First published in 2011 by
The Crowood Press Ltd
Ramsbury, Marlborough
Wiltshire SN8 2HR

www.crowood.com

This impression 2012

British Library Cataloguing-in-Publication Data
A catalogue record for this book is available from the British Library.

ISBN 978 1 84797 265 1

Designed and typeset by Focus Publishing, Sevenoaks, Kent
Printed and bound in Singapore by Craft Print International Ltd

CONTENTS

PREFACE

Model making, in various forms, has been an important part of my life for nearly thirty years. Having trained and worked variously as a museum conservator, graphic artist and guitar maker, each of these vocations has helped inform my modelling, be it in practical or theoretical terms. In 2004 I became the in-house Model-Maker and Feature Writer for *Model Rail* magazine and my work has also appeared in *Railway Modeller* and the two volumes of *Detailing and Modifying Ready-to-Run Locomotives in OO Gauge* (The Crowood Press, 2009).

Being a professional modeller has afforded me the luxury of access to a broad range of airbrushes, paints and equipment and it is the aim of this book to not only pass on the benefits of my experiences – good and bad – but also to remove the lingering mystique that surrounds the art of airbrushing. Experienced airbrush users should also find plenty here, including an array of helpful tips and tricks that I've learned over the years. In addition, a variety of advanced techniques are covered, all of which can combine to help you achieve highly realistic results.

ACKNOWLEDGEMENTS

Many of the products and materials featured in this book have been generously provided by the following: Alex Medwell and Lisa Munro (The Airbrush Company), Dennis Lovett (Bachmann) and Robin Carpenter (Cammett Ltd). Thanks also to Charlie Petty (DC Kits), Arran Aird (C-Rail), Dave Young (Ten Commandments), plus David and Ron at SMTF model shop, Poynton.

Ben Jones, Chris Leigh and Richard Foster at *Model Rail* have been very supportive of my various book ventures, to which I am grateful. Thanks also to the staff at The Crowood Press and Nick Brodrick of *Steam Railway* magazine.

Jeanne Carr's cottage in Settle once again proved a good place to write a manuscript and Scrivener's Books of Buxton supplied much useful reference material. Special thanks to my equine brothers, Jim and Mikey, plus the staff at Bank Farm and last, but by no means least, to the Dent Collective: Julie-Marie, Maude, Leonard and Hannah.

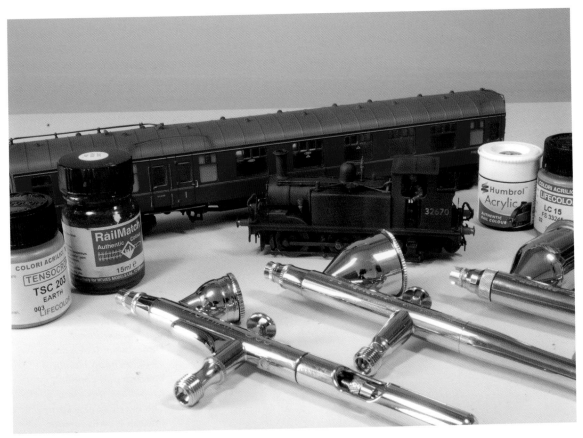

Airbrushing not only offers the chance to improve our modelling output but is an enjoyable pastime in itself.

INTRODUCTION

The technique of airbrushing remains something of a 'Dark Art' to many modellers, akin to the mysteries of low-temperature soldering or brass rolling. However, successful use of an airbrush is within the reach of any modeller, provided that he or she seeks to gain a basic understanding of the materials and equipment involved. Additionally, a good degree of practice is vital.

Contrary to common belief, airbrushing is not a practice reserved for those with deep pockets. Happily, the cost of both airbrushes and compressors has fallen considerably in recent years and the boom in cheap imported goods has also forced established brands such as Badger and Iwata to bring down their prices in the face of stiff competition. Naturally there will always be a need to pay for precision instruments, which is what a lot of 'high end' airbrushes can be classed as. But these are not always suitable purchases for an occasional hobbyist and the introductory chapters aim to help you choose spraying equipment that's right for your own particular needs.

Given prior knowledge of paint thinning, an understanding of how an airbrush works and access to a source of compressed air – even a car tyre – anyone can get to grips with airbrushing. It is, after all, just another skill that has to be learnt through practice. Indeed, my own early experience of spraying model trains consisted of using a bargain basement airbrush, given away free with a magazine subscription. Once I'd learned how to mix the paint correctly and achieve the right air pressure, the strengths and limitations of the tool soon became clear. From then on, airbrushing proved to be an enjoyable exercise.

One of my first attempts at airbrush weathering can be seen on this Hornby Pacer. Undertaken way back in 1990, a cheap Humbrol airbrush and canned propellant was used. The overly coarse spray pattern is symptomatic of poorly mixed paint and incorrect air pressure.

WHY USE AN AIRBRUSH?

The benefits of airbrushing can be summed up by the following adjectives:

- Speed
- Consistency
- Quality
- Accuracy
- Convenience
- Uniqueness
- Enjoyment

Portraying a grimy steam locomotive can be achieved far more efficiently with an airbrush; with experience, livery and weathering schemes can be undertaken very quickly. Even the need for masking can be dispensed with, as was the case here: the ultra matt finish of the smokebox was sprayed freehand, while subsequent fine layers of dirt-coloured paint blended in the 'joint' with the factory finish.

The speed aspect is self-explanatory: even if multiple coats are required for each shade within a complex colour scheme, the rapidness of application will always be attractive, whether you're a hurrying professional or a relaxed hobbyist. When the technique has been mastered, the consistency of paint application from an airbrush is almost impossible to replicate, particularly on miniature models. So much fine detail can be obliterated by too thick a coat of paint, especially where numerous layers have been spread onto the surface.

The quality of finish is also dependent upon the painter knowing what he or she is doing, but the results can be superb, even with only a modest set-up and level of experience. Ditto the accuracy facet, as a well-handled tool can get paint where it's meant to be without the invasiveness of a brush. The ease with which an airbrush can be 'flushed' between paints depends to a degree upon the design of the tool but, generally speaking, they are simple to clean.

Certain paints, particularly cellulose, acrylic or metallic finishes, perform at their best when sprayed. Additionally, there are a number of paint effects that can only be achieved by airbrush, such as 'fogging' or 'misting', where overlapping colours blend gently rather than meeting with a hard edge (see Chapter 14). Many weathering techniques are also unique to airbrushing, such as exhaust staining or streaking effects.

With each of the above benefits comes the pleasure of seeing your treasured modelling project finished to a high standard, rewarding all the hard work expended prior to the painting stage. Whenever a new technique is learnt, there is bound

Airbrushing allows models to be customized, enhanced or refinished with a greater degree of consistency. Indeed, even the most practised brush-painter will struggle to match the quality of finish possible with even a budget range airbrush. This OO gauge Class 31 has been repainted and weathered using a mid-priced Badger airbrush and Railmatch enamel paints.

to be a degree of frustration when things go wrong, but persistence is the key. With this in mind, the most essential background information is presented in the opening few chapters of this book: firstly, the main forms of airbrush, spraying equipment and paints are considered, before moving on to demonstrate basic spraying techniques away from any models. In this way, with only scraps of paper or card to waste, we can develop our proficiency without the worry of making expensive mistakes.

THE BIG 'P'

There is only one way of becoming proficient in the art of airbrushing and that is by practice. The same can be said about developing any new skill, be it learn-ing to drive or play a musical instrument. The other important 'P' is patience and this is one virtue that all of us modellers are meant to possess. This isn't always the case and if you're getting fed up, then stop and do something else instead. This is, after all, a hobby and is intended to bring relaxation and enjoyment to partici-pants. Unless you enjoy making a martyr of yourself, come back with a clear mind and don't give up. Also, don't set unrealistic targets: it will take time to master the technique. It can't be rushed, but it can be fun.

Throughout the following chapters, I have tried to convey just how many facets of railway modelling can benefit from the use of an airbrush. Locomotives, rolling stock, scenery, buildings, track and infra-structure are covered, adapting painting techniques and equipment set-ups to cope with each.

In the space of a couple of hours, a ready-to-run locomotive can be transformed with a little weathering, taking away the 'plasticky' look of the original model. While weathering powders can produce similar 'smoke' effects, nothing compares to an authentic misting of oily enamels over a diesel's roof.

Every element within this miniature scene has received some degree of work with an airbrush. The track, scenery and buildings have been treated collectively, to blend all of the individual components together for a natural-looking appearance.

CHAPTER ONE

CHOOSING THE RIGHT AIRBRUSH

Finding an airbrush that suits your particular needs is an important step on the road to proficiency in spray painting techniques. There are countless brands and model specifications to draw from and choice will depend on a number of factors. Price is obviously important, as is the type of work envisaged. Or, more precisely, what scale are you working in and how much use is the tool likely to see?

Issues such as comfort and balance can be subjective and it helps to try out any airbrush before buying. Competing brands aim to offer a better ergonomic experience and various novel ideas have been introduced over the years, some more successful than others. Most respectable dealerships will permit trials of specific products and offer unbiased advice, based on their own expertise in the field. It's not in their interest to sell you something you don't need as they will be aiming to attract repeated custom and hope for a recommendation to friends. Therefore, a quick telephone call to a firm such as The Airbrush Company will be worth the effort (see Useful Contacts).

Before browsing catalogues or websites, it will be advantageous to learn some basic facts concerning the main categories of airbrushes, how they work and how they came to exist in the first place.

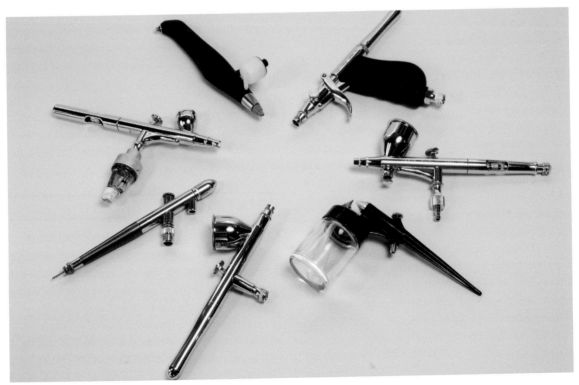

With so many different models on the market, choosing the right airbrush can be a daunting prospect.

A BRIEF HISTORY OF AIRBRUSHING

Since the development of commercial and industrial paint formulas, the means of speeding up application and consistency of finish had been sought. However, it wasn't until the end of the nineteenth century that a solution presented itself, developed by an American shopkeeper from an air-powered contraption built to spray whitewash. Initially agriculture was the main outlet for this machine, although within a decade the principle was developed to form what we now know as the Spray Gun. In turn, this invention allowed factory production volumes to increase, assisted by the introduction of nitrocellulose paints in the 1920s. Indeed, it allowed Henry Ford to offer motor cars in colours other than black!

On a smaller scale, artists and draughtsmen had also been looking into ways of projecting paint onto surfaces without the use of brushes and, in the 1880s, both British and American inventors were hard at work developing what would become known as the Airbrush. At the same time, a similar tool was being developed for medical applications by a certain Dr DeVilbiss. This American practitioner desired a means of treating throat infections in a non-invasive way and such was the success of the 'atomizer' that his company eventually branched out into artists' airbrushes. DeVilbiss remains one of the most respected brands in the airbrush market today.

By 1895 the first internal mix, dual-action airbrush was released, aimed squarely at water colourists. Using the same basic principles that are still in use today, these early tools would not look out of place on a twenty-first century modeller's workbench. Indeed, the airbrush has changed relatively little over the decades, with innovations being concerned more with refining the brand rather than revolution. That said, one of the biggest departures from the established 'method' has been by the Testor Corporation, which has pioneered the use of interchangeable plastic nozzles in its Aztek range.

It remains that the big players in the twenty-first century airbrush market are of North American origin: DeVilbiss (established Ohio, 1888), Paasche (California, 1904), Badger (Illinois, 1963) and Testor (Illinois, 1929). Iwata, a Japanese concern, has established itself as a highly respected manufacturer over the last thirty years or so, although the company has been in existence since the 1920s. Curiously, the influx of airbrushing equipment from other Far Eastern countries has come relatively late, although this situation has since changed dramatically. Indeed, the market is now awash with cheap airbrushes, compressors and accessories of varying quality.

While we're on this subject, I must add a word of warning. The growth in the hobby airbrush market has also seen the proliferation of pirated goods, trading on the reputations of established firms. Mostly selling over the Internet for rock-bottom prices, these fake goods are not only inferior in material and build quality, but are probably supporting dubious working practices in poor and developing nations. If such ethics don't worry you, then that's fine. You can have a so-called Iwata, for instance, for a 'tenner' and it will last a few years under occasional use without ever giving the level of performance that a 'real' one would. However, I like to know where my money's going and would rather save for a bit longer than settle for substandard goods. The reassurance of quality-controlled production, a long warranty, spare part availability, technical support backup and the option of compatible accessories make it more economical, in the long term, to plump for a well-known brand, especially if you intend to get a lot of use out of your airbrush.

WHAT IS AN AIRBRUSH?

All airbrushes are designed to atomize a liquid before projecting it onto a waiting surface. Compressed air is required to achieve this and the propellant must come from an external source. The pressurized air is released through the tool by the depression of a sprung trigger, whereupon it is forced into a narrowing chamber at the nozzle. The velocity of the air is thus increased (known as the Venturi effect), creating a force sufficient to collect particles of paint being fed into the airstream by gravity or suction.

If you desire a tool that can create subtle effects at close quarters, such as shading in and around complex surfaces, then an internal mix, double-action airbrush is required.

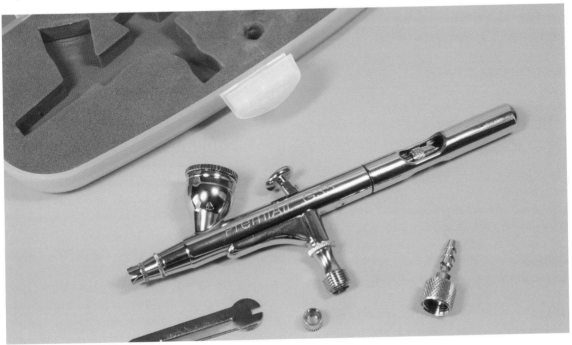

A double-action airbrush package need not break the bank. This Premi-Air airbrush is a perfect entry-level tool, offering the ability to produce great levels of finish both in terms of overall livery coats and delicate weathering tasks.

Provided the liquid is of the correct viscosity, the paint particles will become evenly dispersed within the airflow (known as atomization) as it is released from the nozzle of the airbrush. If all of the necessary factors are correct – air pressure, paint mix and distance from surface – a highly consistent and even paint job can be achieved.

Until about 1980 airbrushes were seen as precision instruments for artwork or photo retouching, not least as the equipment was very expensive. Developments in cheaper tools and the advent of canned propellant subsequently opened up the use of airbrushes to the hobbyist market and they are now used for all sorts of things. As well as modelling and custom automotive art, there has also been massive growth in spray tanning, make-up application, nail art and cake decoration. The possibilities are truly endless.

The proliferation of airbrushing away from the more obvious art and hobby realms is worth keeping in mind, as it may help in sourcing unusual accessories or paint formulas that may not be marketed directly to your own hobby sector, but may still be of use. Not that I'm recommending using skin-tanning paints to weather your locomotives!

AIRBRUSH TYPES

It can be said that there are two main classes of airbrush and their description denotes where, in the spraying process, the paint and air are brought together.

EXTERNAL MIX

Sounding fairly self-explanatory, external mix airbrushes pass a jet of air over a paint reservoir on the outside of the tool and the resultant vacuum effect works to draw the liquid into the airstream. Paint flow can be altered by adjusting the distance between the paint reservoir nozzle and the air jet, although this can only be achieved when no air is being emitted and, according to brand, may require the use of a small spanner.

Generally of a cheap and cheerful nature, these tools are usually constructed of tough, solvent-proof plastic with a demountable paint reservoir. Particularly suited to beginners, there's only one thing to think about when painting: the control of the air. Also, as no paint enters the tool itself, cleaning is confined to the paint jar and its nozzle, greatly speeding up the job. There is also very little to go wrong with these tools, nor many parts to wear out.

Results can be acceptable after a degree of practise, although thinning the paint to the right consistency is paramount for an even finish. Even then, the paint is not atomized as well as it is in an internal mix airbrush, making it impossible to achieve the same degree of finesse. Indeed, they are not suited to fine detail work, not only because the paint flow cannot be controlled, but for the fact that the tool itself is usually quite unwieldy.

External mix tools blur the line between what is strictly an airbrush and what could be more accurately referred to as a mini spray gun. Although they were once marketed as the latter, these tools lately have come to be bracketed together with the former. Manufactured by various brands such as Humbrol, Expo, Revell, Badger or Testor, they are commonly offered in starter packs, complete with a plastic hose and a small can of liquid propellant. A decent example of this type of airbrush will certainly provide a good introduction to spray painting for a very modest outlay. However, don't expect top of the range results from a bottom of the range package.

INTERNAL MIX

Internal mix devices, on the other hand, make use of either gravity or siphon-fed paint cups, feeding the paint into an internal chamber where the particles of liquid are mixed with the air before being emitted through the nozzle.

Originally devised for applying watercolour paints or inks, the use of quick-drying modellers' enamels or cellulose was not what the original designers had in mind. As a result, paints must be mixed to a thinner viscosity than with external mix 'brushes. On the other hand, the system allows for lower air pressures to be used successfully, thus lending them well to hobbyist use with small air compressors or bottled supplies (see Chapter 2).

Containing a typical budget-priced airbrush, this kind of package retails for under £20 and can offer a cheap route into the hobby. Although acceptable results can be achieved with practise and a good air supply, these tools do have many limitations.

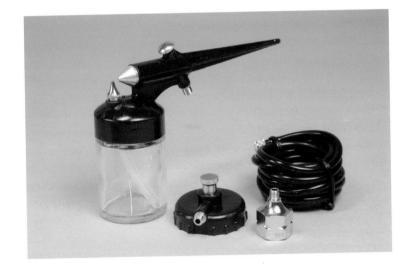

Cheaper airbrushes – or mini spray guns – work in the 'external mix' format, having all the important workings outside of the body, making for easy cleaning and maintenance. The paint nozzle (lower) can be raised to increase the flow of paint being drawn into the airflow.

While acceptable for general use, finer work such as bespoke weathering or small-scale detail work is beyond this type of airbrush. Variation in width of spray is only achieved by altering the distance between the tool and model's surface: a wider line is achieved by moving further away, which also provides a mistier finish. However, working further from a subject can be risky, especially with acrylic paints, as the paint will dry before it hits the surface, leaving a rough finish.

Internal mix airbrushes can also be defined by their 'action', or more explicitly, by how far the paint and airflow can be adjusted.

Single Action. The majority of single-action airbrushes have an adjustable needle inside the nozzle, moved back and forth within the tool by means of a hand-wheel at the rear of the instrument. Painting usually has to be interrupted while an adjustment is made and the further back the needle is moved, the more paint is admitted into the nozzle to mix with the air. This explains the singular 'action' in the description; the airflow cannot be adjusted – it's either 'on' or 'off'.

Double Action. Sometimes also referred to as dual action, both paint and airflow is governable. Press the trigger to release the air, while pulling back on the same control will also emit the paint. The further back the trigger is moved, the more paint is released and the harder the trigger is depressed, the higher the air pressure will be (within the limits of the supply).

Offering extra versatility, these tools do take a little time to get used to, hence why single-action

airbrushes are more popular with beginners. Cost is a factor too, as double-action airbrushes incorporate more sophisticated workings and are naturally more expensive. Results can be far superior, however, as the control of both the air and paint permit the creation of a greater range of effects, perfect for ultra-detailed work at close quarters. Paint flow is automatically cut off before the airflow (as the trigger is released, the cycle of the internal components shut off the paint supply before closing the air valve, and vice versa) meaning that the risk of splattering at the end of each stroke is minimized (see Chapter 4).

Semi-double Action. Semi-double (or 'fixed double') action airbrushes offer something of a halfway house between the two formats, with the trigger movement controlling the flow of air and paint in fixed proportions only. The maverick Testor Corporation has taken control options further by offering an airbrush (the Aztek A470) that can be used in either single-, fixed double or double-action modes. In this case, the trigger operates in the familiar lateral way, while a roller control on the top of the tail end 'dials in' the amount of paint flow.

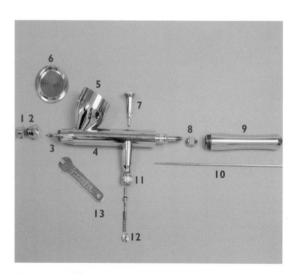

This dismantled Iwata airbrush illustrates a typical dual-action, gravity-fed internal mix tool: (1) nozzle rim; (2) nozzle; (3) needle packing; (4) airbrush body; (5) paint cup; (6) paint cup lid; (7) trigger; (8) needle chuck; (9) tailpiece; (10) needle; (11) air hose connector; (12) air/trigger valve; (13) needle packing spanner.

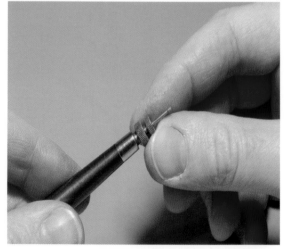

The paint flow from most single-action airbrushes is adjusted by means of a thumbwheel, usually at the rear of the tool. The further back the needle is drawn, the more paint will be released. Painting must be interrupted while adjustments are made.

Double-action airbrushes allow the paint and airflow to be controlled from the same trigger. Pressing down governs the air, while moving the trigger backwards increases the amount of paint released. An airbrush should also be comfortable to hold and operate, especially if you expect to be spending a few hours at a time operating one.

The popular Badger single-action, siphon-fed airbrush – in this case a 200NH model – is a nice tool to use. Well balanced and comfortable to grip, the underslung paint jar leaves a clear view of the subject for the painter and a choice of jar sizes is available. Although lacking the versatility of double-action airbrushes, excellent results can be achieved with this and similar specification tools.

The Aztek airbrush is of a quite different concept to all other airbrushes, showing some laudable innovations in materials and operation. Produced in the US by the Testor Corporation, the durable acetyl resin body is solvent-resistant and the air supply is fed into the tail end, allowing the tool greater freedom of movement. Various sizes of paint cup can be fixed on either side.

Due to the unusual shape, the Aztek airbrush must be held in a slightly different way to a more 'traditional' airbrush, but it remains comfortable and easy to use.

PAINT FEEDS AND CUPS

Siphon paint feeds work on the same principle as a drinking straw, the paint being drawn into the nozzle by suction. Locating beneath or to either side of the airbrush body (most allow for left- or right-handed users), keeping the top of the nozzle free helps with close-up work, maintaining a line of vision between the eye and the subject.

Gravity feed cups may be fixed or interchangeable units and fitted either atop or to the side of the airbrush. Paint simply runs down into the chamber, waiting for the trigger to be engaged before it is admitted into the nozzle. I have no hard and fast evidence to back up my experience, but I've found gravity-fed airbrushes to work more effectively.

Regardless, unless the paint reservoir is permanently fixed, interchangeable jars and cups are usually a friction fit, allowing for quick colour changes and easier cleaning. Having a few spares to hand speeds things up further, especially if a number of paints are prepared beforehand, with just a quick flush with thinners in-between. The other benefit of separately fitting paint cups is the choice of sizes available, the capacity being chosen to suit specific tasks.

Fixed cups are not a problem, although some models, such as the Premi-Air G35 budget airbrush (illustrated below), offer only small capacity receptacles. Frequent topping up during larger painting tasks is not the greatest hardship, but it does add to the time involved and increase the spillage risk. The likelihood of the paint going 'off' before the job is complete is also increased, leading to potential blockages or a compromised paint finish.

Airbrushes with separate paint cups offer the convenience of both quick colour changes and the use of different-sized receptacles for various tasks. Most paint bottles and cups feature small vent holes: do not block these as they provide a pressure release in the event of the airbrush being blocked. Without them, the lid can be blown off with the paint following it!

NOZZLES AND NEEDLES

Internal mix airbrushes have their needles matched to the size of the aperture in the nozzle. Unless the needle is a perfect fit, the tool will not operate properly. Needles are precision-ground components and must be treated with the utmost care when dismantling for cleaning. A bent or damaged needle tip cannot be fixed and must be replaced (see Chapter 7).

Airbrushes are sometimes specified in terms of either the nozzle or needle size, but this means more or less the same thing. However, for the purpose of standardization, this book will refer to the 'nozzle' size. Generally speaking, the size of the nozzle dictates the type and viscosity of fluids that can readily pass through it; the smaller the nozzle, the thinner the paint must be. It also follows that the fineness of spray also increases as the nozzle size decreases. A general-purpose airbrush will have a nozzle size of around 0.5mm and this will suit the majority of tasks that a railway modeller will ask of it.

However, a smaller nozzle (such as 0.3mm) will give a more refined spray that is perfect for creating fine lines, close-up detail work and bespoke weathering jobs. It would also be well suited to painting models in N gauge and below. Iwata produce airbrushes with nozzle sizes down to 0.18mm (Custom Micron B) for the most exacting precision work but, not only are these expensive, they are also less suited to many 'general' tasks as the maximum width of spray is so narrow. Fine nozzle airbrushes are also less forgiving of incorrectly thinned paint and poor levels of cleanliness. The smaller aperture is far more prone to blockage and fast drying cellulose, super enamels and acrylics may all cause problems in this respect, unless thinned and applied correctly.

Interchangeable nozzles are a recent innovation, most popularly endorsed by Testor Aztek airbrushes. Maintenance free, these durable plastic nozzles screw into the front end of the tool and need no form of adjustment or dismantling to clean (they can simply be flushed through with thinners or left to soak to remove stubborn build-ups of paint). Colour coded as to size, they can be used across the Aztek range for a variety of specific tasks.

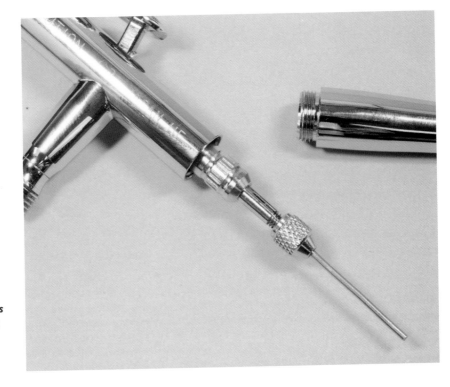

On most double-action airbrushes, the needle and chucking screw are accessed by removing the tailpiece cover. Ease of dismantling is an important factor in choosing an airbrush as regular cleaning will be rewarded with optimum performance. The insides of an airbrush are also a good indication of how well the tool has been machined.

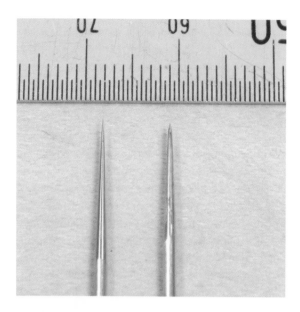

The delicate nature of airbrush needles can be appreciated in this view of 0.3mm (left) and 0.5mm diameter tips. Damaged tips render an airbrush unusable and are difficult to repair; replacements usually being necessary.

The finer the nozzle, the finer the spray pattern can be. This PremiAir tool sports a 0.3mm needle and a nozzle arrangement allowing the panel lines on this Class 14 to be weathered freehand – just a steady hand is required.

A shaped needle chuck screw is a rare but welcome feature as it permits easy refitting of the needle after cleaning, without the risk of damaging the fine tip.

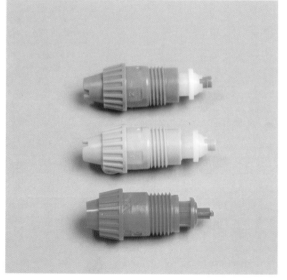

Aztek airbrushes feature interchangeable plastic nozzles that are easy to clean and virtually maintenance free. Offering incredible versatility, simply swapping nozzles allows anything from the broadest strokes to the finest detail to be achieved with a single airbrush.

The shape of the nozzle's rim also has a part to play in how the airbrush works at close quarters. Those fitted with a castellated (or 'crown') rim permit the tool to work much closer to the subject, as the air rebounding from the surface can escape harmlessly through the gaps. With a solid rim, this 'blow-back' causes rough edges to fine lines and an increased risk of paint runs. The majority of airbrush ranges offer a choice of rims, as either separate accessories or supplied as part of an airbrush package.

Another useful feature added to some double-action airbrushes is adjustable needle travel. Here, a grub screw is utilized to limit the lateral travel of the needle, thus forming what is essentially a 'paint flow limiter'. A worthwhile addition for those who will be doing lots of close-up work, it can prevent too much paint being released by any involuntary movement of your finger on the trigger. Setting the 'limiter' further back also produces more consistent broad strokes.

Having a choice of nozzle rims is also helpful, increasing an airbrush's versatility. These are both supplied with the cheap Premi-Air G35.

Nozzle rims can dictate how well an airbrush performs at ultra-close quarters. Despite this Iwata HP-CR sporting a 0.3mm needle and nozzle assembly, the round rim is a limiting factor, although spraying with the rim removed is an option explored in Chapter 14.

Crown-shaped nozzles allow the airflow to escape through the sides of the rim rather than blowing back against the airbrush, resulting in a finer finish. The delicate needle tip on this Paasche Talon TG is, however, rather more exposed to damage with such an open nozzle rim.

Adjustable needle travel screws are helpful for fine detail work as they limit the amount of paint emitted even when the trigger is pulled back fully. Presetting the travel distance before spraying will avoid some nasty accidents.

OTHER CONSIDERATIONS

Comfort is a vital factor to consider before settling on a particular airbrush model. It has to be a pleasure to hold and work with, without causing tiredness in the fingers, wrist and arm. Triggers can sometimes be stiff (although this may be down to the 'newness' of a tool) and dual-action devices may require not a little strength in your finger.

Pistol grip triggers (as illustrated on the Iwata TR2 shown here) offer heightened comfort, especially for larger projects where repeated strokes will be necessary over a long period. They are also very helpful for those with less physical dexterity or who suffer joint or muscular problems. The larger trigger requires much less strength to operate, being squeezed with two or three fingers as opposed to a single one.

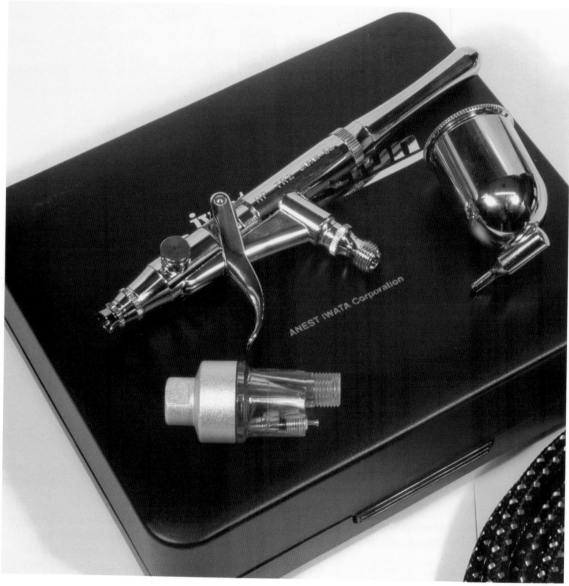

Pistol grip triggers offer a comfortable alternative to the more common button-type trigger.

Although a little less manoeuvrable in tight spots due to its larger size, this Iwata TR2 is great for repetitive tasks such as overall livery applications. The demountable paint cup can be mounted on either side to suit left- and right-handed users and an inline moisture filter is supplied.

Inclusion of a pressure regulating valve in the body of the airbrush can be found on certain 'higher spec' models, allowing a greater degree of fine tuning of the airflow without having to reach over to a control on the compressor or air bottle: a handy feature to possess. We'll look more at pressure regulators in Chapter 2.

Availability and compatibility of accessories within a range, allowing for the upgrading of particular models or to create a more versatile tool from a 'basic' model, is another pertinent fact to consider. A look through the catalogues of different airbrush suppliers or manufacturers will give a hint as to the breadth and ease of supply of extra parts or spares.

Assess the build quality of a tool before you buy one. If the sales blurb in the catalogue does not tell you what an airbrush is made from, ask the dealer. It may not be a make-or-break factor in a prospec-

tive purchase but it should give some idea of how well it has been built and how long it is likely to last. Iwata tools are built with a lifetime's use in mind and incorporate stainless steel throughout the interior of every airbrush, hence they come with a free ten-year warranty. High-quality chrome plating of all exterior surfaces is also important as it permits easier cleaning.

The materials forming the various internal fluid and air seals is also worthy of investigation. They must be able to withstand years of being exposed to harsh thinning and cleaning compounds. A cheaper tool will see these fittings perish quickly, while better quality tools will sport ultra-durable materials such as PTFE or Teflon. Finally, packaging may not seem an obvious factor, but having a nice padded box to keep the tool in will help it last longer and avoid damage.

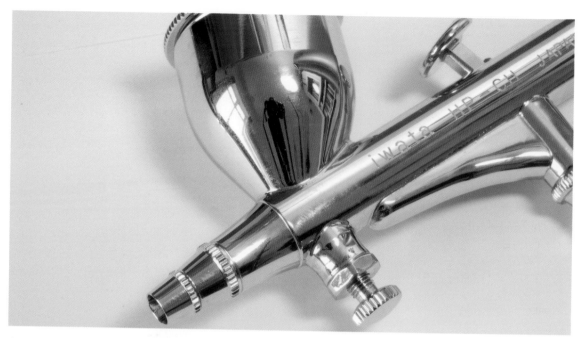

Air pressure adjustment valves (the screw on the underside of this Iwata airbrush) are fitted to higher specification airbrushes, although inline valves can also be obtained as cheap accessories (see Chapter 2). Although not essential features, they do allow for instant fine tuning at the tool end, rather than at the compressor.

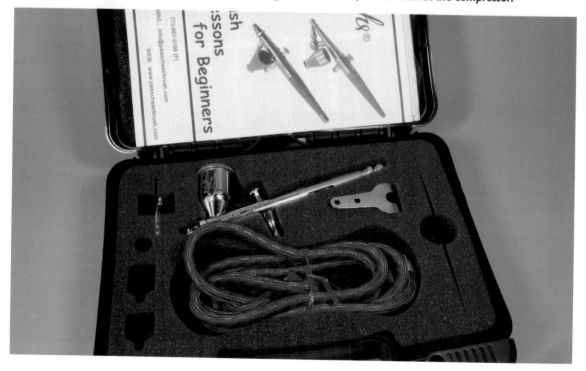

The packaging of an airbrush may not be your first concern but a padded, tough plastic case is not to be sniffed at, not least as it will keep your precious tool clean and protect it from damage. This box contains a mid-range Paasche airbrush, braided hose, airbrush holder, tools and a useful instructional booklet.

WHERE TO GO FROM HERE

When searching for an airbrush, don't confine your-self solely to modellers' outlets. Instead, try looking in art shops as the same brands are often aimed at artists, craftsmen and modellers alike; there may be price differences across different stores and it helps to shop around. On the other hand, firms such as The Airbrush Company or Graphic Air Supplies make life much easier, providing one-stop shops for all your airbrushing needs. Having a source of expert techni-cal advice on the end of a telephone and a full spare parts and repair service also provides peace of mind.

It may not be possible to find a single tool that will cover a whole lifetime's airbrushing requirements, but there are a few specific models that offer a greater amount of flexibility. Interchangeable nozzles and needles, paint cups and compatible accessories all help to provide more scope to develop an existing product. Consider the fact that cheaper brands may not be around in ten years' time, so locating spares will prove difficult.

Finding an airbrush that is comfortable, reli-able and does the things that you need it to do is a rewarding experience. The act of spray-ing paint should be something to look forward to and feeling frustrated with the limitations of your tools is not a recipe for success. Take the time to form your own decision about what you need, making an informed choice rather than an impulse buy. There are hundreds of models out there, produced in large numbers and available from countless outlets in the UK and abroad, so if you're not sure, try somewhere else. Consider other modellers' recommendations too, asking around at modelling shows or by seeking impartial advice from the large online modelling community (such as www.rmweb.co.uk).

An airbrush is nothing without a suitable air source and in the following chapter we shall discuss various supply options. Also, a variety of tools and accesso-ries will be outlined that will help us to develop our skills in spraying paint.

CHAPTER TWO

ASSEMBLING A SPRAYING KIT

An airbrush is nothing without a source of air. That much may be obvious, but ensuring a plentiful and reliable source is not as simple as it may seem. While making a carefully considered airbrush purchase, extra funds must also be provided to procure the compressed air as well as other vital accessories such as a moisture trap, air hose, tool holder, paint strainers, gloves and face mask. There are also cleaning agents, thinners and paint mixing tools to remember.

There are ways of lessening the burden, perhaps by choosing one of the many Starter Packs offered by various manufacturers and dealers, which usually include an airbrush, hose, filter and air supply. This will get you started and allow for upgrading of individual components as you go, thus spreading the cost.

AIR SUPPLIES

Any airbrush, no matter how expensive and finely constructed, is only as good as its air supply. To get the best out of even a cheap beginner's tool, a consistent supply of air is essential. The air must be both clean and free of water vapour when it meets the paint at the airbrush, as well as being supplied at a constant, steady pressure. Inline filters can see to the first requirements, but the latter is not so easy.

CANNED PROPELLANT

A sealed container of compressed air cannot recharge itself, so any usage will see the pressure decrease irretrievably. Only a fairly weak pressure is generally required to spray paint onto miniature models and some form of regulation of the air is essential. But then, as the supply wanes, even that pressure will not be maintained and a new source will have to be found.

Such finite sources include the canned propellant commonly seen in model stores alongside budget airbrush sets. These can be used successfully in very short bursts but the cost can be high in the long term. Offered in various sizes, they are certainly handy, ultra-portable and are suited to very quick painting jobs such as touching-up work and weathering tasks.

One of the easiest ways to start airbrushing is to make use of 'canned air', available in various sizes from brands such as Humbrol, Badger or Premi-Air. While they have their advantages, they also have some serious limitations.

Don't forget that a good deal of air is used simply to clean the airbrush after every colour change and this can swallow up the best part of a can, especially as it helps to flush cleaning fluids through an airbrush at a higher pressure. Because of the cost factor, it can be tempting to scrimp on air while cleaning, but this inevitably leads to paint building up within the airbrush, eventually clogging it up.

As air is released from the can, the pressure drops, especially if the air is 'on' for more than a few minutes at a time. In use, the temperature of the can's interior begins to fall, reaching sub-zero temperatures alarmingly quickly, caused by a reaction of the liquid propellant gasses. Ice then begins to form on the can's exterior, irrespective of the ambient temperature, leading to an interruption in the flow of air.

A means of minimizing this effect is to stand the can in a bowl of warm (not hot) water while spraying. Furthermore, having one or two spare cans, also immersed in warm water, allows for rapid changeovers when a pressure drop is experienced. This all sounds fine until the cost of each can is factored into the equation, especially in relation to the short working time that each will provide before freezing up.

Cans are generally filled with air pressurized at around 70 pounds per square inch (psi), which is far too strong for airbrushing work. Therefore, valves are incorporated into the hose connection, featuring a regulator screw that permits some adjustment of the air pressure. In practice this may be fairly arbitrary, but it does prevent all of the supply disappearing too quickly.

As mentioned above, making use of canned air is a cheap way of getting started in airbrushing. However, the downside to this arrangement is that a beginner is bound to need time to practise with paint mixes, thinner-paint ratios, air pressures, spraying distances and techniques. Couple this with the air needed for cleaning and it can be a recipe for disappointment. Another important note to consider is that canned air supplies are not suited to bleeder type spray guns or airbrushes (see below), as the air will simply disappear through the bleed hole in the tool or connector.

A different option in terms of canned air is to make use of industrial bottles of compressed air or carbon dioxide, as supplied by firms such as BOC (in the UK); even a diver's set of oxygen tanks will do if you have one to hand, as long as pressure regulating valves are fitted along with suitable hose connections.

These large bottles will provide enough power for a few hours' constant operation, although this is not a route to take lightly. Firstly, there's the cost of the delivery and recharging, plus the weight of the canisters that must be stored in a secure location without the risk of them falling over. Also, using carbon dioxide in a confined space is far from healthy and the bottles, filled to pressures of a few hundred psi, are potentially explosive if not treated with care.

TYRES

A car's spare tyre (a bicycle tyre would be insufficient) is also a potential source of compressed air. What's more, it's the ultimate economical option, provided of course that you have a car with a spare tyre in the first place! Small brass ring adaptors are freely available to match airbrush hoses to a standard tyre valve. Inner tubes are not suitable as they simply continue to expand while being pumped up, unrestricted by a steel rimmed tyre and wheel hub.

An average tyre inflated to around 30psi should provide enough 'oomph' for a few small painting tasks and the provision of a pressure regulator at the valve end or on the airbrush itself will permit fine tuning to create a more reliable paint flow. The drawbacks, however, include the need for regular reinflation, although this is made easier by using an electric tyre inflator. The weight of the wheel is not to be forgotten either, and it should be propped securely to prevent it tipping over onto your toes.

Despite offering silent operation and smooth, controllable pressure, the advantages of bottled air or car tyres can be outweighed by the drawbacks (the constant falling in pressure, for instance) and, with a decent electrically powered compressor now costing less than £100, the short-term outlay may actually save cash in the long run.

Making use of a car tyre is an option for providing a free and silent source of air. Always use an inline moisture filter and be prepared for regular re-inflations as the pressure will drop fairly quickly, even with a regulator valve fitted.

Ring adaptors are available to connect an airbrush hose to the tyre's valve and a pressure gauge is a handy accessory.

COMPRESSORS

My first encounter with a compressor was the loan of a fairly elderly unit that was not only noisy but also had a habit of walking about the workshop while chugging away. Without a reservoir tank or regulator valve, the airflow tended to pulse in time with the machine's piston, the effect of which could be seen in the paint spray from the airbrush.

It served its purpose for a while, although the quality of my painting was compromised by the compressor's limitations, and it wasn't long before I upgraded to a new machine from Axminster Power Tools that included a generous reservoir tank and pressure gauge. All it lacked was a regulator valve, although I soon made use of an Iwata MAC inline valve and, latterly, of a separately available moisture trap, pressure regulator and gauge (see page 36). What a treat it was to have a quiet machine, standing still as it purred away, switching itself on and off automatically to maintain pressure in the tank. The difference in my output was marked in both quality and quantity and the machine soon repaid the initial outlay (around £130).

Compressors fall broadly within two distinct types: 'piston' and 'diaphragm'. Diaphragm compressors work in a similar manner to our lungs in that they suck in air from the surrounding atmosphere. However, instead of exhaling the air, it is then ejected forcibly into a small chamber, where it is literally squeezed. The operation is achieved by an electric motor forcing the flexible diaphragm to oscillate back and forth. The squashed air is then either pushed into a reservoir tank (if fitted) or straight down the hose to the waiting airbrush. Diaphragms can be formed of various materials (including metal) and have a finite operating life. Although no lubrication is necessary, there will still be substantial moisture content in the compressed air produced.

Piston powered compressors, also known as reciprocating compressors, are more akin to an internal combustion engine with a ringed piston, powered by an electric motor, moving within a cylinder. As the piston descends, a spring-loaded one-way valve is drawn open, inviting air to enter the machine. On the upwards stroke, the inlet valve is forced closed as the air is compressed and the outlet valve opens, allowing the air to be pushed into a tank or down a hose.

Older-style machines have the pistons oil-lubricated within the cylinder. However, more recent advances in self-lubricating materials have seen the emergence of oil-free machines. Oil lubrication may be good for reliability and longevity, but if the seals or piston rings begin to fail, the lubricant will enter the airflow, leading to potential paint contamination. A complete strip-down and rebuild is necessary to cure the problem, which will prove expensive. A new hose will also be needed as the contaminated one will have to be discarded.

All compressors take in air from their immediate surroundings, so it's a good idea to keep these as clean as possible. If the machine is kept on the floor, ensure that it is kept free of dust, moisture and debris. Also, keep paint overspray away from the compressor or this vapour will be drawn into the machine, which can lead to problems. Compressing air is a tough job and a machine is naturally subject to wear and tear. Avoid leaving it pumping away when no work is being carried out and allow it to rest at regular intervals.

In common with choosing an airbrush, deciding on a compressor is another matter of finding what best suits your own needs. Choice will depend on the size and regularity of painting tasks envisaged. Upgrading later is an option if a cheap machine is to be trialled initially, although there are a number of good quality machines that will suit most, if not all, modelling scenarios in the £100–200 price bracket and which should provide years of reliable service.

A good example of an entry-level compressor is illustrated in the form of the Premi-Air Baby Mobile. At under £70 (2010 prices), it's a great way to get started, amounting to the same cost as a half dozen cans of propellant.

Although a pressure gauge is not fitted to the Baby Mobile, there is an adjustable bleed valve to dial-in the desired air pressure.

A more compact solution is this desktop Silver Jet compressor, by Iwata. Both a pressure dial and gauge is provided, along with an integral airbrush holder and an inline moisture filter.

Mid-priced compressors, such as the Iwata Sprint Jet, produce a smooth, virtually pulse-free air supply while running quietly and efficiently.

A pressure gauge and regulating valve are handy features to look for in a compressor and this Sprint Jet offers both.

The Sprint Jet's pressure gauge is clearly visible and, by adjusting the relief valve, the desired pressure can simply be 'dialled in'.

Keep your compressor clean, especially around the inlet area, to keep out dust and paint overspray. This Sprint Jet incorporates a filter protecting the small air intake and this should be periodically cleaned or replaced; a spare is provided with the machine.

RESERVOIR TANKS

To avoid the pulsing effect of air being sent straight down a hose from the diaphragm or piston, which can create uneven paint coverage in extreme circumstances, choosing a compressor with an integral reservoir tank provides a much smoother flow of air. If fitted with an automatic shut-off valve (as all such machines should be), this arrangement also allows the motor to kick in only as it is required to replenish the tank. Not only does this minimize wear on the mechanical parts, but it also keeps the noise and electricity consumption down.

Hobby compressors usually offer a tank capacity of around 3 or 4 litres, which should be more than sufficient for any modelling application in O gauge and below. For anything larger, however, a more generous tank may be desired. The larger the tank, the longer the working pressure can be maintained, meaning less work for the motor. Working on bigger subjects may also require a higher pressure setting,

especially if a spray gun is in use. In this case, not only a larger reservoir is needed but also a more powerful motor to keep up with the demand. Try sources such as Axminster Tools or your local Machine Mart store for larger compressors.

Reservoir tanks are, however, far from essential. If working in nothing larger than OO gauge, the low pressure needed for most airbrushing work (less than 25psi) means that a good quality compressor, fitted with a pressure regulator, should more than suffice.

TO BLEED OR NOT TO BLEED

A compressor without a reservoir tank is constantly producing a supply of air and this output has to be released somehow. There's no problem if the airbrush is constantly asking for air, but this is seldom the case. Pausing between strokes causes the pressurized air to build up in the hose, leading to fluctuations in air and paint flow from the airbrush. Alternatively, if spraying halts for more than a brief

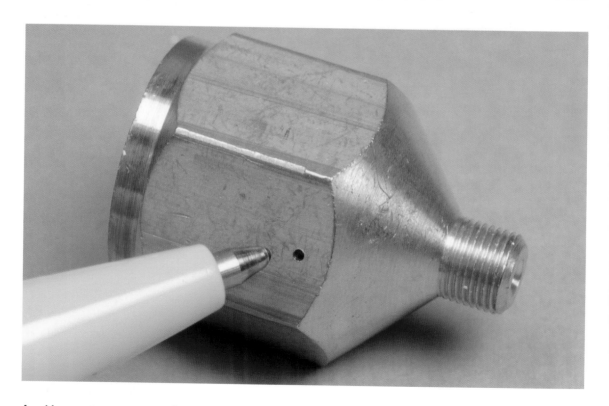

An older compressor or a machine without a reservoir tank or automatic bleed valve will require the use of adaptors in the airline, fitted with small holes to allow excess air pressure to escape.

moment, then there's the possibility of more disastrous consequences, such as a burst hose.

This is why a bleed valve is often fitted to a compressor, allowing excess air to leak away harmlessly and this feature is usually incorporated into the pressure regulating valve, exhausting the excess air to maintain a constant level as selected by the user. If the airbrush is not calling for air, then a safety valve is forced open and enough air escapes to keep the pressure in the system at a safe level.

Machines without the facility for pressure regulation will require a bleeding point elsewhere in the chain, either in the air line connections or on the airbrush itself. These commonly take the form of a tiny hole, constantly leaking air and these apertures must not be covered.

Most modern airbrushes are produced in non-bleed form and compressors are now regularly fitted with the necessary pressure relief valves as standard. However, it's important to check that your choice of airbrush and compressor are suited. If neither component has a bleeding valve, then an air line adaptor with bleed hole must be fitted and these are relatively cheap and freely available from airbrush suppliers.

The moisture filter, drain and pressure regulator (the small dial) of the Iwata Sprint Jet also incorporates an automatic bleed valve, expelling excess air pressure into the atmosphere, thus maintaining a smooth flow of power to the airbrush. However, as any moisture extracted by the filter is also emitted from this drain, it's a good idea to place a cloth or a piece of kitchen towel beneath it.

PRESSURE REGULATION

The general rule goes that the thicker the liquid, the more air pressure is needed to spray it: finding an optimum air pressure to suit a specific paint formula or viscosity can often be a matter of trial and error. While the majority of small-scale modelling applications will require pressure between 10 and 25psi, the ability to make small adjustments within this range is highly desirable. Indeed, it can often be the matter of just 1 or 2psi that makes the difference between a grainy finish and a perfect application. By opting to airbrush a model, we are making a conscious decision to aim for a higher quality finish, but this will not be possible if the air supply cannot be controlled.

Compressors aimed at hobby users now offer some form of pressure control as standard, be it with or without a gauge, according to specification. A gauge, while offering a visual read-out of the pressure in use, is not essential as fairly accu-

A simple and cheaper alternative to a compressor-fitted pressure regulator is the inline valve, such as this Iwata MAC valve, compatible with any airbrush via screw thread adaptors. Such a device also helps when using canned air or a car tyre, smoothing the airflow and prolonging the supply.

rate adjustments can be made 'on the fly' by simply starting at the lowest setting and turning up the pressure gradually until the paint is emitted in a satisfactory manner.

Regulating valves restrict the flow of air in the hose and some airbrushes are fitted with similar controls on the tool itself, as briefly mentioned in the previous chapter. Available as separate accessories, external valves can be added between the airbrush and any air source – compressor, car tyre or gas canister. The Iwata MAC valve offers a cheap and easy way to regulate pressure, although since it offers no bleed-off facility it must be used in conjunction with a self-bleeding or reservoir-fitted compressor. Such valves can be attached to any brand of airbrush provided thread sizes match, although there are plenty of adaptors to convert to your chosen hose and airbrush connections.

MOISTURE TRAPS

The act of producing compressed air by mechanical means results in the air being warmer than the ambient temperature. Once the air is released into a reservoir tank or an air line, it will soon start to cool, producing traces of water vapour. Coiled vinyl hoses are fitted to some compressors that help to cool the air before it passes through a moisture trap. Here the water condenses and falls into a container. Either it will drip away from a drain outlet or it must be purged at intervals by pushing a spring-loaded air valve.

Not all compressors include this feature, but they can be obtained as separate fittings. Alternatively, a small inline filter fitted between airbrush and hose can be a cheaper option. A moisture filter is also highly recommended when using any other source of compressed air. Personally, I work with a filter connected at both ends of the hose – at the compressor and airbrush – to ensure that no traces of moisture reach the 'business end' of the operation.

As a last line of defence against water contamination, an inline moisture filter also acts as an extension to the airbrush's handle. This is an Iwata filter and, by periodically depressing the sprung purge valve, the water trap can be emptied.

OTHER CONSIDERATIONS

Choosing an air hose is another important consideration. Check that vinyl or plastic hoses are certified for use with electric compressors, as some of the cheaper products are designed solely for use with canned propellant and will not withstand the potentially higher pressures of these machines. Even if intending to permanently limit your compressor to lower pressure settings, do not be tempted to fit an unsuitable hose: it's bad practice. Be sure to abide by the specifications listed in your compressor's instructions regarding hoses. Braided hoses are much more resilient to the rigours of workshop use, where they are likely to be trodden on or trapped under furniture or equipment. However, these can be heavier and less flexible, which poses problems when working in confined areas or on very detailed work.

Hose diameter and length has a direct effect on the amount of air pressure lost between the source and the airbrush. No proprietary compressor system delivers 100 per cent efficiency between pump and airbrush nozzle and, even with tightly fitting connectors, the pressure will invariably drop a little, especially if a long hose is in use. This is by no means a serious problem, only that a small amount of compensation should be allowed for when setting the pressure regulator on the compressor. It's also yet another reason why stating a list of hard-and-fast pressure specifications is not worthwhile.

The amount of wasted air can be reduced by sealing all threaded air line joints with PVC/PTFE plumber's tape. Just a little is needed, say two or three wraps around the circumference of the joint, ensuring that the aperture is not blocked by excess tape before tightening the connectors. Hand fas-

tening is usually sufficient, taking extra care not to over-tighten a joint with a plastic thread (such as an inline moisture filter).

Choosing the best site for a compressor within the workshop should take into account where the machine can receive a supply of clean air as well as being well ventilated to prevent overheating. Avoid high traffic areas where trailing power leads or air hoses can cause trip hazards or be damaged. Depending on individual machines, there may be some movement caused by the vibration of the unit in use. If this is the case, mounting it on top of a bench may not be wise, lest it plummet off the edge.

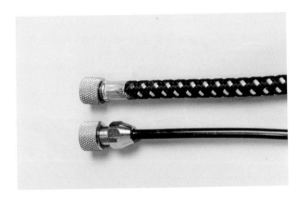

Vinyl hoses allow the compressed air within to cool, helping to weed out the water vapour when used in conjunction with moisture filters. However, they are not as tough and durable as braided hoses.

Don't worry if the hose supplied with your airbrush does not match that of your compressor, as brass adaptors are freely available for only a few pounds each, in a range of sizes and male or female formats.

To prevent air leaking from hose joints and adaptors, wrap a little plumber's PTFE tape around the threads before making the joint. Keep the airway clear, however, or it will impair performance. With the threads sealed, tighten the connectors firmly by hand.

Quick-release valves allow rapid switching between different airbrushes or faster disconnection from the airline after a painting session. This Iwata set also incorporates a MAC pressure regulating valve.

AN EASY COMPRESSOR UPGRADE

There's no doubting that a compressor with a built-in reservoir tank produces a much smoother airflow through the airbrush. Even the better quality 'direct supply' units, such as the Iwata Sprint Jet, still have a vaguely perceptible pulsing of air, most noticeable when working very close-up to a subject or if attempting some very fine, controlled effects such as weathering.

Having obtained a good quality diaphragm compressor with a reservoir tank, the lack of a pressure regulator and moisture trap meant that the machine's usefulness for high-quality, small-scale painting was compromised. Presumably the compressor was designed for larger spray guns as the pressure output was around 30psi, around twice as much as I usually require.

In an effort to widen the usability of this compressor, a separate regulator and filter unit was obtained and connected into the airline. For only £20 (from Expo Tools), the assembly features a gauge and dial valve, with the facility to lock the valve at a specific pressure setting. The moisture filter is accompanied by a generous water trap and purge valve. With a handful of screw-in hose adaptors thrown in, it is great value. A coiled, heavy-duty vinyl hose links the reservoir to the regulator, allowing the air to cool before reaching the filter, thus helping the moisture to condense. A braided hose then links the airbrush to the regulator, proving a more durable conduit to have reaching across a busy workshop.

Combined with the price of both hoses, this entire air system has cost just over £150, yet offers the performance of a much more expensive package. The quality and reliability of the air across a wide pressure range, together with the ability of dialling-in the desired 'psi', makes it a rewarding device to work with.

This portable, oil-less diaphragm compressor is fitted with a 3.5l reservoir tank, providing a smooth, pulse-free supply of air. However, the lack of pressure regulation proved a source of frustration and so a separate regulator and moisture filter assembly was sourced.

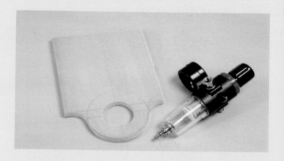

A scrap of 12mm plywood was cut to a suitable size, with a circular hole cut to accommodate the regulator body.

The locations of the four mounting holes must be marked out carefully to allow for a good fit.

In order to safely mount the new regulator and filter, some form of bracket was needed and the best place seemed to be between the motor and reservoir. The four mounting bolts were removed and the motor carefully lifted away.

Having drilled the mounting holes, a set of longer bolts was obtained to allow for the extra material between motor and tank.

When fitting the new bolts, ensuring that they're tight is vital as the full weight of the machine is put onto this joint when lifted.

After choosing the appropriate airline adaptors, plumber's PTFE tape should be wrapped around the threads before fitting.

An adjustable spanner is the best tool for securing airline connectors, although over-tightening them may damage the regulator housing.

The regulator and filter assembly can be seen seated in the plywood bracket.

The pressure regulator is operated by simply turning a dial until the desired value is registered on the gauge. A button on the dial allows any setting to be locked.

A useful addition to the DIY mounting bracket is this simple airbrush holder, formed from a scrap of copper pipe.

FUME EXTRACTION BOOTHS

Depending on where and how often you intend to be airbrushing, it may or may not be worth investing in some form of extraction apparatus. Working in a draughty shed or garage, you can probably get away with wearing good-quality personal protection such as a face mask with the appropriate filter elements. However, spraying paint in a spare bedroom, on the dining room table or in any shared space renders the use of an extractor more of a necessity. The growing popularity of specialist water-based model paints can be appreciated when the issue of fumes is considered, as these are much less harmful than oil- or cellulose-based formulas. However, inhaling any vaporized paint or thinner is not a healthy option.

Spray booth and extractor systems are available from various sources (see Useful Contacts), priced to suit either hobby or professional users. On the other hand, DIY solutions are also possible using a reclaimed cooker extraction hood, for instance. Provided that the system exhausts into a safe area, away from a public space or other open windows, and that the electric motor is of the sealed, brushless type, then it should be safe for occasional use. Cooker extractors should have this sort of motor anyway, designed to prevent moisture or greasy deposits from entering any electrical part of the machine. But it's worth checking, nonetheless.

Extractor booths, like other aspects of modelling equipment, are becoming cheaper by the year and recently there have been a handful of new products aimed at home users and retailing for a double-figured amount. If an extractor tempts you, ensure that it comes with replaceable filters (of the correct grade to deal with the types of paint that you plan to use), and that the working area within the booth is sufficient for the size of projects that you envisage.

A spray booth is an attractive proposition for anyone intending more than the odd dabble with an airbrush. This unit, supplied by Graphic Air Supplies, has served me well for many years. Harmful fumes are expelled via a flexible hose dangled out of an adjacent window. Working in an area rich in natural light is also a bonus, although a few daylight simulating lamps are also kept close by to eliminate shadows.

This budget spray booth is produced by The Airbrush Company and, although not as efficient as a professional-grade unit, it's more than suitable for the occasional hobby user. It can also be packed away flat when not in use.

NOTES ON SAFETY

Compressed air, however it is created or stored, can be dangerous. Commercial compressors or pressure vessels must be certified to strict standards and they should not be tampered with in any way unless by qualified technicians, not only to protect the validity of a warranty, but also to avoid any potential hazards. Propellant cans are equally dangerous if misused, pierced or exposed to high temperatures. Hoses or connectors that may appear worn or show signs of splitting should be replaced immediately; repairing hoses is difficult and not to be advised.

Compressed air also poses a threat to human and animal health if directed at any part of the body. There is a risk of air entering the bloodstream via the eyes, skin wounds or through soft tissue areas (such as the nostrils) and ultimately causing heart failure. This may sound like extreme health and safety paranoia, but it is a real danger that must be kept in mind.

Regardless of the types of paint in use, or in what quantity, you must take precautions to protect the health of yourself and those around you. Always work in a well-ventilated area and wear a face mask at all times. Cheap DIY dust masks may filter out some of the dry paint particles that are likely to be airborne but will have little chance of preventing the fumes from entering your body. Vaporized paint is inhaled in a wet state and will dry inside the lungs. Being largely synthetic substances, they cannot be absorbed and processed by the body, thus laying the seeds of future respiratory problems. It's also worth noting that some specialist model paint brands contain lead chromate, which is highly toxic.

For the occasional airbrush user (say 30 minutes of spraying every couple of weeks), choose a mask designed specifically for the filtering of paint fumes

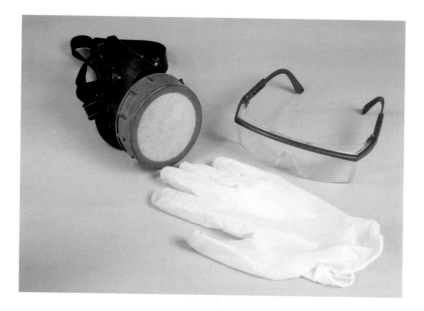

A face mask should be worn at all times when spraying paint, even when using an extraction booth. Choose a good-quality mask with the correct grade of particulate filters, available from good paint and hobby suppliers. Protecting your skin and eyes from paints and chemicals is also a serious business. Disposable gloves and eye protection should be considered, especially when mixing paints.

and particulates, available from most hobby paint and airbrush retailers. For frequent painters, a more robust mask should be obtained, preferably with interchangeable filters that must be replaced regularly. These are also available from hobby outlets or DIY stores. A rubber face seal is preferred; if you wear a beard, make use of a dampened cotton handkerchief to create a more effective seal between your face and the mask. Not surprisingly, the higher a mask's specification, the more expensive it's likely to be. However, it must be weighed against suffering chronic chest complaints a few years down the line.

WORKSHOP ISSUES

Locating your painting zone in as dust-free an area as possible is crucial. Sheds or garages with unsealed concrete floors can be particularly problematic. Areas where animals are likely to carouse are also to be avoided. Simple housekeeping measures can help: wiping all surfaces with a damp cloth and vacuuming before painting is worthwhile, although be sure to use a vacuum cleaner an hour or two beforehand, as they tend to emit dust particles into the air while they work.

Wearing the right clothes is also important. Avoid woollen jumpers in particular, while cotton

garments can also cause problems with fibres being released as you move. It is an established fact that if any particles of material are shed, they will invariably descend and lodge themselves into a fresh coat of paint. Synthetic materials such as nylon are recommended for painting wear, with disposable overalls (as sold in DIY stores) also being well suited.

In the interest of health, windows should be opened to admit a supply of fresh air, but this also leads to an increased risk of dust particles settling into wet paint. To overcome this, I drape scraps of light material over the opened windows of my shed, permitting the flow of air, while also acting as filters to insects and debris. It's not a perfect system, but it does help.

Painting should never be attempted in a cold environment as this will only lead to condensation forming on metal or plastic surfaces. Besides, paints do not perform well in the cold. The optimum temperature for painting is around 20°C and a small portable heater will help when painting in an outdoor or unheated space, employed to pre-warm the room, along with the model, paints, tools, airbrush and compressor. A small thermometer on the workbench is also handy for gauging when is and when isn't a good time to paint.

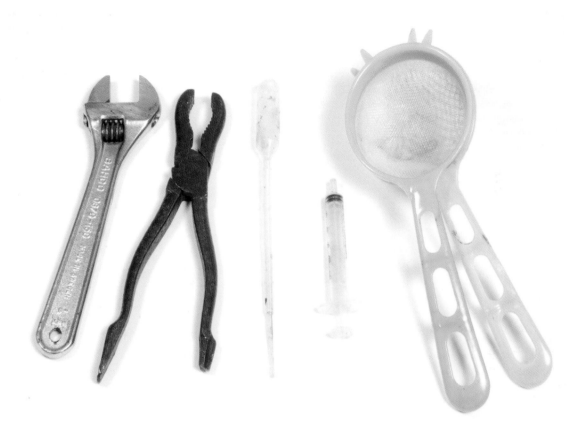

Some useful ancillary tools to have at hand: adjustable spanner for hose connection joints, round throat pliers to aid removal of stubborn screw-top paint lids, pipettes and syringes for measuring and decanting paints and thinners (separate ones for different paint and thinner formulas), and cheap tea strainers for sifting out lumpy paint before mixing and loading into an airbrush (for more details see Chapter 4).

A small work area is all that's needed for mixing and thinning paints. Aim to have everything you may need close at hand before starting work. Painting can be a messy business, so ensure that surfaces are protected from spillage, including the floor; my multi-coloured shed floor offers a lesson in how easily paint can be spilled.

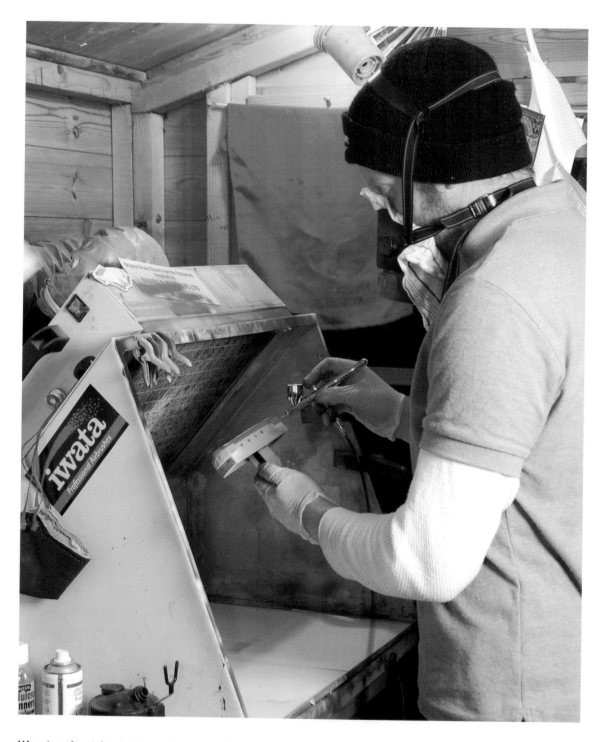

Wearing the right clothing will reduce the risk of errant fibres being shed and falling into wet paint. Here is my regular painting uniform: an old top (man-made fibres) and jeans, latex gloves and face mask with handkerchief to seal the gaps around my beard. As this was taken in winter, note the hat and long-sleeved thermal vest (both of polyester, not wool or cotton). The shed had been pre-heated to around 20°C before work commenced.

Never spray paint in proximity to either naked flames or electric heaters with exposed elements, due to the risk of fire. Paint fumes and vapours can spread over a surprisingly wide area so it pays to err on the side of caution and switch electric heaters off while spraying and for some time afterwards.

Ensure that there is adequate lighting – natural or artificial – to make painting a comfortable experience, avoiding shadows on the workplace by having lights fixed ahead of you. One or two lamps, with daylight simulating bulbs, pointing onto the work area will help with colour matching and prevent eye strain. However, natural light provides the best source of illumination and painting in daylight hours, close to a large window, is recommended.

Finally, keep the workspace tidy and well ordered, with all necessary tools and devices kept close to hand. Unless working on large models, a vast area is not essential; just ensure adequate room in which to accommodate the various pieces of equipment as well as the space to mix and spray the paint.

READY TO PROCEED?

It is to be hoped that all of this background information hasn't induced boredom or confusion. While it's not necessary to have an encyclopaedic knowledge of all the various bits of equipment on the market, understanding the purpose of various tools and accessories – and how they work – will assist you in making informed choices regarding your airbrushing setup.

As with the previous comments concerning airbrushes, gaining expert advice from dealers on air supplies, filters, hoses and accessories is recommended, not least as there are so many new products regularly coming on the market.

CHAPTER THREE

PAINT

One of the most versatile aspects of the airbrush as a finishing tool is its ability to work with a great variety of liquids: primers, paints, varnishes, inks or dyes, even adhesives can be sprayed. All that is required is that the liquid is thinned to a suitable viscosity before spraying.

Moreover, the thinning aspect of a liquid medium is a crucial factor: not all finishing compounds are suited to being diluted below a defined viscosity, as their chemical structure may be broken down to such an extent that the paint will not perform as it should (see below). Having said that, the vast majority of liquid paints that are marketed at art, craft and hobby users will be compatible with all types of airbrush, as long as they are used within their limits.

What must be borne in mind is the importance of choosing the correct paint for a specific job. Indeed, this is just as vital a decision as finding the right airbrush or air supply. Paint is, after all, just another tool in the model-maker's armoury. But how do we decide which paint to use when there is such a vast array of products at our disposal? It certainly helps to have some prior knowledge of the various paint 'types' and their associated properties, so that an informed choice can be made. Of course there's nothing wrong with learning by trial and error – most of my experience has been built in this way – but it can waste valuable modelling time!

The modeller in the twenty-first century is spoilt for choice in terms of paint products in various formulas. There are shades for almost any livery as well as countless 'general' colours for scenic or weathering use.

WHAT IS PAINT?

Paint has been around in many forms for thousands of years and throughout all of that time two common ingredients have remained important, namely the solid pigments and liquid medium. Indeed, these two main factors are co-dependent: the coloured or clear pigments rely on the medium (or 'solvent') to help them disperse evenly over a surface. To allow the paint to dry, the medium must evaporate into the atmosphere once the solid pigment has been deposited. Water is a useful medium, but a minimum temperature is required for evaporation, while mineral or synthetic solvents will vanish much sooner.

Pigments should be finely ground to produce a smooth finish and this can often be the difference between a good quality and an inferior paint brand. Each particle of pigment must be surrounded by particles of liquid solvent in order for the paint to flow freely, proving the necessity for paints to be mixed thoroughly before application. While thinning is often necessary to enable a paint to be brushed or sprayed satisfactorily, it can also weaken the molecular bond between the solvent and the pigment resulting in poor performance. Simply adding more paint to an over-weak mixture will not restore its chemical balance and therefore it is best discarded (for more on thinning paint see Chapter 4).

Other than pigments and solvents, paints also contain one or two other ingredients, depending on type and brand. Additives may include resins, emulsions or plasticizers, each of which promote a tough, durable finish, while matting or glossing agents affect the final sheen. The type of drier added determines how soon the paint will 'go off' and some formulas deliberately offer slower drying times to aid application by hand. Conversely, other paints may be designed to dry almost instantly. Inevitably, ingredients differ between brands and this must be borne in mind when mixing paints: even if they are of the same 'type' they may not be compatible.

Modellers will probably have encountered the terms 'solvent' and 'thinners' before, but their use in the modelling media can sometimes be misleading.

Therefore, it's worth getting this straight from the beginning: a solvent is a liquid medium employed to dissolve solids, while a thinner is a means of diluting the mixture.

The solvent, as the term suggests, carries a selection of dissolved pigments and it's likely that a thinning agent will already be present to reduce the viscosity of the mixture. Adding more thinners breaks down the paint further until a workable consistency is achieved. Consequently, correct choice of thinners for diluting paint is vital as it must suit the thinning agents already present in the solvent.

The confusion surrounding solvents arises from the common use of the term to describe non-organic substances, such as white spirit, xylene or other noxious chemicals. Without wishing to sound too pedantic, a look in any dictionary will reveal that the word simply refers to any compound that is able to dissolve other materials to form a solution. Therefore, in terms of paint manufacture, a solvent can be anything that helps the pigments to flow, including water.

PAINT TYPES

There are three main types of airbrush-friendly paint: acrylic, enamel and cellulose. Each has its peculiar foibles and hazards, the former two formulas being by far the most commonly encountered by modellers. At the risk of boring you with more scientific detail, it really doesn't hurt to know a little about how each paint is formulated as it will help to understand – and anticipate – how a paint will behave when thinning, mixing, spraying and drying. It will also help us to understand their various limitations.

ENAMELS

The term enamel has become somewhat corrupted in the modern modelling lexicon, the main ingredients bearing little resemblance to what originally formed these oil-based paints. Dating back over centuries, enamel formulas had been largely unchanged until the 1940s when wartime conditions led to the development of synthetic resins to replace the natural solvents hitherto employed, such as linseed

Enamels will be familiar to anyone who grew up building plastic kits, with well-known brands such as Humbrol and Revell offering large and economical ranges.

oil. These resins work not only to disperse the super-fine ground colour pigments in a more effective manner, but they also evaporate far quicker and provide reduced drying times, leaving a superior and incredibly hard-wearing finish.

Deep, lustrous enamel finishes are hard to beat; although some brands may still take up to a week or two to dry completely (especially gloss coats), the potentially excellent results are worth the wait. Water- and oil-resistant, enamels can also be polished (when dry) with petroleum distillate and, depending on the brand, thinning can be achieved with either high-quality white spirit or fast-evaporation thinners aimed solely at airbrushing use. White spirit will also remove enamels before they dry completely, while common DIY paint stripper works on fully cured paint. Such strippers will, however, destroy most plastics (see Chapter 5).

Due to the presence of chemical solvents and pigments, enamel paints and their vapours can be extremely harmful to both our health and the environment and suitable precautions must be taken. They are also highly flammable and certain specialist brands contain lead chromate, making them doubly toxic.

ACRYLICS

Modellers' acrylic paints, as their name suggests, contain a variety of plastic compounds, mostly of the 'thermoplastic' type, drying to a film-like substance, not unlike household emulsion paint. Fast drying, due to the rapid evaporation of the liquid solvent (usually a solution of distilled water and alcohol), these are much less toxic than either enamels or cellulose formulas. Some brands even claim to be entirely non-toxic.

Once thoroughly dry, acrylics possess a good degree of resistance to water, oils or chemical solvents and, depending on the brand, they may also offer a fairly flexible coating that will resist fading and discolouration over time. Water may be used to clean mixing and painting tools as well as acting as a thinning agent, although specific grades of acrylic thinners are available.

Indeed, when airbrushing, the use of air-drying acrylic thinners is recommended over water for superior results and faster drying times. Such thinners are often formed of distilled water and iso-propyl alcohol, the former ingredient removing the problem of mineral content in bottled or tap water (especially in hard water areas), while the alcohol promotes speedier evaporation. Much less liable to combustion, only acrylics with high alcohol content are classed as flammable.

Some hobby acrylics require a slightly higher air pressure to produce quality finishes, the extra power being needed to atomize the paint compound sufficiently. The standard of the airbrush itself can also be instrumental in the performance of acrylic

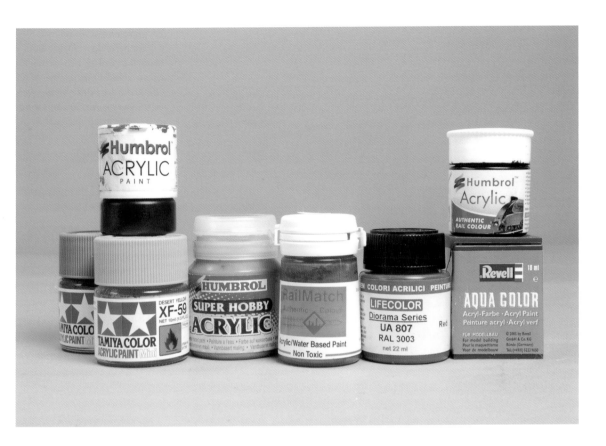

Acrylic paints have become increasingly popular with modellers and the majority of brands can be applied to a high standard using an airbrush. Formulas differ wildly in performance, however.

paints; cheaper, less refined tools tend to hinder the atomization process.

While easy to remove when wet (with water), dried acrylics are exceedingly difficult to budge and, given their rapid curing time, this can prove something of a mixed blessing. Some model paint strippers, such as Superstrip from Phoenix Precision, will lift acrylics as long as the model is left to soak in the solution for a few hours. The speed of drying also leaves airbrushes prone to clogging if not flushed through with cleaning agents at regular intervals.

Synthetic acrylics, as contained in many modern automotive finishes, offer supremely hard-wearing and lustrous finishes coupled with ultra-rapid drying times. However, they are far more hazardous than hobby or artists' acrylics, with a higher risk of combustion

and more harmful vapours. They're also expensive and most commonly offered in aerosol form. Colour choice is limited to specific car finishes although generic shades of black, grey or white can be easily obtained. Additionally, some automotive colours are a close match to certain railway livery elements, for example Land Rover Deep Bronze Green is a very close match to BR Standard Loco Green.

While talk of aerosol paint may seem a little 'off message' in a book on airbrushing, these paints can be decanted into a container for use in an airbrush. It's a potentially messy business, but a drinking straw, some cling film and a glass jar is all that's required (for a demonstration see the accompanying illustrations overleaf). Aerosols have their uses but cannot offer the same finesse as an airbrush, so this method is worth experimenting with.

Formulas used in aerosol paints offer fast drying and superior results, especially those acrylic and nitro-cellulose types produced for automotive use. While spray cans have their attractions, they cannot offer the same standard of finish as an airbrush.

Pete Waterman's company Just Like the Real Thing (JLTRT) produces exquisite cellulose-based paints for use with the same firm's O gauge kits, although they're offered in aerosol form only. It's a shame that spray cans are not suited to intricate applications on to small scale models.

There is a viable method of decanting paint from an aerosol for use in an airbrush, but it can be a messy and smelly business. By fixing a drinking straw to the can's nozzle, the contents can be sprayed into a glass jar. Cover the top of the jar with cling film, with a hole for the straw, to minimize the potential for spillage and to contain the nasty fumes. Be sure to wear gloves, an apron, face mask and safety glasses.

If necessary, modify the can's nozzle with a knife to achieve a good fit with the straw, although this should only be done with the nozzle removed. Thin strips of duct tape will help keep the straw in place for the short time that it takes to fill the jar.

Remove the cling film and leave the lid off the jar for a few minutes to allow the propellant gases to disperse from the paint – you will see them bubbling away – and the paint should be used in the airbrush without too much delay. Thinning should not be necessary, but acetone or good-quality cellulose thinners will be suitable for most formulas, as well as for cleaning up afterwards.

CELLULOSE

Cellulose is a naturally occurring substance forming the main constituent of cells within all plant matter. Organic solvents, such as acetone, are employed to dissolve refined cellulose compounds and colouring pigments to create paints and clear lacquers (sometimes also referred to as 'dope'). Drying times are extremely rapid and a superb quality of finish is possible if the paints are applied correctly.

Cellulose paint also provides an extremely tough finish that is completely waterproof and resistant to oils and most chemical solvents. Today, hi-tech nitro-cellulose finishes contain various plastic compounds (similar to some synthetic acrylic formulas) that offer more reliable results, yet they can be especially hazardous to health. In bygone days, manufacturers recommended painters to consume plenty of fresh milk to counteract the drowsiness and nausea caused by cellulose fumes. However, it's far safer to take every step to avoid inhaling any of the vapours in the first place and the utmost care should be taken with these paints. As such, they are better suited to the more experienced modeller and, not surprisingly, cellulose finishes are not as freely available as enamels or acrylics.

Due to the high volatility of solvents in cellulose paint, the formula can literally dry in thin air while being sprayed, before it even reaches the model. It takes practise to ensure a finish befitting the strengths of the paint and the correct air pressure and spraying distance – between airbrush and subject – is crucial. Certain plastics, such as polystyrene, are vulnerable to damage by cellulose paint, or more specifically by the solvents. Thus, testing on a scrap of the same material first (such as the sprue from a plastic kit) is recommended. Having said that, building up numerous ultra-thin coats of a cellulose primer can often be possible on polystyrene models, provided that each layer dries thoroughly in between (for more details see Chapter 6).

COMPATIBILITY

A general rule of thumb that I've heard now and again is to keep to a single type of paint during any one project, although not necessarily to the same brand. Why? Cleaning airbrushes between coats may entail using a different solvent for different paints and any residual traces of paint or thinners may react adversely with the next load. I've never had any problems in this respect as I endeavour to be fairly fastidious as far as airbrush cleansing is concerned.

Another reason is the inevitable inconsistency of surface finish that may result. Colour matching becomes difficult (swapping brands can also cause problems here) and, in some cases, paints will actually react against each other. For example, a layer of cellulose over an enamel or acrylic base coat can have disastrous consequences: both paints will simply blister and peel off. Any paint can be applied on top of a dry cellulose coat, however, and most hobby enamels are suitable for spraying atop acrylic and vice versa, as long as each previous layer is completely dry. To be certain, leave at least a couple of days between coats. If there is a need to mix paint media, testing for compatibility on scrap material beforehand is recommended.

There may always be exceptions to rules and, in blatant defiance of the above, I regularly use a cellulose primer, followed by acrylic livery shades and finishing with an enamel varnish. Alternatively, an enamel livery may be followed by an acrylic varnish. The key to success is that the cellulose only ever lies on the bare surface of the model (no previous paint traces remaining unless they are also of a cellulose formula) and that each separate stage is carried out with adequate drying time in-between. In theory, all livery shades should be applied using the same paint type although, again, this is not always so. However, such a mix-and-match approach can lead to an inconsistent appearance, especially if mixing matt, satin and gloss paints. In cases such as these, the varnishing coats then become an essential device for blending everything together.

It should be noted that all of the paint products featured in this book are known to be safe for use on plastic, resin or metal models. As mentioned, only cellulose paints pose a potential risk to some plastics but, in my experience, as long as care is taken in their use, there should be no problem.

When in doubt, read the guidelines on the paint packaging, call the advertised helpline, or test on a scrap of the same material.

DRYING TIMES

Performance of enamel paints tends to vary across different brands (and within the same brand in some instances), depending on their chemical make-up. The fastest drying types offer a 'touch-dry' time of around thirty minutes, although virtually all still insist on a break of twenty-four hours between layers. Gloss and metallic enamels require considerably longer and full hardness may not occur until a week or two later. If spraying with white spirit as a thinning agent, drying times may be increased, hence specific airbrushing thinners are available that evaporate far more quickly and can reduce drying times considerably.

Acrylic paints also offer rapid 'touch-dry' times and these can usually be recoated after between twenty and thirty minutes. However, most brands take up to a week to dry completely and, again, the type of thinning agent plays a role in drying time. Water takes much longer to disperse than alcohol-rich acrylic thinners, while in contrast some cellulose finishes are completely dry in an hour or two and can be abraded, filled, polished and recoated without further ado.

The painting and drying environment also plays an important role, a warm ambient temperature being crucial to successful painting. Wet models, stored carefully in a lidded (but vented) container and left in a warm airing cupboard, for example, will be dry much sooner than those left out in a cold shed overnight.

MATT, SATIN OR GLOSS

As Chapter 10 will confirm, a clear varnish coat is the best way of finishing most paint jobs, particularly rolling stock projects that have involved decals and multi-layered livery schemes. With this in mind, it can seem rather pointless to use gloss paints in advance of the clear coat. No real advantage may be

gained and good quality varnishes, built gradually to a high sheen over several thin coats, will look just as effective (if not better) whether matt or satin paints have been applied below.

Moreover, using gloss paint at the livery stage not only dramatically increases the drying time of each phase, but also lessens the effectiveness of a subsequent layer that may not adhere as well to a shiny surface. Achieving a high-quality gloss finish is not an easy task and can prove something of a litmus test to how well an airbrush has been manufactured. Unless a near-perfect layer of paint is deposited onto a surface, the sheen will be uneven, something that will be especially visible on a gloss finish.

Gloss paints and varnishes certainly have their uses, particularly when working on larger scale, live steam or petrol-driven models as they impart a very tough finish that can be cleaned and buffed without detriment to the appearance. Models requiring hand lettering or lining will greatly benefit from the use of gloss enamels for the base colours: as long as the paint is completely hard, any mistakes with the lining can simply be wiped away with white spirit.

In contrast, matt paints tend to absorb the light, rather than acting as a reflecting surface as gloss finishes do. Thus the attention of the eye may be drawn away from any minor deficiencies in a matt coating. There is much variety in the degree of 'flatness' of different matt paints, those with larger proportions of matting agents tending towards a dusty appearance. Moreover, manufacturers' descriptions can be a little vague. For example, some products marketed as 'dull' will nonetheless maintain a slight sheen when dry, rather like 'eggshell' household paints. Conveniently, matt finishes tend to build up to full opacity sooner than gloss and, with fewer coats, delicate detail and sharp edges are preserved.

Satin paints are intended to offer something of a halfway house between 'shiny' and 'dull', although different brands interpret satin in different ways. Indeed, many of them veer too close to gloss, although this is largely a subjective matter. It is possible to inter-mix each type of paint in order to achieve the exact level of finish to suit your own tastes: adding a little matt to a gloss paint or varnish,

Choosing between matt, satin or gloss paints is a subjective issue. Matt is usually favoured when layering multiple livery elements, while a gloss coat alleviates the need for a coat of varnish prior to adding decals. With this in mind, kit-maker C-Rail Intermodal offers all of its commissioned paints (from Phoenix) in a gloss formula.

for example, will tone down an overly shiny finish. For best results, intermix paints from the same brand and formula and be aware that drying times will be affected; adding gloss will lengthen the hardening process. Clear matting agents are available from some suppliers (such as Phoenix Precision) for mixing with any paints or varnishes from that range, just a tiny amount usually being needed to take the edge off a gloss finish.

SHAKEN OR STIRRED

Ensuring that paint has been thoroughly mixed is one of the most crucial steps in the painting process and cutting corners here will only serve to produce a substandard finish. When paint is left standing, the solid pigments will begin to settle at the bottom of the container and sections of the liquid medium, such as matting agents, may also separate. Ensuring that all of the ingredients are intermixed before starting work will allow the paint to be at its optimum performance.

Different brands and formulas demand different mixing techniques, so it pays to read the information on the labels. In general, thin acrylics can simply be shaken for a few minutes as can cellulose lacquers, some brands of which include metal mixing balls within the jars to help break up any sediment and ensure an even dispersal of pigment.

Stirring is the best form of preparation for both thicker acrylics and all enamels, preferably using a dedicated paint spatula rather than a screwdriver. Indeed, anything small or purely round in section is pretty useless here as it will not disperse the paint constituents as well as a paddle-shaped spatula, especially at the speed at which a human can physically stir it. Be prepared to spend between five and ten minutes on this task, although a more convenient option is to invest in a powered stirring tool. Dedicated battery or mains-powered devices are freely available, while a cheaper alternative is to mount a short length of shaped brass rod into a mini electric drill. Care must be exercised, however, to prevent spraying the entire room with paint.

Don't forget to intermittently restir or shake the paint while you work, especially before topping-up the airbrush, as things soon start to settle after standing for a moment or two. A less obvious factor to consider is how to open and reseal a tin of paint without contaminating the contents or reduce the shelf life. Moreover, the design of the container can have a marked effect on the usefulness of the paint inside and, having trialled a vast range of paints over the years, it's been fascinating to note how manufacturers have chosen their styles of packaging: some have been incredibly ill-suited to the task while other makers have thought up innovative solutions to this problem.

In short, a jar with a screw lid is fine as long as the threads are cleaned of paint every time it is opened, while flip-top lids have an annoying habit of trapping paint around the hinge and rim, which dries and flakes back into the jar the next time it is opened. Push-on covers, such as those found on Humbrol, Revell or Phoenix tinlets, are acceptable as long as the lid and rim are cleaned scrupulously before closing. The trough around the rim is handy for stopping minor spillage but, when decanting into a mixing jar or airbrush, it is difficult to clean up. Dried paint around a lid not only leads to risks of blockages, but also shortens the useful life of the paint as the airtight seal is compromised and the paint will begin to dry out. Another important point to remember is to clean the container of dust before removing the lid, lest any debris fall into the paint.

THINNING

Virtually all hobby paint formulas require thinning before applying by airbrush. Some acrylics can be thinned with water alone, while others need a dilute mix of water and alcohol (usually isopropanol), and the ratio of alcohol to water varies according to brand. Enamel formulas also differ, especially those 'super enamels' that offer faster drying times, as do different brands of cellulose lacquers. Therefore, for reliable results always use the same brand of thinner as the paint at hand. This is not always possible, however, and a little prior experimentation will determine which paints are happy with various

Using a dedicated stirring tool is far more effective than a screwdriver. The flattened end works as a paddle for agitating the paint in the jar and can also be used to decant small amounts when mixing different colours.

Stirring paint is an important but onerous duty that can be accelerated with the use of a minidrill. This cordless Dremel tool is perfect for the job, with variable speed control and a stirring paddle improvised from a length of thick brass wire.

Some paint brands are supplied in packaging that can be prone to clogging around the lid and this can cause problems if flakes of dried paint enter and block the workings of the airbrush.

brands of thinner. For example, Lifecolor acrylic thinner is also compatible with Railmatch, Vallejo and Humbrol acrylics. On the other hand, Phoenix Precision enamels are best diluted with the same brand of thinner.

The process of airbrushing requires a particular formula of thinner to enable the paint not only to flow sufficiently through the device and be atomized satisfactorily, but also to evaporate much more quickly than thinners aimed at hand brushing, a process that generally requires a longer curing time. Quick-drying airbrush thinners are marketed by many paint-makers to speed up the painting process and these are a welcome innovation, although rapid curing is not always desirable. Cellulose paints, for example, may offer short drying times, but unless the paint can flow over the surface sufficiently before 'going off', it will be impossible to achieve a smooth coating. Enamels, too, can dry too quickly if used with some airbrushing thinners and, if aiming for a gloss finish, such products should be avoided.

The Superflow brand of thinners is recommended for use with cellulose formulas as it offers the right balance of drying time and better control over the paint flow. Cheaper cellulose thinners, on the other hand, should be used for cleaning purposes only as they evaporate far too quickly. As already mentioned, the volatile chemicals that cellulose thinners contain can cause damage to some plastics. With this in mind, the choosing of thinners is an important step, not only to ensure a match with the paint but also for safe application onto the model.

It is common to read how modellers use a set ratio of paint-to-thinners, but I've always been wary of stating such specifications as paint performance tends to differ wildly by brand and formula. Indeed, it's not uncommon for two tins of the same paint to react quite differently from each other, due to the quirks of different batches, storage conditions, ambient temperatures and so on. Manufacturers constantly update their products to maintain a competitive edge and formulas may change from year to year. All of these variables lead to a modeller having to use his or her own discretion and experience when thinning and the following chapter will look in detail at this process.

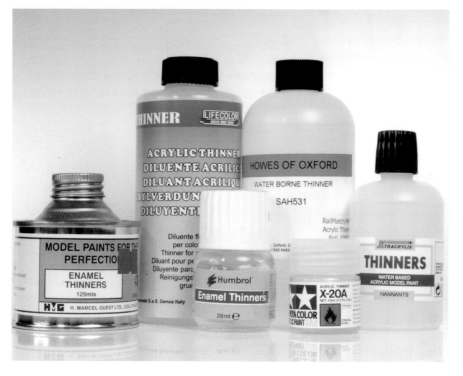

Choosing the correct thinners to suit a specific paint formula is crucial. A useful rule of thumb to remember is to make use of the same brand of thinners and paint wherever possible.

PAINT PAST ITS BEST

When I know that a paint job is to come under severe scrutiny, whether via a publication, display or as a commission, I want to ensure that the finish is as good as I can manage. With this in mind, I'm very fussy over using paint that has been hanging around for some time. As mentioned, different forms of packaging has the implication of affecting shelf life and, if a paint has begun to look a little lumpy or has formed a skin over the surface, I usually either ditch it or save it for rough scenic work, to be applied by hand.

This may be wasteful on my part as, especially in terms of enamel paints, it may still be serviceable once a film has been removed and the paint strained into a separate mixing/thinning jar. However, I find that the paint tends to behave differently once a skin has formed, usually in terms of unpredictable curing times. Additionally, the sheen may be slightly different once the paint has dried, which can be a problem if attempting to match to a previous coat of the same paint.

Some acrylic brands suffer ageing worse than others. In particular, Humbrol acrylics tend to thicken in consistency and the same pot can require thinning to a far greater degree when used a few months apart. Similarly, Lifecolor paints can take on a gritty consistency if the lid has been left off for too long. Indeed, storage conditions play an important role in the shelf life of paint, as recently illustrated by the harsh winter experienced during the writing of this book. Housed in my garden workshop, my stock of water-based paint suffered particularly badly, with some formulas freezing solid and threatening to burst their plastic jars as the contents expanded. Curiously, some remained usable once thawed while others were reduced almost to a coarse powder. Either way, I learned the lesson of storing all of my paints indoors over winter.

PAINT BRANDS

Here we shall take a quick look at the major players in the general hobby and rail-themed paint market, with a digest of their main properties, limitations and advantages. Some brands, such as Humbrol, have been around for a long time, while others may not

be widely known in model railway circles, being marketed more towards military or aviation enthusiasts. Not all may be available from your local model shop so it may be worth looking through the Useful Contacts at the rear of this book to source suppliers.

There are still many other brands out there that offer general shades or military-themed colours – Gunze Sangyo and Xtracolor, to name but a few – as well as the Chris Wesson range of cellulose-based railway paints. However, I've limited my comments to cover formulas that I've actually used in quantity over the years.

HUMBROL
Enamels
- Huge range of colours and clear varnishes
- Thin with white spirit or standard airbrushing enamel thinners
- Drying times: 1–2 hours (touch); 6–12 hours (recoating)
- Inconsistent in performance but generally provide good results

Acrylics
- Water-based equivalent of many of the enamel shades, plus small range of railway and weathering shades, mostly of Big Four, BR and Privatization eras; mostly accurate
- Thin with water or acrylic thinner
- Straining is essential before spraying
- Drying times: 20mins (touch); 6 hours (recoating)
- Reasonable results but flip-top lids liable to clogging

During the 1980s Humbrol offered a range of rail-themed enamels, but these proved short-lived, being eclipsed by the growth of specialist brands such as Railmatch and Phoenix. Instead, a spiral-bound mixing guide was published, detailing how to achieve certain rail shades by mixing existing colours. A small range of acrylic rail paints has recently been reintroduced, although the accuracy tends to be a little inconsistent.

REVELL

Enamels
- Similar range to Humbrol
- Synthetic resin enamel: thin with Revell thinners only
- Drying times: 30mins (touch); 4 hours (recoating)
- Viscosity and performance inconsistent but can produce a good finish

Acrylics
- Contain virtually no organic solvents
- Thin with water
- Drying times: 1 hour (touch); 2–3 hours (recoating)
- Results are good, as long as the paint is thinned correctly
- With no thread or hinge to the lid, decanting of the paint can be done without the risk of spillage or clogging

VALLEJO

Acrylics
- More than 200 colours, plus clear and metallic finishes
- Thin with water or acrylic thinner
- Drying times: 30mins (touch); 2–3 hours (recoating)
- Handy eyedropper style dispenser
- One of the best acrylic paints around

Among the finest of acrylic paints is the Spanish Vallejo range. Although not dealing with specific railway livery colours, there are countless options for scenic and weathering work. Vallejo also offers its paint in Flames of War-branded packs, aimed at war gamers.

TAMIYA

Acrylics
- Large colour range, but just a single clear coat option
- Use of Tamiya's own brand of thinners is essential
- Drying times: 1 hour (touch); 6 hours (recoating)
- Varying performance, but acceptable finish possible
- High alcohol content, noxious fumes and highly flammable

LIFECOLOR

Acrylics
- Large range of colours, plus clear, weathering and metallic paints; also Tensocrom translucent pigments. Small but highly accurate selection of BR and Danish Railways colours
- Dilute with Lifecolor acrylic thinners or water
- Drying times: 30mins (touch); 6–8 hours (recoating)
- Fairly consistent and good results

Despite the claims of manufacturers, not all rail-themed livery paints are entirely accurate. Lifecolor's small range of acrylic BR shades, however, is highly regarded.

Lifecolor also offers various innovative weathering and diorama packs of acrylic paints: Dust and Rust, Weathered Wood and Rail Weathering are among the most useful to railway modellers. Tensocrom weathering paints offer a unique, semi-opaque finish and can be sprayed without the need for thinning.

RAILMATCH

Enamel or acrylic
- Huge range, mostly modern, BR and Big Four, highly accurate. Also 'faded' and weathering shades available
- Thin with Railmatch enamel or acrylic thinners
- Drying times vary
- Semi-satin finish, provide excellent results
- Some paints contain lead chromate

Railmatch authentic livery and weathering shades are available in both enamel and acrylic formulas and provide excellent results. The glass jars are ideal for airbrush work as they permit decanting into a mixing/thinning container with little mess.

PHOENIX

Enamel or acrylic
- Largest – and arguably most accurate – railway livery range, including pre-Grouping and overseas liveries, also general colours, weathering shades, primers and varnishes
- Thin with Phoenix's own brand of thinners
- Drying times vary
- Dull matt, satin or gloss finishes, excellent quality
- Some paints contain lead chromate

Boasting the largest range of authentic railway shades is the Phoenix Precision Paints brand, available in 14, 50, 125 or 250ml tins. A full selection of thinners, primers, varnishes and masking products is also offered.

COM-ART

Acrylics
- Range of general and weathering colours
- Supplied ready to spray but can be thinned with water
- Drying time: 30mins
- Convenient and high quality

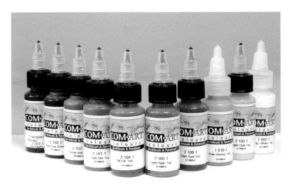

Com-Art water-based paints are pre-thinned ready for spraying, making them highly convenient. A good range of general colours is available, along with this useful pack of weathering shades.

SAFETY ISSUES

No matter what type of paint is being used, or in what quantity, you must take precautions to protect the health of yourself and those around you. As mentioned in the previous chapter, working in a well-ventilated area and the use of a face mask at all times is vital. Where possible, avoid skin contact with paints, thinners and airbrush cleaning solvents by wearing disposable latex gloves, while there's always a risk of paints and thinners splashing into the face when decanting and mixing, so eye protection should also be considered. I once managed to get cellulose thinners in my eyes and the discomfort was, to put it mildly, extreme. Serious damage could have arisen had I not had quick access to clean water to immediately rinse the affected eye, proving the worth of having a small First Aid kit in the workshop.

REFLECTIONS ON PAINT

Each paint brand and formula has its own quirks, whether in terms of viscosity, sheen, opacity or even in the type of container in which it is supplied. Faster drying times are either a blessing or a curse and it pays to build up a little experience of a brand or formula before embarking on a modelling project, familiarizing yourself with its performance and limitations. Some brands can be frustratingly inconsistent and the knowledge of how to compensate for these shortcomings is borne of practice and persistence.

It's easy to fall into brand loyalty, favouring a paint whose properties have become familiar. However, it doesn't hurt to broaden your horizons a little by trialling some new formulas or brands. It's not that long ago that I only ever used enamels for the vast majority of my modelling work, but I've come to appreciate the advantages of acrylics and, having built a proficiency in airbrushing, embraced cellulose primers and lacquers too.

Ensuring a sufficient supply of paint is another important consideration, as running out halfway through a project can be very frustrating. On average, a typical 15ml tinlet of paint will provide enough to cover two average OO locomotives in an all-over livery. More grandiose projects may need a larger supply and approaching the manufacturers directly may reveal that bulk quantities can be ordered.

Another easy trap to fall into is relying on a paint brand's description of its colour. Just because a tin is labelled as 'British Army Reflective Green' doesn't mean that it can only be used to recreate a military uniform: it may have a multitude of uses in scenic or weathering tasks. This opens up a broader range of paints that may be marketed purely at military or aircraft modellers. Your local art shop will doubtless have numerous liquid paints, inks and dyes that can easily be applied via an airbrush to good effect. Experimentation is, after all, part of the fun of this hobby.

CHAPTER FOUR

GETTING STARTED

Now that we've covered the most pertinent background information relating to airbrushes, equipment and finishes, it's high time that we made a start in spraying. There are, however, a few important factors to consider. Firstly, take a moment or two to check that your chosen spraying set-up is prepared properly, with hose connections made, moisture filters in place and plenty of compressed air on hand. Adequate paint, thinners and cleaning materials should also be provided along with plenty of ventilation and a means of preventing fume inhalation.

Secondly, paints must also be suitably prepared and achieving the right consistency is one of the most fundamental aspects of airbrushing. If the paint is too thick, the airbrush will not atomize it properly. Conversely, if it's too thin then the paint will run over the surface in an uncontrollable flow. These factors do not exist in isolation, but are interdependent upon the air pressure also being correctly set. If the pressure is too high, the paint will be projected so quickly that it will either dry in mid-air and give a rough finish, or disturb the paint on the surface, literally blowing it off the model. An excessively low pressure will mean that the paint is not mixed with the air sufficiently to achieve a fine and even mist, leading to the paint 'spattering' out of the airbrush.

Add to this the importance of the distance between airbrush tip and subject and the whole process begins to sound highly complicated. Moreover, the fact that all of these variables must be borne in mind for even the most mundane of spraying tasks, explains why so many people are turned off by airbrushing after only a limited time and without adequate practical guidance. However, practice and perseverance will soon pay off.

WHY THIN?

As we discussed in the preceding pages, paint preparation can be something of a challenge to the unwary, not least because there are few hard and fast rules for thinning paint for airbrush use. Variations in formulas and the type of finish required (flat coats, high gloss or weathering mists, for instance) all play a role in how the paint must be treated. Experience will bring with it a degree of intuition as to how and when paint can be prepared, but this is only achieved by devoting time to the pursuit of this knowledge.

A modicum of trial and error in paint thinning will reveal some or all of the following results.

If paint is too thick:
- Won't spray at all, clogging the airbrush
- Paint will spatter from airbrush leaving uneven or messy finish
- May clog surface detail
- Take longer to dry
- Harder to spray sharp, fine lines or soft-edged shapes
- Less control
- Airbrush more difficult to clean

If paint is too thin:
- Semi-opaque finish
- Need more coats to build up a flat coat, potentially obliterating fine details
- Risk of runs on surface
- Less control

Reaching something of a middle route between the ills of thicker or thinner viscosities is the goal, although there is no holy grail of perfection in the form of an exact paint-thinner ratio, as air pressure can be tweaked a little to compensate for a thicker or thinner formula. Each factor remains fluid within certain parentheses: if the airbrush is struggling to atomize the paint, dial in a little extra power from the air source and that should solve the problem, but don't be tempted to turn the pressure up further than a few notches as the problems of high pressure and prematurely drying paint will rear its head.

Paint can only take being thinned to a given ratio before it starts to lose many of its important properties, most notably the ability of the pigments and solvent to adhere properly. Again, a little tinkering with the air valve can help with a thinner liquid, lowering the pressure as far as possible until good results are achieved.

MIXING AND THINNING

Our primary concern is to ensure that the paint is thoroughly mixed within its container, shaking or stirring to disperse the pigments, whereupon decanting into a separate mixing jar will offer many advantages: cleaning-up will be easier and wastage minimized. Additionally, if using a lidded container, the prepared paint can be stored for a short time without detrimental effects (it will just need stirring or shaking again before reuse).

Airbrush makers invariably offer various mixing jars with matching screw-top lids, although empty paint containers, such as Railmatch jars, can also be pressed into use. Glass or clear plastic vessels are preferred as it's helpful to be able to see inside the jar to gauge the viscosity of the fluid.

As paint packaging varies wildly in its convenience, the simple act of pouring some of the contents into a different receptacle is not always easy. Steel tinlets with anti-spill troughs around the edge of the lid actually create more mess. Other jars can be equally annoying and the use of a pipette, syringe, spatula or even a small spoon will eliminate much of this hassle. Some paints, on the other hand, offer assistance by sporting the eyedropper style of packaging (as seen on Vallejo and Com-Art acrylics) that is especially suited to airbrush use.

Straining paint at this stage is not compulsory, especially if a fresh jar or tin is being used, but if there is any suspicion of solid matter in the paint, then it will likely reveal itself in the stirring stage. Both acrylics and enamels can be prone to 'lumpiness' and if there is any dried paint visible around the rim of the jar, then some of it is bound to fall into the mixing vessel. Proprietary paint strainers are widely available, although one or two tea strainers can be a cheaper alternative.

Using a separate container to mix and thin paint is a convenient way of ensuring that the fluid is in optimum condition before loading into the airbrush. Lidded jars are freely available, while empty paint containers can also be cleaned and given a new lease of life. Having a tight-fitting lid allows thinned paint to be kept for a short time between coats.

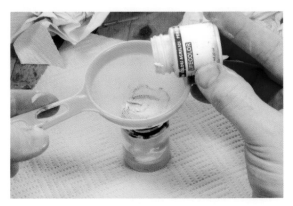

Straining paint is not always necessary but it can save a lot of frustration as airbrushes are easily blocked by even the smallest of solid particles. Paint filters can be expensive, but a cheap tea strainer is equally effective. To ensure that even the smallest particles are intercepted, place a couple of strainers on top of each other to reduce the size of the perforations.

It's amazing what can be extracted from a seemingly healthy jar of paint. The strainer can then be cleaned in thinners.

Cylindrical paint filters such as this Badger unit are offered for siphon-fed airbrushes and are a last line of defence against paint impurities. The fine steel mesh offers more resistance to harsh cleaning solvents than cheap tea strainers.

With the paint now in the mixing jar and in tip-top condition, thinner can be introduced by means of a pipette or syringe, adding just a few drops at a time. Stir for a few moments and then add a further amount. Repeat this process, intermittently checking the viscosity by waggling the jar from side to side (not too vigorously as to cause a spillage), looking out for the point when the paint takes on the thickness of semi-skimmed milk.

My own tried-and-trusted method involves watching how the paint drips from the end of a spatula: if it falls in small self-contained blobs then it's ready for use. If it runs off the tool slowly in long, thick droplets, then further thinning is needed. When the paint flows off the spatula in an uncontrollable torrent, then it has been thinned too much. The accompanying images perhaps describe this test better than mere words can. This decidedly un-scientific method is nonetheless a fairly accurate and reliable guide.

The amount of time and thinners needed to reach the correct viscosity differs widely according to paint brand and formula, while the age of the paint and ambient temperature also play a role. Paint can be thinned directly within the airbrush's paint cup, but I rarely do this, even when in a hurry. I know of a few other painters who do it with no problems but it smacks of bad practice to me.

If you are tempted to try it, make sure the thinners go in first or the airbrush will quickly clog up. Follow with the paint and then a little more thinners as necessary, stirring or agitating until happy with the mixture.

Gauging how much paint will be needed for a particular exercise is another skill that comes with experience. In keeping with my slightly haphazard approach to specifications, I know that I can usually cover a OO gauge locomotive in an overall coat of BR blue or green with a three-quarter full 250ml jar of thinned enamel, giving me enough to build up several light coats.

Running out of paint midway through a job is not the end of the world, especially when working with enamels whose slow drying time is more forgiving of such temporary hitches. As long as you don't take too long about mixing and thinning a fresh supply, acrylics shouldn't be a problem either. Having an excess of thinned paint is a worse sin; unless it's used within a week or so, it will lose its 'goodness' and prove unreliable. Indeed, draining unused leftovers back into the original container is not recommended as it will affect the performance of the entire tin.

Once you're happy with the paint mix, add it to the airbrush paint cup or jar and then we're ready to go.

The ease of decanting paint into the mixing jar depends largely on the design of the container. Eye-dropper style bottles (as offered by Com-Art and Vallejo) are the most convenient, with screw-top jars a close second (Railmatch and Lifecolor among others). However, the familiar little tinlets with their anti-spill troughs can prove tricky unless the paint is extracted by means of a syringe, spatula or a 'dropper' tool such as this from a Lifecolor Master Mixer pack.

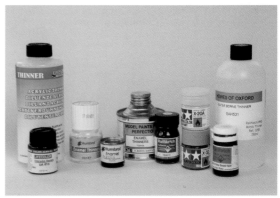

Choosing the right thinner to suit the paint is critical and the only route that offers 100 per cent success is to employ thinners of the same brand and formula as the paint.

Add thinners to the paint a few drops at a time using a syringe or pipette and stir vigorously. Keep a few different pipettes at hand for dealing with different types of thinners to avoid cross-contamination.

Getting the paint to the correct viscosity is one of the keys to successful spraying. The paint should be thinned gradually until it reaches the consistency of milk, although various types and brands of paint will take a different amount of thinners before this is achieved. One of the best ways of gauging the mix is to employ a 'drip test', regarding how well the fluid falls from the end of the stirring tool. If it struggles to drip – like this – then the paint is too thick.

If the paint falls freely in small, self-contained blobs and clings to the spatula in a light film, as depicted in this view, then it's ready for spraying.

If it pours off the spatula in an uncontrollable torrent, then it's too thin. Also, the metal of the tool appears clean as the paint pours off the surface. This method may seem a little primitive but it has proved reliable over the years.

When happy with the thickness of the paint, it can be poured into the receptacle of the airbrush, taking care not to spill any. Wipe away any paint from around the rim of the cup before fixing the lid in place.

THE PAINT-AIR MIX

The vast majority of craft and hobby paints require a pressure range of 10–25psi for correct atomization and delivery from an airbrush, provided that the liquid is thinned to the right consistency. As mentioned in Chapter 2, small electric compressors can provide anything from 1–100psi depending on the capacity of the machine, but it's the lower end of the range that we need for model-making purposes.

I'm reluctant to assume that all readers are equipped with a pressure gauge, but such a device does make the whole process simpler, especially for beginners. As a basic reference point, I usually start a session by setting the compressor to an output of 15psi and, after loading the airbrush with paint, a test is made on a scrap of card, making a small increase or decrease in pressure until I'm happy that the paint is flowing correctly. If a gauge is not available, a basic but effective way of working is to turn down the pressure as far as possible until no paint is emitted; then gradually increase the pressure until the paint starts to flow, stopping when optimum performance is reached. To put things more succinctly, we're basically aiming for the paint to flow at the lowest pressure possible.

GET TO KNOW YOUR AIRBRUSH

In order to gain the best results from an airbrush, the tool should feel familiar and comfortable, leaving your mind to concentrate on the task in hand rather than the apparatus. The late football manager Brian Clough is reported to have encouraged his players to sleep with a football in order to foster a feel and companionship with the object and it's not too fanciful to draw a similarity here. Any experienced craftsman will tell you how he or she has favourite tools that become almost an extension of their limbs, permitting total focus on their work. Therefore, getting used to holding an airbrush is an important factor and it won't hurt to sit and pretend to paint with it for a time, moving it about gently and operating the trigger to gain an understanding of how the various parts move under gentle pressure. Virtually all spraying techniques require gentle movements of the arm, so a little practise will help.

While the basic design of airbrush is fairly universal, there are still enough minor variations to differentiate between individual models. Apart from the budget-priced external mix spray guns, most airbrushes are designed to be held and controlled in a similar manner to a pen. The thumb and fingers steady the tool, while the index finger should sit lightly on the trigger (pistol grip tools differ slightly as the device is held like a gun). Whatever the airbrush, the hand and wrist must be kept fairly relaxed at all times.

The location and size of the paint jar or cup plays a major part in how the tool is handled, not least if the user's view is obstructed by it. Such appendages also dictate how easily the tool can reach into narrow spots or, if using a bottom-feeding jar, how high the model will have to be sat above the work surface to permit an upward angle of attack. Additionally, it can be helpful to pass the air hose over your wrist to keep it out of the way and permit freer movement.

Another important comfort factor concerns your standing or sitting position during painting. Personally, I prefer to stand for most jobs as it allows free movement around the subject, although I will pull up a stool for longer, delicate tasks such as weathering or detail work. Incidentally, my workbench and spray booth are set quite high above the workshop floor to suit my standing position and to minimize the need for leaning over, which can soon prove fatiguing.

With everything connected and all valves open, switch on the air supply and depress the trigger, aiming the nozzle away from you. If air is being emitted properly, then add a little clean water into the paint cup and watch how the jet appears when the trigger is pressed. Adjust the flow of fluid, according to the specific workings of your airbrush, regarding the change in the volume and shape of the emissions. Additionally, varying the air pressure where possible will also cause a visible change in the airbrush's output. Not only will this exercise reveal whether your set-up is operating properly, but will help in the familiarization of your airbrush's workings. If there is something amiss, refer to the troubleshooting guide on page 72 for help in identifying the possible cause.

Take time to familiarize yourself with the feel of your airbrush as well as working out what all the buttons do! Read the instructions fully and practise dismantling and rebuilding the tool, appreciating what each part is for and how it works. Such knowledge will smoothe our path through the waters ahead.

Keeping the airbrush steady in one hand is not easy for most people and a helping hand can be added by supporting the ball of the painting hand and resting an elbow on the work surface. Just be sure that you relax and are able to move the tool around freely. Passing the air hose over the wrist keeps it out of the way.

BASIC EXERCISES

Talk of air pressure and paint-thinner ratios can seem bewildering to a novice, so, when setting out on your first spraying forays, why not make life easier and eliminate one of these factors. The use of pre-thinned paints, formulated especially for airbrush use, leaves us to concentrate solely on the matters of air pressure and spraying distance. There are plenty to choose from in the ranges of Com-Art or Badger and even a few drops of food dye can be mixed with water to make a suitable painting medium.

Propping a sheet of paper or card on something akin to an easel makes for a good proving ground. Mount the paper as close to vertical as possible to mimic how we will usually paint a three-dimensional object and take up your seated or standing position in front of the subject. With paint loaded and the air switched on, start spraying onto the blank 'canvas' in freeform fashion to see what happens. Play around with different air pressures and volumes of paint flow, as far as your set-up permits, noting how these changes affect the patterns emerging onto the paper. Note also how distance affects the width and shape of the spray pattern landing on the surface.

Pretty soon an appreciation of the tool's behaviour will be obtained and, when you're ready, moving on to trying out some specific tasks will help to cement a few basic skills. Attempting to form rows of straight lines is a good task to start with, teaching control of the hand and an appreciation of the importance of both distance and air pressure. Use your other arm to help steady the airbrush if necessary, cupping the left hand under the right wrist (or vice versa for those readers of a 'south paw' leaning), which will also act as something of a height gauge if the elbow is rested on the work surface and moved from side to side in tandem with the airbrush.

Progressing to freehand patterns teaches not only control of positioning but also use of the trigger, introducing paint when and where it's needed without depositing blobs or runs of excess paint. Meanwhile, working with the airbrush set at an angle to the subject also creates its own effects and, furthermore, masking a variety of basic shapes will help in the practice of shading and highlighting.

Eliminating the need to judge paint viscosity as well as other vital factors such as air pressure, paint flow and spraying distance makes learning the basics much easier. While inks and food dye can be used (added to water), there are also certain paint formulas designed specifically for airbrush use without the need for thinning. Badger and Com-Art are among those who offer such paints.

Taking your first steps in spraying paint onto a subject is best done on a sheet of card or paper, preferably propped up on an improvised easel. Tape the corners of the paper down to prevent it blowing around and support your painting hand to keep the tool steady.

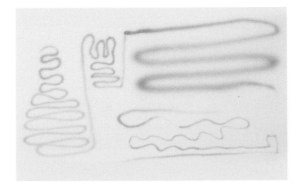

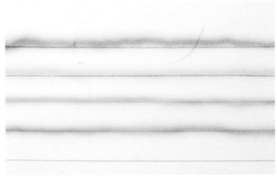

With paint in the airbrush and the pressure set fairly low (around 15psi), play around by creating shapes and lines, simply to see how the paint goes onto the surface. Note how changes in pressure and paint flow affect the output. Start about 150mm (6in) from the surface and see what happens when you move the airbrush closer and further away.

Practising painting straight lines is a good starting point for learning control and an appreciation of both distance and air pressure. Use lined paper or rule pencil lines onto a sheet of card before attempting to follow them, maintaining the width of each line by keeping paint flow and distance between airbrush and surface consistent.

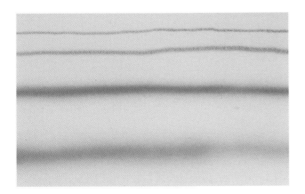

Create narrow lines by getting up close to the surface. The upper line in this view was created with the nozzle around 6mm from the surface. Only a small amount of paint is required, so adjust the flow accordingly and keep the air pressure as low as possible to prevent the paint being blown back against the nozzle at such a close distance. The tool has gradually moved further away (keeping the same level of paint and airflow) and so the thickness of the lines has increased while also losing their definition.

While creating this pattern, the paint flow has been increased gradually at the same time as the airbrush was being moved further away – a tricky technique to master. Note how the corners of each line appear darker as the airbrush dwells slightly before changing direction. Ideally, the paint flow should be eased momentarily at these points.

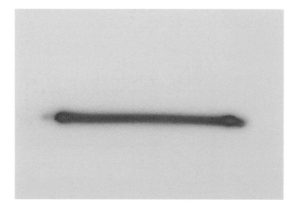

Dumb-bell shapes such as this are produced by the airbrush momentarily standing still at the end of each sweep. From this it can be appreciated why it's best to carry on past the end of a subject before returning in the opposite direction, avoiding excess paint build-up and promoting a more even coating.

Layering multiple coats over the same area will increase the paint's opacity, although each coat should be given a short break of a minute or two to dry out. Angling the airbrush away from the edge of the paper introduces a fading effect.

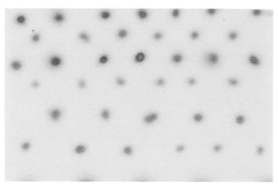

If using a double-action airbrush, then another useful technique to learn is how to lay small spots of paint accurately onto the surface. Begin by holding the nozzle about 100mm from the subject and introduce the air by pressing the trigger. Momentarily draw back the trigger to release a small amount of paint before moving the trigger back again, but without cutting off the air altogether for a second or two. This latter instruction will help to prevent any paint spattering at the end of the cycle, thus ruining the intended effect. It may take a little practise to master, but this will prove handy during many weathering tasks.

Attempting to write words in a script style is another good way of mastering control of paint flow and hand movement. With the nozzle up close to the surface, the airbrush must be kept moving to avoid an excess of paint building up.

FLAT COATS

Creating unique painting effects such as those described above is only part of the airbrush's repertoire and, unless you envisage using your set-up only for weathering purposes, then the process of achieving even coats of solid colour should also be mastered. Practise on a flat surface to begin with, building up the paint in numerous light coats with the nozzle remaining a consistent 150–200mm (6–8in) from the surface. Allow each layer to dry before recoating and work until the colour is fully opaque, keeping the airbrush moving constantly at a steady pace.

After the first two or three coats, it now becomes crucial to get the paint on the surface looking slightly wet. There can be a somewhat fine line between the wetness that we seek and an excess of paint that will start to run: hence why low air pressure and light individual layers are important. Additionally, working in a position where light is reflected from the subject's surface greatly helps the eye to discern how wet the paint is looking. A dull reflection means that the airbrush is too far away, the air pressure too high or that the paint has not been thinned sufficiently. If it has a uniformly moist look, even just for a few seconds before it

starts to dry, then we're on the right track. Unless this wet-look is achieved during application, a smooth, even finish will not result.

Progressing from a flat surface to a three-dimensional object will introduce different challenges. Sourcing some scrap toys, models or plastic packaging will provide suitable test-beds for your technique, noting how internal corners require the airbrush to be moved from its usual perpendicular angle from the surface. Ensuring that excess paint does not build up in recesses is also important.

Please be patient and practise these basic steps repeatedly and you shall be rewarded with a better grounding in the theory and practice of airbrushing. Indeed, everything from now on is but a variation and development of these techniques. Hopefully, the importance of air pressure and its relationship with paint performance should now be appreciated. So too should be the practical effects of distance between airbrush and subject as well as the angle of approach and rate of movement across the subject.

Incidentally, the water-based paint recommended for use during these exercises is simple to flush out of the airbrush using plenty of clean water. For a more thorough discussion on cleaning the airbrush, see Chapter 7.

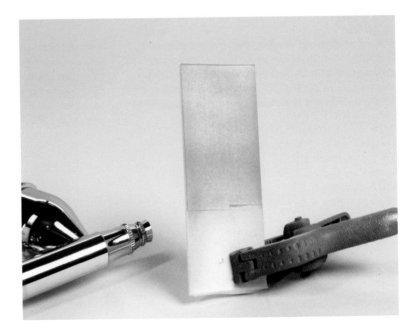

For flat coatings, an even layering of paint is needed, built up over a succession of light coats. Allow sufficient time in between for each to dry out and work the airbrush from side to side in straight passes, rather than random movements that will create an uneven surface. The initial coats will appear misty and translucent, but this is natural and the temptation to rush must be ignored.

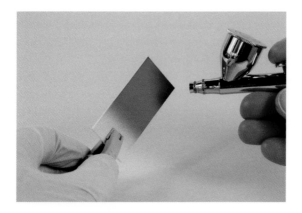

Be prepared to apply many light coats before the colour starts to build. At this stage, the swatch has already received around six layers, with many more necessary.

As the paint finally begins to achieve opacity, it's necessary to get the paint going onto the surface looking slightly wet. Remember to keep the layers light and the spraying distance constant, repeating until the colour is satisfactory.

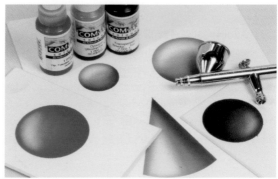

Cutting shapes into masking film creates stencils and using these gives the opportunity to practise a different set of techniques, such as shading. Use a sharp blade to cut the film and apply it to paper or card (masking film is discussed further in Chapter 8).

Areas of light and shade can be built up using a single colour of paint, relying on the density of coats to create tonal variety. Try a selection of circles, cones, cubes or other shapes: this is how I learnt how to use an airbrush at art school and I can vouch for its usefulness.

Concentrating the layers of paint in areas of shade – in this case around the edges of the circle – builds the colour to full opacity, while the highlights are achieved by simply limiting the amount of paint applied. This simple exercise will teach you a lot about how an airbrush works and how the movement of your arm and hand directly affects the way that paint reaches the surface. For shapes such as this, the tool must be moved in a series of smooth arcs in both a clockwise and anti-clockwise direction.

When you feel confident enough to start work on a three-dimensional object, making use of spare bodyshells or defunct models is a good way to practise your technique without fear of ruining an expensive model. Obtained either from swapmeets, exhibitions or via eBay, anything will do as long as it looks something like a train! Die-cast models, such as old Tri-ang products, are especially handy as the metal bodyshells can be painted and stripped (with Nitromors) as often as you like.

This trusty old Lima wagon has been my test surface for years, allowing paint, air pressure and colour shade to be checked before working on the main subject. Now and again a bath of model paint stripper restores the vehicle to its naked state for further use.

QUICK TROUBLESHOOTING GUIDE

Having problems? The solution could be one or more of the following:

No paint emerging
- Nozzle or fluid paths may be blocked: clean the airbrush and try again
- Check air supply, connectors and valves
- Breather hole in the paint cup may be blocked
- Not enough paint in cup (if using a siphon-fed airbrush)
- Air pressure too low

No air
- Check air source is 'on' or gas canister is charged
- Check all hoses, connections and valves
- Ensure trigger installed properly (refer to airbrush's instructions)

Paint spatters
- Poorly thinned paint
- Clogged nozzle
- Trigger being released too quickly
- Needle may be damaged

Runs and puddles
- Paint too thin

- Spraying too close to surface
- Spraying too much paint at once – ease off the paint control
- Airbrush not kept moving during spraying

Rough paint finish
- Air pressure too high
- Airbrush is too far from subject
- Paint too thick
- Nozzle may be blocked

Paint creeps out in a 'spider' effect
- Airbrush is too close to the subject
- Paint too thin
- Air pressure too high

Bubbles appearing in the paint cup
- Fluid paths or nozzle may be blocked or restricted, causing blow-back into the cup
- Needle lock nut may be loose

Dumb-bell shaped lines
- Airbrush remaining static at beginning and end of sweep

If the paint is too thick or the air pressure insufficient, the paint will not be sufficiently atomized to ensure a smooth flow through the airbrush nozzle. A 'spatter' effect is the result.

When too much thinner has been added, the paint will be at risk of running when it hits the surface. This can also happen if an excess of paint is applied too soon, regardless of how well it has been thinned.

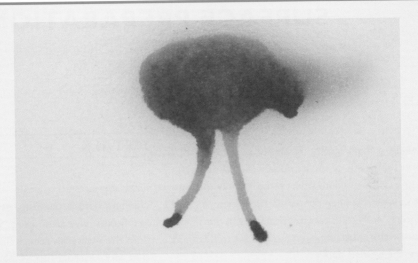

High air pressure leads to the paint drying too quickly, often while it is still in mid-air. This, along with an excessive distance between the nozzle and subject, produces a rough, uneven finish known as 'orange peel'.

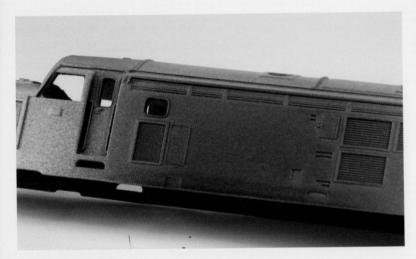

This 'spider' effect is caused by an excess of paint being applied too close to the surface.

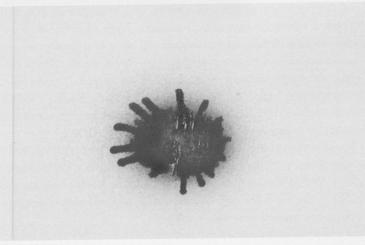

CHAPTER FIVE

SURFACE PREPARATION

Achieving a high-quality airbrushed finish is not beyond the reach of most modellers, although the level of success depends on how thoroughly the subject's surface has been prepared. Moreover, a good paint job is likely to draw attention to even the slightest flaw in the substrate, so it pays to get things right before the paint is applied.

Whether over-painting a factory finish, stripping away old paint or starting with bare materials, various common principles apply. Along with cleanliness and attention to detail, all glue joints must be clean and tidy, while any modified areas should be abraded to a super-smooth finish, especially where filler has been applied. Wherever abrasives are used, dust and debris must be washed away from all nooks and crannies. Similarly, deposits of grease, oil or adhesive residues must also be removed to help subsequent layers of paint adhere to the surface.

PLASTICS AND RESIN

The use of polyurethane resin in kits and components has increased markedly over recent years and anyone who works with this material will soon learn a few valuable lessons regarding painting and finishing. Firstly, thorough cleaning is essential, even before construction begins, as there will be chemical residues present from the casting process. Such additives are introduced to the material to aid removal from a mould and it is this 'non-stick' coating that interferes with both adhesives and paint. Everything should be washed again after assembly and left to dry for a few days before the first primer coats are applied. Injection-moulded plastic kits are prone to similar problems and the same precautions should be observed.

METALS

Cast or etched metals also require thorough cleaning before painting, especially where solders and fluxes have been used, as they contain acids to help the molten material flow freely, it is essential that any residual flux is neutralized. Additionally, deposits of limescale, oil and grease will cause problems, some of which may not surface until after the paint has been applied. Metals such as brass, copper and nickel silver tend to tarnish when left exposed to the atmosphere and the surface coating that develops may also hinder the painting process. Therefore, if a kit has been stood for some time in an unfinished state, be sure to clean it again before work resumes and again upon completion, prior to preliminary primer coats.

If the model has not been treated sufficiently, then patches in the paint will appear soon after spraying. Usually looking like dark, wet puddles on the paint's surface, there is no other recourse than to strip away this paint and start again. Never succumb to the temptation to believe that a further layer of paint will cure any problem: it won't. In fact, it will often make matters worse and simply leave more paint to remove before the job can be restarted. Frustratingly, signs of trouble may take a day or two to manifest, especially where trapped moisture has started to seep out of a restricted space or a trace of acidic flux begins to degrade the paint coating. As a precaution, it may be wise to leave a model for a week or so following the first primer coat to check that nothing untoward happens before progressing.

Without thorough surface preparation, followed by cleansing and degreasing, the painting process can prove frustrating. This white-metal kit proved just so, with a mixture of my own laxness and suspected impurities in the alloy causing the paint to refuse to set. I hadn't noticed any patches in the grey priming coat and continued the painting process until these dark patches appeared.

Instead of opting for completely stripping the paint back to the bare metal and going through the cleaning process again, I chose to strip only the affected areas and cleansing as best I could. This half-hearted approach was not rewarded by success.

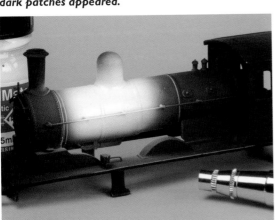

While the problem seemed to have been cured in most places, the side of the boiler still persisted in shedding its paint. Another local rub-down followed, along with the application of plenty of strong solvents (cellulose thinners). A small area of primer followed and the strength of a good airbrush revealed itself with its ability to seamlessly blend both this extra undercoat and top coats of black with the original finish, aided by some light work with Micromesh abrasives.

Happily, this particular project worked out well, but a few important lessons were confirmed. Taking shortcuts invariably leads to further problems down the line; if the model had simply been stripped back and deep-cleaned again, I would have saved myself two or three days' extra work.

FILLERS

There are few modelling tasks where some form of filling putty will not be required. Basic kit assembly, rolling stock modification and countless other jobs all see the need for small (or large) gaps to be filled.

Choosing the right filler for the job is important, not least as many single-pack fillers are designed to chemically soften the surface of a plastic model to encourage proper adhesion. Such action can have a drastic effect, especially if applied over a pre-painted surface. Although any disturbed paint or softened plastic will eventually harden, the finish will have been damaged and the only solution is to rub down the affected area, reprime and repaint.

Brands such as Humbrol, Revell, Vallejo and Squadron each offer good quality single-pack (ready-to-use) filling putties for use on plastic models. Each of these can also be applied with good results to pre-primed metal surfaces. Certain automotive filling compounds, such as knifing putty, are also ideal for modelling use as they're designed to take a highly polished surface from abrasives. Being cellulose based, curing times are short, although they can be more aggressive towards plastics or painted surfaces than hobby-grade fillers. Testing on a scrap of similar material beforehand is advised.

Twin-pack formulas, such as Milliput epoxy putty, have the minor disadvantage of needing to be mixed before use, but they set much harder and thus can be carved, drilled, machined, filed, sawn or tapped. They are also water, oil, fuel and heat resistant while the curing time differs between brands and ambient temperature. Whatever brand is used, it's often best to wait around twenty-four hours before attempting to work the putty with tools, especially if applied to more than a millimetre in depth. Epoxy putties adhere well to bare metals and employing water as a lubricant when mixing and sculpting will produce a smoother finish.

Virtually all fillers shrink while setting, so attempting to create a perfect finish before the putty dries out is a waste of time. Rather, leave the material slightly proud of the surface, to be worked back flush with files and abrasives later. Allow the stated curing

time to elapse before sanding or filing and build up deeper layers (more than 2mm depth) in stages, with each previous application having cured completely.

The slightly porous nature of fillers will become apparent when the first layers of primer or paint are applied, usually showing as a little darker than the surrounding areas. This is not a problem, merely highlighting the need for adequate primer coats under any new paint. Once the first coat is dry, a light rub down may be required and a little extra primer applied over the affected areas. Priming will be discussed in detail in the following chapter.

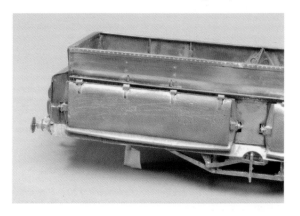

Kits often incorporate more than one type of material, be it different plastic compounds or varying metals. Not only can certain vehicular subjects provide a maze of nooks and crannies in which to trap fluids and debris, so the materials themselves can contain flaws that must be addressed before painting.

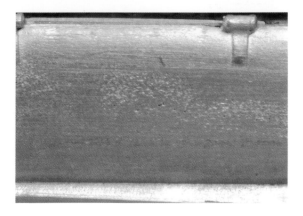

White-metal castings are particularly susceptible to pitting and other irregularities, regardless of the quality of manufacture.

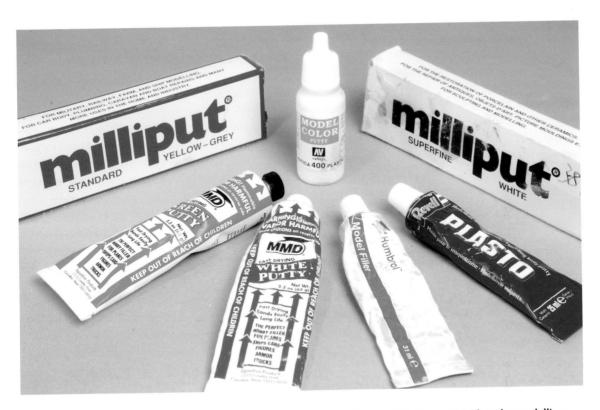

There are many different brands and formulas of filling putty on the market. Those aimed at the modelling and hobby market are recommended as they are likely to be safe for use with most plastics. Some brands simply will not take a highly polished finish, whatever fine abrasives are employed, while others will create a super-smooth surface, sometimes better than that of the surrounding material. Automotive fillers are also handy, although these should be used with care.

Other than epoxy putties and some automotive products, most fillers struggle to adhere well to metal surfaces. This is not a problem, however, as an initial coat of primer will provide a suitable background for hobby fillers. This green putty from Squadron is useful as it is highly visible against dull priming paints, being a helpful feature when rubbing down and checking for flatness.

ABRASIVES

Abrasives are necessary for many tasks, from repairing scratched or rough surfaces, levelling and smoothing areas of filler or 'keying' a previously applied finish to allow further coats of paint to adhere. A vast choice of abrasive papers, sanding sticks, polishing cloths and wire wool is available, in a variety of grades.

Wet-or-dry paper is, perhaps, one of the most commonly known abrasives and is suitable for work on virtually any material. Used wet, the paper's grit is kept free of blockages (regular rinsing with clean water is essential), thus prolonging its useful life and helping to produce a finer finish. It will be helpful to have a choice of grades at hand, ranging from 200grit (coarse) down to 4,000grit (fine), with the finer grades always used with water as a lubricant. Be sure to work through each grade in turn, as jumping to a finer grit too soon will produce a poor finish.

A drawback of regular wet-or-dry is that the paper backing will begin to degrade with repeated wetting and folding. A more versatile alternative is Micromesh, a range of ultra-fine abrasives backed by a rubberized cloth. Being both waterproof and highly flexible, Micromesh is offered in a choice of grades or in multi-packs of different grits. It must always be used with water and the manufacturer recommends that the abrading action should be carried out with movements in one direction only, rather than the more usual circular motion.

Self-lubricating abrasives can also be found, such as the Lubrasil range of paper-backed, silicone impregnated sheets. Without the need for wetting, the sheets are long-lasting and durable, producing a supremely smooth surface to virtually all materials. Available in a wide range of grit grades, these papers are not so freely available, being confined to specialist cabinetmaker and luthier suppliers (one such source is listed in the Useful Contacts).

Abrasive paper or cloth benefits from being used with a backing pad of foam or cork, rather than wrapped around a finger. The flat backing promotes a uniform surface on the subject, although this is not always possible in confined areas. Improvising your own sanding stick is not difficult, using double-sided tape to fix strips of abrasive paper to a shaped backing pad. Moreover, having a few of these at hand, with different grits on each, will speed up many a preparation job.

A further option is to make use of manicurists' sanding and polishing pads, as available from cosmetic counters and pharmacists. Often packaged as multi-sided buffing tools, they offer an economical and easy to use alternative with a variety of grades mounted on foam backing that is ideal for delicate tasks.

Wire wool is good for reaching into tight corners and dealing with irregular-shaped objects, although it can be an awkward job to remove all of the tiny fibres emitted during use. Well suited to de-nibbing (removing any small lumps and bumps from previous paint layers), as well as 'keying' a factory finish before repainting, delicate surface detail can also be preserved if used gently. In common with abrasive papers, wire wool is available in various grades, with 00000grit being the most appropriate for model work.

Abrasives come in different grades and forms, from paper- and cloth-backed sheets, to sanding sticks and pads. Keeping a stock of various grits will be worthwhile.

Where possible, using abrasive papers over a cork or foam sanding block will not only produce a more consistent finish, but will prolong the life of the abrasive. Sheets of Micromesh are an excellent resource and, when lubricated with water, produce superb results.

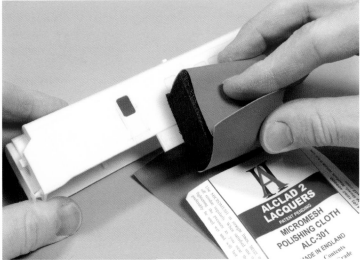

It's not always possible to use a sanding block, especially in confined areas, but you can make your own easily enough. This old paintbrush handle has been shaped and fitted with a small pad of 240grit wet-or-dry paper, fixed with superglue. The shape of the pad allows it to fit into awkward corners. I have a few of these, with varying grades of abrasive attached.

Manicurists' sanding and buffing sticks are freely available from chemists and cosmetics counters and are a cheap and versatile form of abrasive.

Patient filling and rubbing down, with various grades of sanding sticks and Micromesh sheets, followed by thorough cleaning, is rewarded by a super-smooth finish. This will form the basis for a quality paint job.

With livery colours and varnish coats applied, this wagon has received a finish befitting the excellence of the kit (a Dave Bradwell product).

Wire wool is another excellent abrasive resource, especially for flattening and 'keying' factory finishes for subsequent refinishing. However, it creates plenty of mess and the small metallic particles can prove damaging to any electrical or mechanical parts.

Of special note is the importance of keeping wire wool – and the debris produced from its use – away from all mechanical and electrical components. The fine particles can easily find their way inside electric motors or circuit boards and, being metallic, will cause short-circuits. Unexpectedly, wire wool can also be highly flammable, something that I only discovered after setting fire to my workbench a few years ago. After discarding a handful onto the bench top, the wool came into contact with the exposed terminals of a standard 9V battery. The wire instantly glowed incandescent, heating the bundle to an extreme temperature that not only scorched the wooden bench but also ignited some sheets of paper nearby. Luckily, I noticed the burning straightaway and took emergency action but, given that there were plenty of highly flammable solvents in close proximity, it could have been very serious. Therefore I'd recommend storing all wire wool in sealed bags and away from any sparking hazards or electrical outlets.

Fibreglass scratch brushes are handy implements, offering the ability to work the abrasive into very tight corners. The tough bristles are also capable of removing the most stubborn deposits of excess glue or solder while also acting as a burnishing tool on metal surfaces. The problem of countless fibres being shed all over the workpiece (and within the tightest of recesses) is similar to that experienced with wire wool, save for the fact that fibreglass particles are much more insidious and can easily find themselves settling into your skin, causing severe irritation. Wearing gloves is a wise precaution and cleansing of the work area after use should be scrupulous.

On the subject of protective clothing, do remember to wear a dust mask when abrading plastics, resin or fillers as the fine dust is easily inhaled. Following with a gentle rub from a toothbrush will help to remove most of the waste material before thorough cleansing. The nylon bristles will also impart a burnished sheen to plastic or metal surfaces.

Fibreglass scratch brushes are also potentially messy, although they are very helpful on uneven surfaces and great for burnishing metal components.

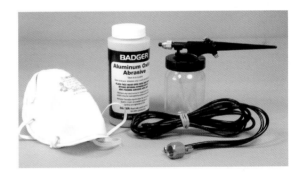

This Badger abrasive gun is designed to spray aluminium oxide powder. Good for general cleaning and stripping of grease, oil and loose paint, the tool is supplied in a set that includes the gun, hose, face mask and abrasive. Always wear the mask when using such devices, along with gloves and eye protection and work into a spray booth to contain the fine grit.

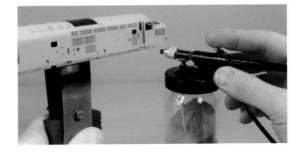

Working in a similar way to a basic external mix airbrush, the Badger abrasive gun is handy for many tasks such as cleaning up this bodyshell, which has already been in a bath of paint stripper. The fine powder shifts stubborn paint traces from awkward areas, especially when sprayed at a high pressure.

Factory finishes often incorporate several, non-uniform layers of paint. Logos, numbers and livery elements are printed separately, such as the band of EWS 'gold' along the sides of this Class 37. However, surfaces must be absolutely flat before refinishing or the previous design will show through the new livery.

A tack rag is useful for cleaning up after abrading a surface, especially between coats of paint where a little de-nibbing may be required. It's not a substitute for a good wash, however.

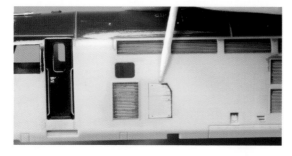

Some manufacturers use the method of building up layers of paint to mimic specific raised details, such as this small panel on a Vi-Trains Class 37. When stripping or rubbing down, it can be hard to retain such items, although they can be reinstated using the same method of masking and application of extra paint layers.

FACTORY FINISHES

Factory finishes, as applied to locomotives and rolling stock, are invariably made up of numerous layers, according to the peculiar aspects of the livery in question. Not all manufacturers employ priming coats and it doesn't always follow that lighter colours will precede darker elements. Moreover, the prevailing use of tampo printing, whereby finer livery elements such as lining, stripes, logos and numbers are applied, deposits fairly thick layers of paint onto the model's surface.

All of these variables result in ready-to-run models containing a medley of paint layers that must all be flattened to a uniform level before refinishing can commence. Without a thorough treatment at this stage, segments of an old livery will start to reappear through the new paint.

As far as compatibility is concerned, most manufacturers employ either cellulose or synthetic acrylics and, as long as the surface is given a suitable 'key' (and thoroughly cleaned and degreased), cellulose, enamel or acrylic paints can be sprayed on top with confidence. Ready-made buildings in the Skaledale and Scenecraft ranges may be treated similarly and can be sprayed with any paint formula, providing the surface is clean.

PAINT STRIPPING

Instead of hours spent rubbing down with abrasives, it may be preferable to strip a model back to its base material before refinishing. This will certainly remove the risk of damaging any fine details or clogging areas of delicate relief with numerous layers of paint. Starting with a blank canvas is often more convenient and any danger of paint incompatibility is avoided.

Unless dealing with a wholly metal subject, DIY paint strippers should never be used as they will destroy virtually all plastics. Model paint strippers, including those marketed by Modelstrip, Phoenix Precision, Finishing Touches and Expo, are formulated specifically for use on plastics or other delicate materials (they can also be used on metal surfaces).

By way of a disclaimer, they each recommend testing on a particular material beforehand to make sure nothing untoward happens, but I've never had any problems with any of these brands on ready-to-run or kit-built models.

Modelstrip is a very thick paste that must be spread over the model with a spatula. Sealed in a plastic bag and left overnight, the majority of the paste can then be peeled off, taking most of the loosened paint with it. Rinsing in water and scrubbing with an old toothbrush should remove any lingering traces. Modelstrip will work on most enamel paints but will not budge either acrylics or factory finishes.

Phoenix Precision's Superstrip, on the other hand, will shift most paints. Consisting of a thin, clear liquid, best results are achieved by soaking a model for a few hours before scrubbing with a toothbrush. The stripper is only available in fairly small bottles and a few will be needed to fill a modest-sized stripping bath. Good quality Tupperware-type boxes make perfect 'baths', especially those with air- and water-tight lids that allow the fluid to be retained indefinitely. Many stripping operations are possible with the same fluid, although sifting out the worst of the floating paint debris is recommended.

It helps to be aware that all model paint strippers will destroy glue joints, especially cyanoacrylate (superglue) bonds, so be ready to salvage any detail components that will come loose in the paint bath or whilst being rinsed. Thorough cleaning is essential after stripping, with all traces of the chemicals and loose paint removed before any new finish is applied.

CLEANING AND DEGREASING

As already suggested, cleaning is a fundamental part of the preparation process, potentially making the difference between a poor and an excellent finish. Plastic dust or metal filings can be very difficult to remove completely without a thorough wash in water and detergent, helped by a gentle scrubbing with a clean toothbrush. However, the choice of detergent is important as many household products, especially washing-up liquids, incorporate lanolin to leave hands feeling soft and dishes shining.

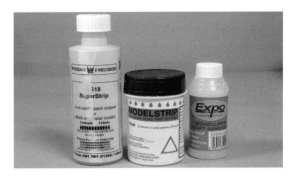

A choice of model paint strippers exist, with some brands being better than others. Phoenix Superstrip is the best all-rounder and it can be used again and again. Never use DIY paint stripping solutions on plastic models.

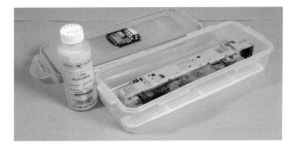

Liquid paint strippers can offer excellent results if the model is left to soak for a few hours. This plastic tub is just long enough to accommodate an average locomotive bodyshell and, after soaking in a couple of jars' worth of Phoenix Superstrip, the factory finish has been successfully removed. Leave the model submersed for about six hours to loosen enamels, acrylics and cellulose factory finishes and always wear gloves and eye protection as the liquid can easily be splashed into the face.

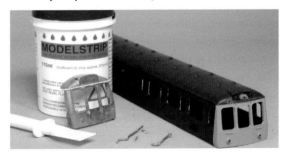

Modelstrip is a thick paste that is good for removing enamels, but not for acrylics or factory finishes. This old Lima DMU conversion was originally finished some decades ago with Railmatch enamels but has since been stripped ready for a better-quality paint job. All paint strippers will attack glue joints, so be prepared to salvage any parts that come loose.

General-purpose liquid detergents, such as Cif or Flash, should be acceptable, as long as they're thoroughly rinsed away with clean water. Soda crystals, while seen as a rather old-fashioned cleaning medium, are still readily available from hardware stores or supermarkets and are far cheaper than modern detergents. When dissolved in water, following the mixing instructions on the packet, the solution will work just as effectively without any of the unwanted residual problems of so-called 'hi-tech' cleaning products.

Household detergents invariably lean towards an alkaline nature and are, therefore, perfect for neutralizing the acids present in soldering fluxes. Cream cleansing fluids, containing small abrasive particles, are great for cleaning metal kits, imparting a burnished appearance to the surface and removing limescale and flux residues at the same time. However, a powdery deposit may remain unless followed by a scrub in diluted soda crystals and a good rinse under the tap for a few minutes.

Intricately shaped objects, such as locomotive boilers, can be awkward to clean with small brushes, so a soak in a bowl of diluted detergent, followed by a thorough rinse with clean water, should suffice. Stubborn deposits may still need some mechanical means of removal, however, and cotton swabs, cosmetic buds, cocktail sticks and pipe cleaners all have their uses.

Washing will remove all loose material and most unwanted residues, but it takes the use of something a little stronger to complete the cleansing procedure. Solvents such as white spirit, turpentine substitute or methylated spirit are helpful for removing grease, oil and chemical residues (including flux) before evaporating away completely. However, washing articles in such fluids is not to be recommended, especially plastics. Instead, wiping a surface with a spirit-soaked swab or cloth will be sufficient, although the process should be repeated a handful of times; just one or two wipes will simply spread any contaminants around rather than removing them completely. Allow the surface to dry out naturally for an hour or two between each swabbing and again before applying any paint. Never use any form of solvent cleaner on clear plastic components as they will be irrevocably damaged.

Well-known metal kit-makers DJH Kits recommend soaking metal components or assemblies in acetic acid (or good-quality white vinegar) before priming, although I've never tried this myself: I detest the smell of vinegar! Personally, I find that cellulose thinners will do the trick admirably, although it's not suitable for use directly on plastic materials. Again, repeating the cleaning at least two or three times is essential to ensure that all traces of grease are removed.

Enough time must be allowed for the model to dry after being washed. Liquids will likely become trapped inside any recesses or voids and may take hours – or days – to evaporate. Storing in a warm, dry environment, such as an airing cupboard, will speed things up to a degree, but it's worth leaving it there for a day or two to be sure. Cover the model or place it in a lidded, but vented, container to keep away dust and fibres and avoid handling the subject as much as possible without wearing gloves. Indeed, after degreasing, the model should not be touched by bare hands again. Or, if it is, then another degrease will be necessary before further painting.

While many household detergents are suitable for cleaning models prior to painting, some may contain ingredients that will actually prevent paint from sticking to a surface. Soda crystals are a good, traditional form of detergent with no fancy chemical ingredients. Simply dilute with water and rinse away thoroughly after a good scrub with a toothbrush.

Chemical cleaners and degreasers are recommended to follow the washing stage, once the subject has dried out thoroughly. Ensure that the product is safe for use on plastics, such as this tin of water-based Model Clean from Just Like the Real Thing. White spirit or turpentine substitute will also work well if used sparingly. Apply with cotton swabs while wearing latex gloves and avoid handling the model with bare hands before painting.

OTHER CONSIDERATIONS

If building a kit, take the time to consider whether painting will be more straightforward if done before assembly is complete, with any finer details fitted later and touched-in if necessary. Many modellers finish coach sides, for instance, while they can be laid flat on a workbench for lining, before assembling to form a bodyshell. I often assemble and paint wagon bodies before adding the self-coloured plastic underfames, which are subsequently treated only with weathering shades, greatly speeding up kit-building tasks.

The same applies to other models that can be disassembled in some way, such as ready-to-run locomotives, rolling stock or scenic items. Steam locomotives, in particular, can prove troublesome when masking and lining-out, with all the myriad pipes and handrails getting in the way; refitting these later makes for a smoother project.

Once again, it's worth reiterating the importance of thorough preparation before any paint is applied. It can be tempting to rush into the finishing process, especially if you're pleased with a freshly assembled kit and the eagerness to see it 'in colour' is understandable. However, in order to do our models justice, we must take the time to ensure all surfaces are smooth, clean and properly receptive to a coat of paint.

Consider how the painting process can be made easier by dismantling models or leaving a kit part-assembled until the finish has been applied. Treating these wagon bodies separately negates the need for the awkward task of masking up when painting the underframes, which will be added from self-coloured black plastic. When complete, the weathering process will colour the new parts and remove any contrast between the two separate assemblies.

CHAPTER SIX

PRIMING AND PAINTING

Having discussed the preparation of surfaces in the preceding pages, we must now move on to consider another fundamental preparatory stage. Primer application provides the ideal platform for refining our spraying technique as it's vital that a flat, even coverage is achieved. The paint must also reach into all nooks and crannies while being applied to a depth sufficient for full opacity without obliterating delicate surface relief. Moreover, the quality of these base coats will dictate the standard of the final finish: if it doesn't look right at this stage, then it will only get worse.

WHY PRIME?

Primers do not necessarily contain an increased adhesive quality over ordinary paint, although etching primers (see below) do possess specific ingredients to improve their 'grip'. They are, however, an invaluable first stage in the painting process. Not only do primers offer a uniformly neutral shade, over which colours can be built to their full opacity, but they also contain a higher proportion of solid pigments, producing a consistently flat surface. Indeed, some primers even contain micro-fillers that help to even out any minor imperfections.

Therefore, all modelling projects may benefit from a priming coat, whether an overall paint job is needed, or merely a little touching-in of new or modified components. Many modellers' enamel and acrylic paints boast of needing no undercoat but, in my experience, this is far from the case. Card, plaster and wood all benefit from an undercoat of some description, while paint struggles to adhere to most plastics, metals and resins without such a priming layer. The longevity of a finish is also dependent upon the quality of a priming coat, dictating how easily paint may be chipped or worn away.

Furthermore, the manifold benefits of priming can be distilled into the following statements:

- Primers help to seal porous surfaces
- Different base materials and textures will be unified
- Provides top coats with a 'key' to adhere to
- Promotes an even final finish
- Helps to identify surface imperfections
- Acts as an adhesive to seal delicate detailing components in place

There are, on the other hand, some instances when applying a primer is either impractical or unnecessary. Painting and weathering track is a task that springs to mind, as it would be counterproductive to spray primer over ballasted track before the rusty red rails and murky sleepers are treated. As the railheads must be kept clean of paint and the sides of the rails will see little handling or movement, in this case achieving a resilient finish is not as vital. Any problems of adhesion can be solved in such cases by ensuring that the surface is clean and degreased beforehand and by applying a preliminary 'tack' coat of paint, which should be sprayed very finely and left to dry before adding further coats.

In general priming terms, grey is often the preferred shade as the neutrality of the colour helps the eye to discern any telltale shadows or peaks caused by gaps, scratches or debris on the surface. White and red primers are also available and are helpful when applying subsequent top coats of light or dark colours respectively. White primer, in particular, can render minor imperfections almost invisible, but they will soon be revealed by the following coats of paint.

A grey priming coat will help to reveal surface imperfections far better than white or red shades. Primer also provides a barrier between fillers and awkward materials such as resin and metal, enhancing adhesion. Be prepared to fill and reprime a number of times until the surface is perfect.

There's no real need to keep a specific airbrush solely for priming jobs, although it does help to have a slightly larger nozzle size if working on subjects in OO gauge and above. Tools with fine nozzles (0.2– 0.4mm) are not totally inappropriate, however, but it will require more time to cover the surface and demand greater care to produce an even finish when so many separate passes of the tool will be needed. Some airbrush makers offer tools with interchangeable nozzles (such as the Aztek range outlined in Chapter 1) and this is one situation when the value of this facility is appreciated, speeding up the process and ensuring a more consistent priming coat.

PRIMERS

Virtually all brands of hobby paint include primers of varying descriptions, predominantly in enamel or acrylic formulas. Most are produced with hand-brushing or spraying in mind, although there are a few that come pre-thinned for direct loading into an airbrush. Whatever formula is chosen, it pays to use as good a primer as possible. Cheaper formulas will prove a source of frustration and avoidable remedial work may be necessary before the topcoats can be added.

Enamel primers from both Railmatch and Phoenix Precision are recommended, being suitable for both enamel and acrylic topcoats, while acrylic primers (as offered by Lifecolor, Vallejo and others) can produce decent results with the benefit of quicker drying times. However – and this is just a personal view – I've never been able to achieve total satisfaction with acrylic primers, although I know plenty of expert modellers who do. I just find that I get the results I want much more quickly with enamels and, especially, with cellulose priming paints.

Indeed, one of the best model primers around is that in the Alclad2 range. Sold in 120ml screw-top tins, the formula is pre-thinned ready for use. As it dries in a matter of minutes, a number of thin layers can soon be built up to full opacity and the micro-filler elements in the paint go some way to disguising minor imperfections on the model's surface. Although cellulose based, I've not had any trouble applying it to polystyrene or other plastics, provided only very light coats are administered. Each layer should be allowed to dry completely before reapplication and working in a well-ventilated space avoids a concentration of fumes around the model. It is, after all, cellulose thinners that are hazardous to soft plastics, not the paint, and as long as they can evaporate rapidly then any danger is averted. Because of the rapid drying times, Alclad recommend spraying at low pressure only (around 12–15psi).

Ironically, most of the other high-quality primers that I can recommend come supplied in aerosol form only. Those offered by Halfords and Just Like the Real Thing (JLTRT) are either synthetic acrylic (Halfords) or cellulose (JLTRT and some Halfords products) formulas that can be applied with decent results straight from the tin. Just be sure to shake the can for at least a few minutes

and spray from the specified distance. Also, only ever use them at a minimum of room temperature as a cold and damp environment will create havoc with the propellant.

Halfords, in particular, offer a broad range of aerosol-based primers, some of which are specifically tailored for use on plastic surfaces, such as car bumpers. Others, including 'primer-surfacer' compounds, are designed to help hide minor surface imperfections in a similar manner to the Alclad2 range mentioned above. However, being of a more industrial nature, this particular type of automotive paint is not recommended for use on small models, especially plastic surfaces. 'Primer-surfacers' can, on the other hand, be beneficial to large-scale modellers working in metal.

As shown in Chapter 3, aerosol paints can be dispensed for spraying through an airbrush, producing much finer and more controllable results. Primers are no different in this respect and, although the decanting process can be a little messy, the end results are worth the effort. Just be sure to use the correct thinners to suit the paint formula.

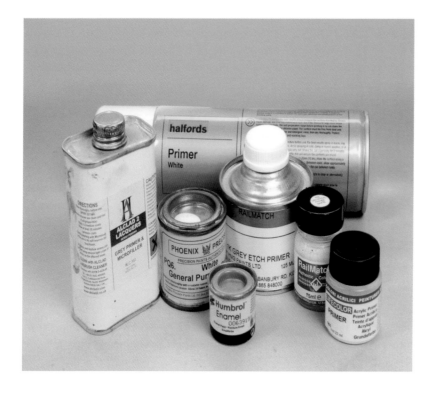

Most ranges of model and hobby paints include primers, mostly in grey or white.

Aerosol-based automotive primers are also excellent for use on metal or plastic models.

Etching primers offer a more robust finish as the paint actually eats into the surface to gain a firm foothold. Mostly used on metal models, some formulas are also suitable for plastics and resins. Just Like the Real Thing offers a choice of primers to complement its range of composite kits that make use of brass, white-metal, resin and plastic.

Etching primers come in two main types: single- and twin-pack. With single-pack products, such as offered by Railmatch, use only the prescribed thinners.

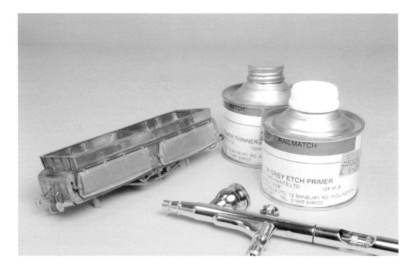

ETCHING PRIMER

If working in brass, nickel silver, copper or white-metal, then making use of an etching primer is a step on the road to achieving an attractive and long-lasting finish. Available in single- or twin-pack formulas, each type contains acids that chemically break down the surface structure of the metal just enough to gain a firm foothold. The etching process begins only as the paint begins to dry and, when fully cured, the acids are automatically neutralized and the surface is ready for a coat of regular primer before topcoats follow as usual.

Brass, copper and nickel silver are all naturally inclined to tarnish when exposed to the air or, especially, when in contact with the skin. A layer of oxide forms on the surface and, although this can be removed by mechanical means (scrubbing with detergent or abrading), the oxide will simply return after a short time. Applying etching primer solves this problem as it not only eats through such oxidation, but it will prevent it reforming.

Of paramount importance is the use of the correct thinners with each brand of etching thinners – use only the specified formula recommended by the manufacturer. The same thinners will also be required to clean out any spraying equipment, so ensure that you have enough at hand before starting work. As mentioned, the etching takes place only when the paint dries out so, provided that the airbrush is cleaned immediately after use (and thoroughly), there should be no risk of the chemicals etching into the equipment.

Single-pack etch primers are the more commonly applied medium among modellers, due to their relatively low cost and ease of use. However, they do have a number of limitations, not least their short shelf life (around a year). Also, single-pack primer must only be applied very sparingly, creating an almost transparent finish to the subject. Only a small amount is needed as the purpose of the paint is to form a bridge between the base metal and the regular primer coats that will follow. If too thick a coat is applied, then the paint below the surface is unable to dry sufficiently, thus not etching to the surface. As a result, the paint is liable to peeling away.

Twin-pack etching primers purport to provide both a better-looking finish and a higher level of performance. While the former is open to debate, the latter is probably true, although the higher cost should be considered. Made up of one-part paint and one-part activating thinners (containing the etching compound), they can be used on both ferrous and non-ferrous metals. Intended for building up into thicker, opaque coats, there is often no need for a subsequent layer of 'regular' primer before the topcoats can be applied.

To avoid the risk of etching primers drying too quickly, low-pressure spraying is vital: a

Etching primers are highly toxic and must be used with the utmost care. Any product that admits to being a potential cause of cancer demands to be treated with respect.

setting of 10psi should suffice. Accordingly, the paint will need to be thinned to a suitable consistency to facilitate this. If a higher pressure is used, then not only will adhesion be poor but the paint is also likely to form into fine string-shaped fibres, blocking the airbrush nozzle in the process. There's also the potential for damage to the inside of the airbrush as the drying paint begins to etch into the metal. With this in mind, only an airbrush set-up with a reliable means of controlling air pressure (with a gauge) is suitable for etching primers. Likewise, it's not possible to apply etching primer via an external mix airbrush due to the higher air pressure necessary to draw the paint from the reservoir.

Drying time is typically around two or three days for single- and twin-pack primers, depending on the brand and, as may be surmised from the acidic nature of these paints, they can be extremely hazardous. Such is the seriousness of this issue that some brands openly warn of the paint's carcinogenic nature. Do not take any risks in the handling, mixing, application and disposal of these paints and, unless you possess an adequate fume extraction set-up then I'd urge you to give etching primer a miss.

Certain etching primers are tailored for use on plastic or resin kits and components, helping to ensure good adhesion onto what can be treacherous surfaces. Among these are the aerosol-based formulas from Just Like the Real Thing, which produce fairly impressive results straight from the tin without the need to decant the paint into an airbrush. Mind you, at around £15 each, you'd expect them to be good!

I have to admit to using etching primers only rarely, not least due to their toxic nature. On the other hand, when finishing a metal or resin kit where a high standard of finish is necessary, I will opt for a single-pack primer. Although it may seem extravagant, I reserve an airbrush solely for applying etching primers (a budget-priced Premi-Air G35) as I'd rather not risk damage to any of my more expensive tools, regardless of how small the possibility may be.

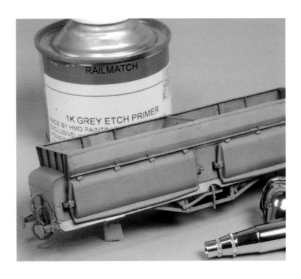

Single-pack etching primers are not designed to be built up to a fully opaque coating. Instead, a handful of ultra-light coats are enough before regular primer follows. As the etching process takes place only as the paint dries, allow a few days for it to cure completely.

Etching primers are not acidic enough to eat into the surface of stainless steel, so red oxide is a better option. And it's cheaper. Automotive aerosols provide a source of red oxide, as do tinned paints that can be thinned and sprayed through an airbrush. These primers dry very quickly, so immediate cleaning of the airbrush is vital.

HOLDING THE WORK

Before spraying any model or component, some thought must be given to how the subject is to be held. It may not be enough to simply place the article onto a flat surface as the air pressure may blow it around. Moreover, a surface must also be checked for any loose debris or dust that will invariably be transferred to the wet finish.

If there is a way of holding the model with your spare hand, then a glove should be worn, although you must make provision for transferring the model to a drying area without disturbing the paint. Alternatively, some form of holding device can be obtained or created from scrap materials. There are plenty of ready-made items on the market, of varying quality and usefulness. Indeed, there are some that can cater for a vast range of sizes and shapes of objects, while a turntable can also be of great value. Illustrated here is a small selection of off-the-shelf holding aids, along with a few home-made alternatives.

Whatever device is used, it must hold the model firmly enough to avoid it accidentally falling off, while not gripping so tightly as to cause any damage. It should also be able to be left somewhere for drying-out, whether self-supporting or capable of being mounted in a vice or clamp.

Another useful painting aid is a drying box or booth, allowing a model to rest securely in a dust-free environment; especially useful when working with slow-drying varnishes or gloss paints. Nothing too sophisticated is required, an upturned box often being sufficient to cover the model, although there must be adequate space for the thinners to evaporate fully. As solvent vapour is heavier than air, propping the box to leave a gap of around 50mm at the base will allow all fumes to dissipate. Alternatively, draping a dust cover over the front of a spray booth forms a good barrier to airborne debris, although it must be clean and dust-free.

Spring clamps are ideal for holding a range of items, both big and small, provided that there is enough material for the jaws to grip onto, preferably where the paint is not to be applied.

Sprung steel work holders are commonly available from paint and sundry suppliers, although they are just as easy to make yourself from strips of suitable material, riveted or bolted together at the base and sprung halfway up by a coil spring and bolt. Sponge pads have been fixed to the outer faces and, depending on the strength of the spring, a range of objects can be held with confidence. Designed to be held in the hand while painting, it must be mounted in a vice while the model dries.

A minor problem with sponge pads is the liability of the sponge to ooze out of any apertures, such as between the boiler and frames of this steam locomotive.

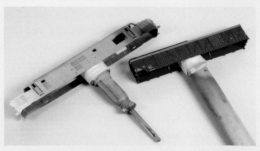

Home-made holding aids are simple to construct from all manner of materials. Timber off-cuts or dowelling are particularly useful.

A turntable will prove itself useful for all manner of painting tasks, from priming and all-over topcoats, to weathering and detail work.

Combining the benefits of a sprung paint handle and a turntable is this rotating clamp from Tamiya. The spring wire can be set in a number of ways to cater for a variety of widths.

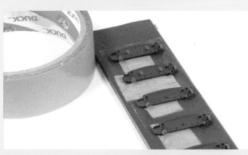

For small items, gently fixing to a strip of double-sided tape may be the best way to hold them.

Awkward objects may need a different approach, such as this pair of intermodal containers. As the flat base will always be out of view, brass hooks were driven into a pre-drilled hole and formed a means of holding the boxes during painting (in a gloved hand).

Other challenging subjects, such as this N gauge wagon and container, can simply be fixed to any spare device with Blu-Tack. In this case, a screwdriver and an aerosol lid have been pressed into service.

APPLICATION

As the accompanying photographs illustrate, the key to a successful primer coat is to build up a number of light layers of paint until full opacity is achieved. The first few coats will not obliterate the underlying colour of the material and it may take up to four or five layers before the primer becomes a uniform shade.

As mentioned in Chapter 5, the use of fillers and composite materials can lead to the primer sitting unevenly over each surface, usually as a result of different degrees of porosity. This can simply be addressed by a few more light coats of primer. If there are still irregularities, than it may be down to the surfaces not being 100 per cent smooth, so a little rubbing down and repriming should remedy the situation.

Ensuring that all areas of the model are evenly covered is important and this can be where an airbrush trumps an aerosol can. Being able to work at a low pressure allows paint to be worked into the tightest of corners and, with care, an even coating can be achieved quickly and effortlessly. Aerosols, on the other hand, can be difficult to control and in order to avoid excess paint building up in confined spaces it can be tempting to skimp on the amount applied, creating a less than perfect coverage.

It helps to work paint into corners and recesses first, particularly on surfaces with a complex array of detail or relief. Keep the airbrush at a consistent distance from the subject, around 150–200mm (6–8in), while working from different angles to ensure that the paint covers every aspect. Moving on to coat the rest of the model, horizontal sweeps should also see the airbrush remain at a constant distance from the surface, passing over the end of the subject before returning in the opposite direction. Remember the basic exercises covered in Chapter 4, thinking about how the paint reacts on a surface in relation to the distance and motion of the airbrush.

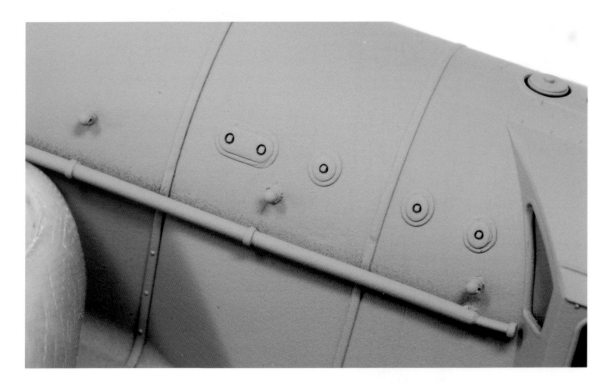

Applying aerosol-based primers has the drawback of a lack of control over paint flow. Reaching into awkward areas can be difficult, such as behind the raised pipework on this locomotive boiler, without the risk of clogging the fine detail or causing runs of excess paint.

Build up layers of primer slowly and gradually. Here, Alclad2 primer is being worked into the corners and recesses of the model first, attacking the subject from different angles to ensure full coverage to the door apertures.

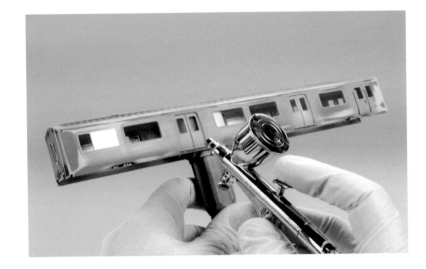

Overall coats now follow, working in repeated passes from side-to-side and up-and-down in alternating layers. Overlap each pass of the airbrush to avoid creating ridges in the paint. It's also important to keep the airbrush at a consistent distance from the subject and to allow a few minutes between coats to prevent paint runs.

Once the coat starts to reach full opacity, ensure that the paint starts to appear 'wet' as it lands onto the surface; this will allow a smooth, even coating to be achieved. If it doesn't, check that the air pressure is not too high and that the tool is close enough to the subject.

Don't forget to work underneath and inside a model, particularly on bodyshells where parts of the interior will be visible. Steam locomotives, in particular, require approaching from countless angles in order to get the paint between the frames, around the boiler and into the confined areas around the footplate, smokebox and cab. Be sure to keep the airbrush moving, while also rotating and tilting the subject to make the job easier. Spray the paint away from your person at all times, preferably aiming towards an extractor booth.

After the initial few coats have been applied, we should be aiming for the paint to look slightly 'wet' as it lands onto the surface, as discussed in Chapter 4. This will tell us that the paint is flowing in the right manner and that the coat is being built to a uniform level. Allow a short time between coats for the primer to dry a little, which may be identified by the surface beginning to appear dull. With acryl-

ics and cellulose, this may take just a few minutes and, if working on a large subject, then one side will have cured by the time the other has been treated. Enamels, too, can be recoated after a few moments' wait, provided that the paint no longer looks 'wet'.

Another challenge to be addressed in the priming stage is the ability to cover large areas evenly, when using a tool that may only offer an effective spray width of a centimetre or so. Resist the temptation to move the device further from the surface to create a wider spray pattern as this will lead to a poor finish. Instead, be prepared to make a large number of passes to and fro, overlapping each as you go. Varying from horizontal passes to vertical and vice versa over several coats will also help to create an even covering. It may take some time to build up a full primer coat but, other than investing in an airbrush with a large nozzle, there are no shortcuts.

Good-quality primers are self-levelling and should produce a flat, even coat. Although touch-dry in a few hours, all primers should be left overnight before rubbing down or recoating.

If an overall priming coat is not necessary, then a series of light mistings over a local area will suffice. A set of new etched brass footsteps have been sprayed with Alclad2 primer, built up over about eight coats, ensuring that all aspects of the parts have been covered.

UNDERCOATING

While the ubiquity of grey priming paints provides a neutral base for topcoats of paint, this may not be a suitable grounding for all colours. Lighter and vibrant shades, such as white, yellow or orange, will suffer if applied over a dull grey, while most authentic livery paints are colour-matched by the manufacturers on white backgrounds. An undercoat is, therefore, an essential next step for many painting projects and an overall coat of white will form something of a bridge between the priming and painting stages (it's not essential to use a white primer over an already primed surface, as regular matt paint will suffice).

However, the surface may well need a light rubdown to aid the adhesion of the subsequent coats.

In instances where only a localized undercoat is needed, such as a base for a yellow warning panel or a red bufferbeam, treating the area alone is acceptable. Applying light coloured paint over a darker background will require a few coats to achieve a fully opaque coating. White, in particular, can be a time-consuming prospect and several light layers must be built up, following the same procedure as the priming stage. Too thin a covering will allow the base colour to show through, especially along edges and around recesses, although this phenomenon can be harnessed for certain weathering effects. (For more on this see Chapter 12.)

Many livery colours are not suited to a grey base, not least as many authentic shades are colour-matched on white backgrounds. For lighter colours, a coat of white undercoat is essential. In this case, Railmatch enamel matt white has been built up to full opacity over several coats to form the basis for the vivid Railfreight red and grey scheme.

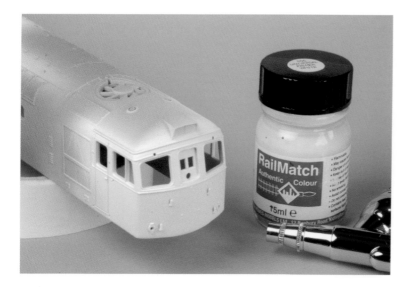

This model has also received a couple of light coats of white before the yellow warning panels are added. Once the relevant topcoat has been applied and masked, the rest of the model can be painted in a darker colour as necessary. However, be prepared to rub down any surrounding overspray, which is likely to be a little coarse. (For more details see Chapter 8.)

TOPCOATS

There is little to be done differently when spraying topcoats, as far as airbrush technique is concerned. Provided the priming and undercoating has been successful, there should be no hindrance to maintaining a smooth, even coverage. Rubbing-down the undercoat beforehand with a very fine grade of abrasive, such as Micromesh, will ensure maximum adhesion. Likewise, avoiding handling of the object with bare hands should alleviate the need for any degreasing.

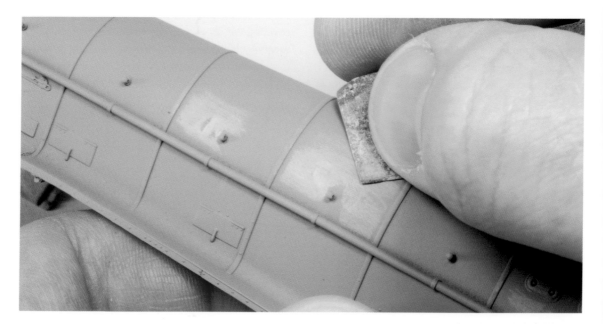

When fully cured, it doesn't hurt to lightly abrade the primer coat to prepare it for the following layers of paint. Only an ultra-fine grade is needed, such as 6,000grit wet-or-dry or Micromesh, used wet. The model will then need to be washed and dried thoroughly before continuing.

Thinning should be carried out according to the peculiarities of the paint brand and formula, erring on the side of a thinner viscosity and backing off the air pressure as much as possible. By building up numerous very thin layers, a quality finish will follow. As before, work the paint into recesses and corners first, going on to cover the rest of the model and aiming for that slightly wet look when the paint lands on the surface.

One of the most common preconceptions about airbrushing models is that the job can be done quickly and effortlessly, simply by pressing the trigger and waving the tool around. Not so, I'm afraid. It may take up to an hour simply to build the paint to full opacity on a locomotive bodyshell, allowing a few minutes' drying time between each layer. This is especially true if covering a white undercoat with a contrasting or darker colour. Furthermore, spraying distance must remain constant and rushing to get too much paint onto the surface will only end in tears.

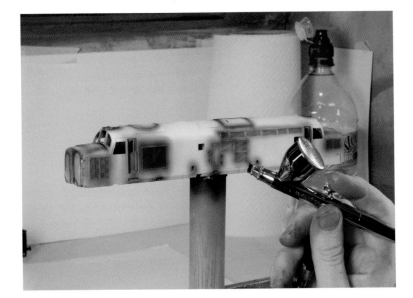

In similar fashion to the initial coats of primer, it's best to start off by getting paint into the corners and recesses first. Don't overdo it as it will take some time to build up the colour completely, especially over a white background. Remember to keep the airbrush moving and to use as low an air pressure as possible to ease working into any tight spots.

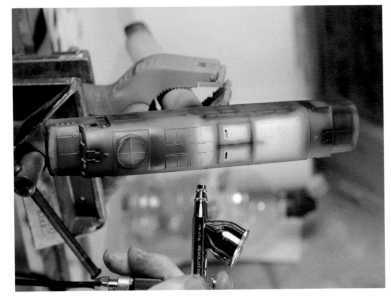

Follow all recessed panel lines and around any raised details, building up a patchwork of lines that will be hidden by subsequent layers.

The rest of the model can then be dealt with, working in straight lines and using your wrist to keep the airbrush perpendicular to the surface. With each stroke, pass over the end of the model before returning in the other direction to avoid building up too much paint at each end.

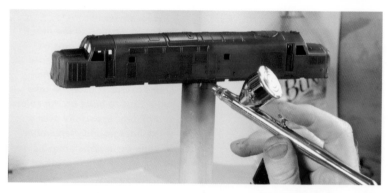

The paint should be looking wet as it lands on the surface and a few minutes should be left between each coat, repeating the whole process each time: recesses, corners, raised details, then the overall coating.

The freshly completed livery coat should look something like this: slightly shiny, even and with a uniform colour.

As the paint dries, it will take on its intended sheen of matt, satin or gloss (in this case a dull matt sheen, as seen on the model in the background).

Without deliberately working the paint into the various recesses, results such as this will occur. Note the lighter shades of purple around the roof details where the white undercoat is showing through. My excuse for such shoddy practices: rushing for a magazine deadline!

Another less than perfect finish: in this instance, a thick coat of enamel has been built up too quickly, resulting in an uneven surface texture. Note also how the area behind the lamp bracket has been missed, due to not angling the airbrush correctly around the various raised details beforehand.

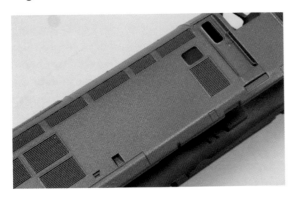

TAKE A BREAK

A full livery coat must be left to dry completely before going any further. Even rapid-drying acrylics or cellulose will need an overnight rest to harden completely and to allow all of the thinners to evaporate. Store the model safely in a dust-free location, preferably somewhere warm and dry. Pressing a fingertip onto the surface to test for dryness is never a good idea and an easier test can be made with the nose: if the model still carries a strong smell of paint, then the thinners have not finished evaporating and therefore the paint is not sufficiently dry to proceed. Once the subject no longer carries a strong odour, then the paint has cured.

Instead of rushing ahead, now is a good time to concentrate on cleaning up your airbrush and equipment, as will be discussed in the following chapter.

What we must avoid at all costs: the dreaded 'eggshell' finish. Easy to do, this coating was staged by simply not thinning the paint sufficiently, using too high an air pressure to compensate for the thicker paint and then spraying with the airbrush too far from the subject. Each one of these factors will produce an unpleasant surface texture.

LEFT: If a poor finish results or a mistake is made, it may be simpler to strip the model back to the base material and start again. However, the deliberately 'eggshelled' model was given a thorough rub-down with wire wool and Micromesh, cleaned and reprimed with an enamel-based undercoat (cellulose would lift the underlying paint). If caught in time, unsatisfactory paint layers can be wiped away while still wet. Enamels are best in this instance as white spirit will wash the offending paint away up to an hour or two after application.

CHAPTER SEVEN

CLEANING AND ROUTINE MAINTENANCE

An airbrush is a precision instrument and, for it to operate properly, it must be kept in optimum working condition. In common with any machine, tool or device, airbrushes must be cleaned, serviced and lubricated on a regular basis. Moreover, a well-maintained airbrush will provide years of satisfactory service, with only the odd 'consumable' part requiring replacing from time to time.

Deposits of dried paint trapped inside the narrow confines of the paint reservoir, chamber or nozzle tip will soon lead to blockages or impaired performance. On the other hand, introducing fresh paint and thinners into the tool may loosen some of these particles, which will then be emitted onto the subject, ruining the finish. If left for some time without being thoroughly cleaned, an airbrush may seize up completely, requiring a lengthy salvage job. When most of us do our modelling in our spare time, it seems senseless to waste hours on avoidable tasks such as this. With just a few minutes' worth of diligent cleansing after each painting session, an airbrush can be kept in tip-top condition and ready for use.

REGULAR FLUSHING

When I worked for Liverpool Museums, we had a scheme called Preventative Maintenance, whereby a short period of our working time each week was set aside for cleaning and servicing the tools and equipment used for handling artefacts. Given that what we handled was irreplaceable (and worth vast amounts of money), this seemed an eminently sensible policy. This approach is easy to carry into model-making, with the focus on how to prevent any problems occurring by maintaining our equipment as best we can. This needn't take long and a little time spent here will save hours of remedial work later.

A policy of regularly flushing the airbrush with thinners or cleaning agents between colour coats is essential to prevent contamination of one colour by another. However, doing the same at regular intervals, regardless of what is being sprayed, will prevent build-up of dried paint within the device. This is important when working with rapid-drying acrylics or cellulose, or for larger jobs where the airbrush is spraying the same colour for long periods. Taking a minute to flush out the tool, perhaps between top-ups of paint, will keep everything working properly. For best results, work the fluid through until the spray runs clear; directing the flow onto a scrap of white paper will help to identify when all of the paint has been cleared.

There are plenty of aerosol-based cleaning fluids available that will shift all types of paint, although the fumes they create must never be inhaled. Commonly based on chemicals such as toluene, acetone or xylene, they can be pretty nasty to one's lungs. If you don't own a spray booth, you can always direct the airbrush out of a window as long as there is no risk of anyone walking past! Alternatively, a sealed cleaning station will contain the nasty fumes and paint residues.

Along with dedicated cleaning fluids, cellulose thinners will also shift virtually all paints, although again the resulting emissions will be fairly toxic. If working with water-based paints, inks and certain acrylic paints, clean water will help to keep the airbrush clear. However, a more aggressive cleaning agent must be used at the end of each session to loosen any lingering deposits. Specific fluids and foaming cleaning sprays for acrylic users are generally less toxic than the previously mentioned products.

Various airbrush cleaning fluids are available in liquid or aerosol form that will shift all types of paint. There are also formulas suited specifically to acrylics, with less toxic ingredients. Check the hazard warnings on each brand before use and wear suitable gloves and eye protection to avoid splashes.

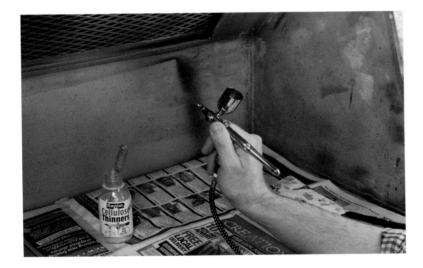

Flushing cleaning fluids – or neat thinners – through the airbrush at regular intervals will keep the device clear of dry paint deposits and prepare the tool for a change of colour without cross-contamination. Spray until the mist becomes clear.

Spraying cleaning solvents creates a lot of nasty fumes and an airbrush cleaning station is a handy option. This unit captures all emissions from an airbrush, while a filter prevents a dangerous concentration of fumes within the jar. A rubber grommet seals itself around the nozzle while the airbrush is being discharged. Periodical emptying and washing-out is all that's required. It also acts as a handy airbrush holder.

Aerosol-based cleaning fluids invariably come supplied with application nozzles designed for accurate dispensing into small orifices. If regular thinners, water or other fluids are being used, then employ a pipette to avoid spillages. It helps to work over a bed of kitchen tissue, rags or newspaper to soak up any excess fluids and paint dregs. Be aware that cleaning fluids are flammable and contaminated materials must be disposed of carefully.

Before refilling the airbrush, always test the spray away from the model, checking that the last of the cleansing fluid has been expelled and that the fresh paint is flowing correctly. Upping the air pressure will help in the cleaning process, forcing out any loose debris and the remains of the liquid, but be sure to reset the pressure before continuing to paint. A good amount of air will be needed to clean an airbrush between coats and especially at the end of a session, and it will soon be appreciated how uneconomical canned air supplies can be; every ounce of air in that can has cost you money and it can be so tempting to limit the amount used during cleaning. However, this skimping can be counter-productive and may lead to problems in performance.

DEEP CLEANING

While it's unnecessary to effect a full strip-down of the airbrush after every painting session, a more thorough cleansing routine will ensure that the tool is ready for use next time. Having said that, if the next session is not to be for a while, it will be worth going a bit further and this will be discussed in due course. For now, after a good flush-out in the way described above, use a cotton swab soaked in cellulose thinners to clean the inside of the paint cup and around the nozzle. For dual-action tools, retract the needle tip from the nozzle by pulling the trigger backwards and push the swab into the recess. Similarly, fill the paint cup (for top-loading, fixed paint cups) and jiggle the trigger back and forth to soak the needle along the length of the 'working end'. This will also encourage any stubborn deposits to be released from around the inside of the nozzle.

Cleaning routines are dictated to a large degree by the design of the airbrush and manufacturers often include a rough guide to keeping it clean. Some brands (usually the cheaper ones) incorporate rubber or synthetic O-ring seals and these will be seriously degraded if over-exposed to solvent-based thinners or cleaning fluids. Similarly, plastic-bodied tools may also be sensitive to certain solvents, so do check the instructions before choosing which cleaning product to use.

Speed up the cleaning of an airbrush by loading the paint cup with thinners, covering the nozzle with a finger or rag and pressing the trigger. The air will be blown back into the paint jar, causing a bubbling effect that also serves to dislodge any trapped paint within the nozzle or paint channels. Take care not to overload the cup with thinners or to create too much blowback with a high pressure setting. Wear gloves and eye protection at all times.

Cut off the air supply and retract the needle before using a thinners-soaked cotton swab to clean out the end of the nozzle.

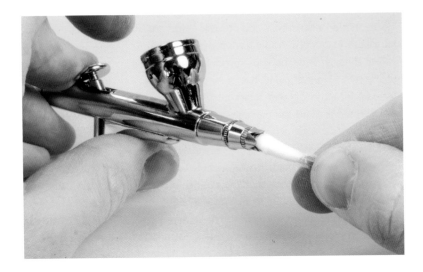

A swab will also help to clean the interior of the paint cup.

Mixing jars, stirrers and filters need cleaning thoroughly if colours are not to be cross-contaminated. Collect all waste paint and thinners in a sealed jar or bottle for safe disposal.

Siphon-fed airbrushes and those with inter-changeable paint cups should have the paint channels flushed through with the cups removed and treated separately. Thinned paint has a way of squeezing itself into the tightest spots and will invariably have formed around the paint port and cup outlet. Personally, I always extract the needle from the airbrush after each session, spraying more cleaning fluid through the airbrush in its absence. A quick wipe with a damp cloth (soaked in cellulose or white spirit) removes any residue from the needle before it is refitted. When doing so, push the needle fully into position and then withdraw it once more, rather like when checking the oil level in the car with a dipstick. If there are new deposits of paint on the tip then the airbrush needs further cleansing. Repeat the process until the needle comes back clear.

On a more infrequent basis, say every ten hours' painting time, it's worth taking the time to break-down the airbrush for a thorough clean. This is also recommended if the tool is unlikely to be used again for a few weeks or more. A cleaning regime should be tailored to your own particular needs, in line with the frequency with which painting occurs in your workshop. My job sees me work with an airbrush for at least an hour or two every other day and, with those old Liverpool Museum ways still ingrained in my psyche, I endeavour to dismantle and clean my airbrushes at the end of each week.

I'm not alluding to a comprehensive breakdown of the whole instrument, rather the removal of the air and paint nozzles (the latter requiring the use of a small spanner supplied with the airbrush) and the needle. If fitted, a paint cup blanking plug (for left- or right-handed mounting) should also be detached and all parts lain on a bed of kitchen tissue. An aerosol cleaning solution, such as Premi-Air Liquid Reamer, is then sprayed over the parts and, while this fluid works its magic, the interior of the airbrush is also sprayed through and left to soak for a few minutes. Cleaning kits, consisting of a variety of pipe cleaners, will work into the tiniest of orifices and it's surprising how much material can be unearthed from a seemingly clean airbrush.

A needle can indicate how clean the interior of an airbrush can be. Carefully withdraw it and wipe on a moistened tissue. If paint is revealed, flush the airbrush through again with cleaning fluid, without the needle. Gently push the needle back into place.

Airbrush cleaning kits, such as this one from Paasche, typically consist of pipe cleaners of various sizes, along with brushes for shifting stubborn stains.

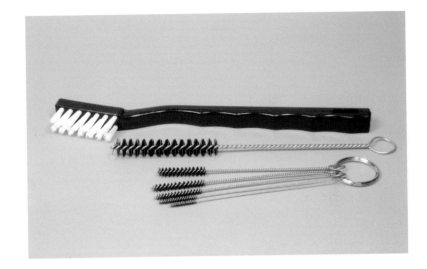

With a little cleaning fluid sprayed into the tool, the pipe cleaners will then dislodge any deposits of dried paint. Remove the paint and air nozzles from time to time to clean out the paint channels thoroughly.

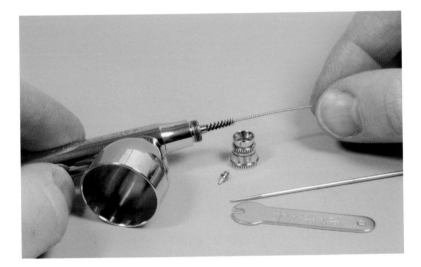

Make sure all of the channels are clear, making use of the different sizes of pipe cleaner. It's surprising how much muck will appear, even when the airbrush looks clean.

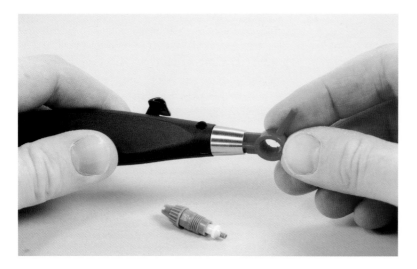

The unusual Aztek airbrush comes supplied with a handy cleaning tool for the paint cup inlets and the nozzle recess. Despite being plastic, the airbrush body is resistant to solvent cleaning fluids when sprayed or flushed through it. However, it must never be left soaking in solvent.

The Aztek's plastic cleaning tool includes prongs of different diameters to ream out any stubborn deposits from all corners of the airbrush.

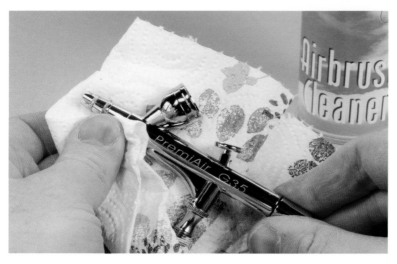

A final step in the cleaning process is to wipe down the outside of metal-bodied tools with a spirit-soaked rag, helping to keep the chrome plating looking like new. Leave to one side for the vapours to evaporate before returning the tool to its case.

This is all very straightforward and, with a well-practised routine, can be achieved in around ten minutes. However, take great care not to lose any small parts or to allow delicate components to be damaged. Needle tips are particularly susceptible to mishandling and can be very difficult to repair (if at all). When the various parts have been cleaned and wiped with a cloth, reassembly can commence. Take care not to overtighten the paint nozzle or the threads will be damaged, especially on cheaper tools. Fastening to just a fraction past hand-tight is more than enough as the paint nozzle will be held in place once the air nozzle is refitted. The needle should also be replaced with care, avoiding catching the tip on the edges of the chuck screw and ensuring that the trigger mechanism is correctly aligned before trying to force the needle through it.

Avoid spraying liquid cleaners or thinners into the rear of the airbrush, around the trigger mechanism or around the air valve, especially if it is fitted with rubber seals. Good-quality tools make use of Teflon seals that are impervious to such chemicals, but there is no reason why paint should be getting into these areas in the first place. If it does, carefully dismantle the tool and clean the affected areas with swabs dampened with a little cellulose thinner and let everything dry out before refitting. Finally, spray a little liquid cleaner onto a clean piece of tissue or rag and wipe the outside of the airbrush to remove any grease and remaining residues. Leave for a few minutes to allow the cleaner to evaporate before replacing the device into its case.

LUBRICATION AND SERVICING

Needles, where fitted, are moving parts that benefit from periodic lubrication. Certain brands supply small tubes of lubricant with their airbrushes and application during a weekly deep-clean is more than enough. Apply a small blob onto your fingertip and run the needle through it, smearing the grease around. Keep excess grease away from the tip, limiting the majority of lubricant to the parts of the needle that pass through the trigger and air seals; this is where the most wear and tear occurs and, besides, we don't want the lubricant to interfere with the paint. Incidentally, Vaseline petroleum jelly is an able substitute for bespoke airbrush lubricants and is applied in the same fashion.

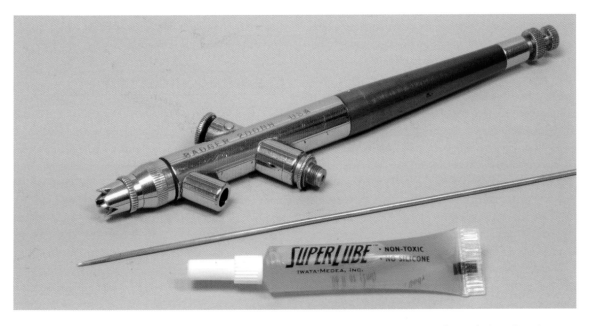

Airbrush lubricants are produced to minimize wear and tear on the moving parts within a device. Certain airbrushes come supplied with a tube of grease, or it can be sourced separately.

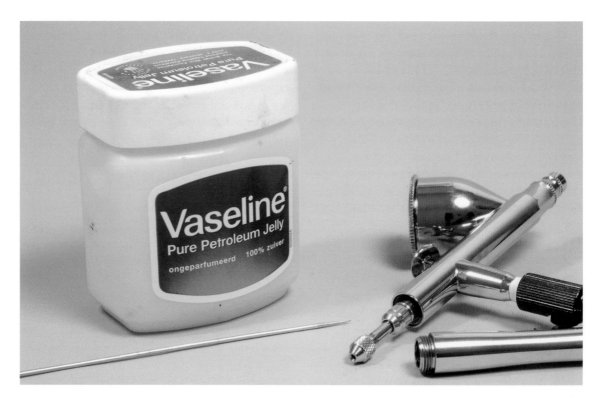

Vaseline is a cheaper alternative to tubes of lubricant, doing the job just as well. Use all lubricants sparingly.

Consumables, or parts liable to wear and tear, will inevitably require replacement over time. The more an airbrush is used, the sooner parts such as rubber washers and seals will wear out. Perhaps understandably, cheaper tools tend to degrade more quickly than others, while using some paint formulas, such as etching primers, can have harmful effects if they're not cleaned out properly. The odd knock or accident may occur and small parts can get lost in a cluttered workshop environment. Happily, spare parts are readily available for all of the popular airbrush brands and it's now common practice to include an exploded diagram, with a list of part numbers, with each device. Many dealers also offer a service and repair facility: if you fancy giving your airbrush a treat, you can always send it off for some professional TLC!

Regular cleaning, dismantling and servicing of an airbrush will help you to form an idea of how each part operates, and with this knowledge comes a better understanding of the processes at work. This, in turn, also helps to develop our technique. Just as a good train driver will know how his engine works, so too a good airbrush artist will appreciate how his equipment functions and how to get the best out of the resources at his fingertips.

CLEANING PROBLEMS

The design of an airbrush dictates how easy it is to dismantle for cleaning. Some models tend to collect paint in all manner of hard-to-reach places, while others are a joy to work with, being devised to promote a seamless channel through which paint and cleaning fluids will flow freely. Indeed, it's only when you've spent time cleaning an airbrush that its inherent quality (or lack of it) becomes apparent. The standard of machining on the inside of the instrument also governs how well paint can pass through it: a rough surface promotes an awkward passage, while a shiny, smooth interior offers much less resistance and fewer areas where residual paint can adhere.

Learning to tell when a device is clean or not is another facet of this hobby that comes with experience, although it doesn't take long to acquire. If, however, you find yourself with a seized airbrush after a period of inactivity, avoid trying to force the affected components apart. Instead, decant a little cellulose thinner or Liquid Reamer into a jar and stand the nozzle end of the airbrush in it. There's no need to soak the whole tool, indeed this may damage any seals around the trigger or air valve. After an hour or two, the nozzles should come loose and the needle can be removed. The whole tool will then need cleaning thoroughly with fluids and pipe cleaners.

Illustrated here is a Badger 200NH that I'd used regularly until a few years ago when I upgraded to a couple of Iwata airbrushes. I had meant to give the Badger a thorough cleanse and lube before putting it aside as an emergency back-up but somehow forgot, presumably due to the initial excitement of receiving my new tools. As I'm still waiting for something to go wrong with my Iwatas, the Badger had been forgotten. Upon rescuing the tool from the bottom of a drawer, it was found to be seized due to a heavy deposit of paint on the needle tip. A good soak in thinners freed things up enough to enable dismantling and a thorough clean followed.

Ultrasonic airbrush cleaners are a recent innovation that can help to shift stubborn build-ups of dried paint, although these units are fairly expensive. While they take away lots of the dirty work, I'm not sure how cost-effective they are. What they are good at is dislodging paint particles in the most difficult areas within an airbrush.

NEEDLE TIPS

It is imperative that the sharp tip of an airbrush needle is not damaged in any way during cleaning and servicing. Don't allow it to roll off the tabletop or use it to unblock the nozzle as any deformation, no matter how minor, will seriously hamper performance. Regularly check the tip by drawing it across your fingertips, while also rotating it. If a slight drag-

If an airbrush is not cleaned properly then it's likely to seize up. Soaking the nozzle end for a few hours in cellulose thinners should loosen the parts enough to aid dismantling.

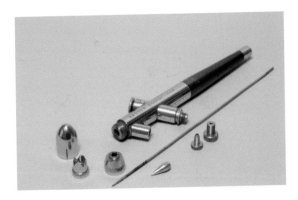

After soaking, this seized Badger airbrush has been loosened enough for dismantling. Build-up of dry paint on the needle was to blame.

Thinners will remove thin coatings of dried paint but this thick deposit needed more persuading. Wet-or-dry paper was used to clean up the needle shaft, working up to a super-fine grade to remove all scratches and blemishes.

ging is sensed, then the tip may be bent; a magnifying glass will help to identify any problems more clearly.

Very minor tip problems may be rectified by pulling the needle tip along a fine abrasive block. However, the tolerances involved with a needle and its attendant paint nozzle can be measured in fractions of a millimetre, so any significant deviation from its intended profile will seriously affect its usefulness. Replacements are available for most reputable brands, although they may not be cheap.

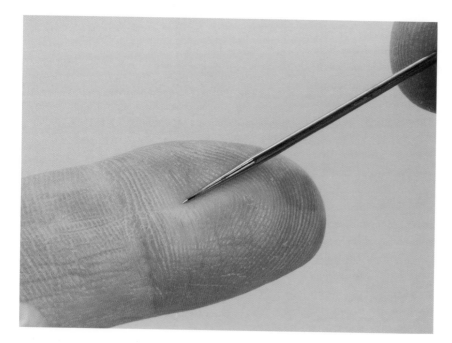

It's not always obvious when a needle tip has been damaged, but drawing it over your skin will reveal a dragging sensation if the tip is bent.

Minor damage to a needle tip can be remedied by drawing it over a flat abrasive pad. Anything more serious will require a replacement needle.

External mix airbrushes offer the advantage of being easier to clean than the internal mix variety. However, the paint cup, lid, siphon tube and nozzle should all be cleaned thoroughly between colour coats.

CLEANING OTHER STUFF

Of course, much of the above discussion concerning the cleaning of airbrushes may be irrelevant to users of external mix devices, as the paint is mixed with the air outside of the tool. However, the paint cup, siphon tube and nozzle must be kept as clean as possible and each part should be easy to dismantle. A spray of Liquid Reamer, or other cleanser, and a little work with a cotton swab and a pipe cleaner will do the job in a few moments. Moreover, keeping a spare paint cup filled with clean thinners can greatly speed up the process of colour changes, using periodic flushes to keep the paint channels clear.

Be sure to clean all mixing jars and tools, both between colours to prevent contamination and again at the end of each session. Cellulose thinners, white spirit or acrylic cleaners will work well in these instances. Additionally, plain old soap and water will do for anything that has been used to mix acrylics or other water-based paint, as long as the paint has not dried. Pay particular attention to the screw threads of paint jars and lids, while paint filters can be scrubbed with an old toothbrush. Finally, don't forget to clean up the work surface. Newspaper covered in overspray should be disposed of, as dry paint particles will be disturbed during subsequent applications, only to settle into the wet paint. Any paint or thinner-soaked rags, swabs and tissues should also be removed and disposed of.

DON'T FORGET THE ENVIRONMENT

Keep an old lidded jar or bottle in which to collect waste paint and dirty thinners, keeping the concoction sealed and out of reach of youngsters and animals. When full, pop along to your local household waste and recycling centre and place it in the appropriate receptacle. Some paints and thinners, if left in an open container in the shed, will evaporate or dry out to a solid mass that is easier to dispose of; just be sure to leave the container in a well-ventilated area and out of direct sunlight.

Do not pour any waste thinners or paints into drains, watercourses or onto land where it may damage wildlife or vegetation. Without wanting to sound preachy, I am aware that the model-making hobby can have a negative effect on the environment. The amount of plastics, metal alloys and chemical solvents involved, most of which demand toxic industrial processes and by-products, mean that we need to be careful with how we use and dispose of our effluvia.

CHAPTER EIGHT

MASKING-UP

An airbrush permits many mundane and complex paint effects to be achieved freehand with the minimum of fuss. However, creating clean 'joints' between different colours can only be achieved with the help of masking mediums and this is an aspect of the painting process where the airbrush really proves its worth: there is no other way of seamlessly layering multiple livery elements upon miniature scale models with such precision.

Masking also serves to protect certain features such as glazing, bearings, electrical contacts and headlight lenses. Ensuring that paint does not creep beneath the covering is vital, as some materials will be forever damaged by contact with paints and thinners. Such instances can be avoided by completely dismantling all at-risk components from a model before starting work, but this is not always possible, nor desired.

Furthermore, making use of stencils and complex masking patterns allows great scope for creative colour schemes and accurate renditions of railway liveries. Fancy or ostentatious schemes are not solely a modern phenomenon and it can be a time-consuming process to recreate the colours of pre-Grouping and post-Nationalization subjects, with the number of individual paint applications easily reaching into double figures. Moreover, prior planning of the order in which schemes are constructed will pay dividends. In this chapter, we shall discuss masking techniques and the wide variety of suitable materials for the job.

PLANNING THE JOB

The planning stage of any craft project is usually one of the most important and the ordering of livery applications is no different. Even a plain black

steam locomotive must have bright red bufferbeams, necessitating a white grounding, although this can either precede or follow the overall coat of black. Moreover, ensuring that each livery element is being applied onto a suitable background is paramount, despite potentially leading to a need for a great many separate paint layers. Provided that each coat is assembled as gradually and lightly as possible, there should be no problems.

Also worthy of consideration is how the model is to be held while painting and whether it will be treated in separate parts. If dismantling is possible, then the masking process may be eased if glazing can be removed, for example. I know from bitter experience how difficult windows and other parts can be to remove from ready-to-run models, with a high risk of irrevocable damage. Instead, simply mask the clear material inside and out: a tedious task at times, but necessary.

Alternatively, omitting certain fine details from a kit-building exercise until after the main aspects of the painting have been completed may also help. Handrails, lamp brackets, piping and other such delicate items may be fitted onto steam locomotives later, while bufferbeam hoses, door handles and windscreen wipers are other fittings that interfere with the masking process.

MASKING TAPE

Masking tape can be found in many different forms, sizes and materials. The most common is the cloth-backed types, which differ in quality and suitability according to maker and cost. It is generally worth sticking expressly to well-known hobby brands for tapes destined for use on locomotives, rolling stock or finescale buildings.

With any livery consisting of more than a single colour, the sequence of painting must be planned beforehand to ensure that each element is applied over an appropriate backing. In general, working with the lighter shades first is preferable, although if this is not practicable then light undercoats will need reapplying over a darker backing. Taking the BR Intercity scheme as an example, a suggested procedure would be the following: white overall primer; yellow warning panels; off-white for bodyside; light grey for lower edges of sides; dark grey upper sides and roof. Finally, the red stripe will finish things off, either in the form of waterslide decals or masked and painted.

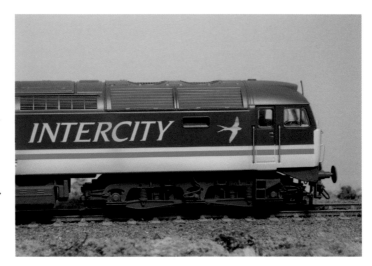

A much simpler prospect is the standard locomotive green scheme, as applied to steam traction: grey overall primer; white grounding for bufferbeam followed by red; green to boiler, cab, tender and wheels; black chassis, running plates, smokebox, cab roof and smaller details. Adding a copper-capped chimney with metallic paint, along with other exposed metal components such as injectors and safety valves would follow. The model would then be ready for lining-out by hand or with decals.

The act of masking may begin before even the first priming coats are applied, especially if any working surfaces are to be preserved in their natural state. Wheel bearings and treads are one example, while clear glazing or lenses, electrical contacts, motors and gears may also have to be protected.

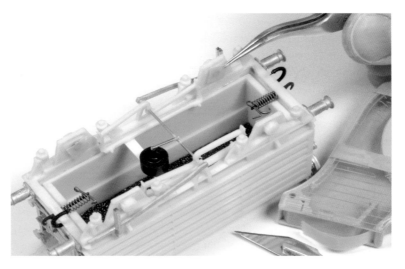

Masking tape comes in many different forms, sizes and materials. Avoid decorator's tapes for anything other than coarse scenic work as it may damage the substrate and will not cope with uneven surfaces. Good-quality, low-tack hobby brands are not too expensive and vinyl tapes, in particular, offer sharp transitions between colours if applied carefully.

Avoid trade or DIY grade decorators' tapes as much as possible, save for use on scenery or fairly crude work. Even then be sure to opt for a quality brand rather than the cheap rolls one can find in the local hardware store or supermarket. Low-quality tapes will turn brittle fairly rapidly and the level of tackiness can be unpredictable, to say the least. If left in place for more than a few days, some of these tapes can become devilishly difficult to remove without recourse to solvent intervention, which may have dire consequences for a part-finished paint job. Lack of flexibility is also an issue and use on uneven or curved surfaces will prove troublesome.

Tamiya produce some of the best tapes around for general modelling use, with a level of tackiness strong enough to keep it in place, yet gentle enough not to lift previous paint layers, provided that they are completely dry. They are also fairly flexible and can cope with gently undulating surfaces or raised relief. Available in various widths, all but the widest tapes come supplied in handy dispensers that keep the tape clean and ready for use.

Vinyl tapes, on the other hand, are more expensive but offer superior results. Ultra-flexible, they can cope with the most complex of surface irregularities and can be stretched and manipulated to a degree to cope with awkward shapes. Easy to cut and offered in various sizes, brands such as Eurostar lead the way in

this field. Other vinyl tapes may not be as flexible and it pays to inspect a reel before buying.

A minor drawback with many masking tapes is the need to clean up the edges after application. Even with the best intentions, dust, hairs or fibres often find themselves trapped beneath the tape and it pays to keep an eye out for this, lest the fragments be sealed in place by subsequent layers of paint. Keeping all reels of tape in a sealed, clean container is also a good idea to prevent dust and fibres from being collected.

A particular foible of vinyl tapes is the tendency to shed some of the adhesive around the paint 'joint'. As a rule, I always follow the masking stage with a wipe-down of the exposed areas of the model with a cotton swab dipped in a tiny amount of white spirit to remove any debris or sticky residues. This is an effective measure, but be sure not to overdo the use of the spirit or it will affect the masking tapes. When the tape is later peeled away, there may also be some degree of residual adhesive left behind and this too can be cleaned away with white spirit when the paint is dry enough not to be damaged.

If high-quality paint finishes are desired then it's necessary to pay a little extra for the best quality tapes. However, effective economies can be made by using superior tapes to demarcate the actual paint 'joint', ensuring a sharp, clean edge with little risk of paint seepage. The rest of the area to be masked can then be covered with general-purpose tapes or even scraps of paper taped in place for larger areas. As long as each transition between tapes is sealed completely, there should be no problems.

MASKING FILM

Produced primarily for graphic artists, masking films have been around for a long time. Trade names such as Magic Marker Film and Artool Frisk Film are well known, while Ultra Mask is another respected brand, especially among hobbyists. These self-adhesive, low-tack films are transparent, allowing for easier positioning onto a subject. Designed for optimum use on flat or gently shaped surfaces, they can prove a little awkward when used on small-scale three-dimensional objects, such as a steam locomotive boiler. However, films do have myriad uses, especially over larger areas where the use of masking tape would be uneconomical.

Films are also easier to form into complex shapes than most masking tapes, greatly aiding the application of many contemporary coaching stock and multiple unit liveries in most scales. For larger scale projects, (O gauge and upwards), films will definitely prove their worth on surfaces with minimal relief.

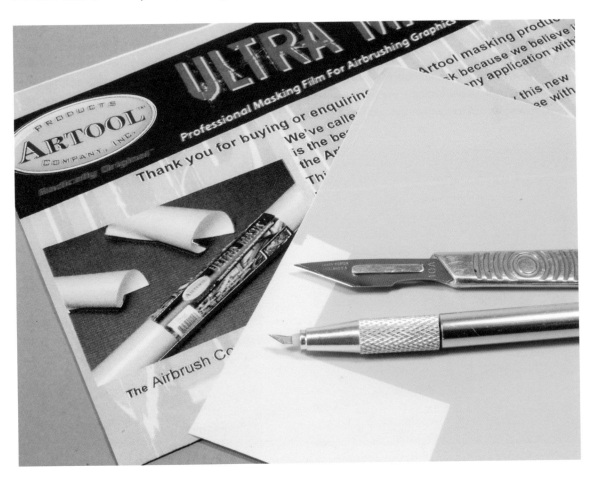

Masking films, such as Frisk Film or Ultra Mask, are supplied in either sheet or roll form and can provide great benefits to model painters. Low-tack, residue-free adhesives are coupled with a translucent, easy-to-cut film material to make application – and removal – easy. However, they tend to struggle with uneven surfaces. A swivel-bladed knife (lower) will help in cutting intricate shapes.

CUTTING MASKS

Masking must retain a clean edge if colours are to be separated effectively. This is all the more vital when applying livery schemes incorporating stripes or other multiple layers. Therefore, whenever cutting masking films or tapes a very sharp blade must always be used, preferably one that is brand new. Scalpels with replaceable blades will prove the most economical tool for these purposes.

Moreover, the smaller the blade tip, the better the tool will cope with curves and intricate shapes, as only a small area of the blade will be in contact with the material at any one time, minimizing friction. However, this can lead to the vital 'point' of the blade dulling more quickly than the rest of the cutting edge, making frequent blade changes necessary for larger projects. An alternative is to use a swivel-blade knife (X-Acto and other specialist makers can supply these tools – see Useful Contacts), wherein the blade actually rotates within the tool. It can take a while to get used to such knives, but the ability to cut out the most intricate patterns will be the reward for a little practice. Compass cutters are also handy for cutting circular or curved masks and can be freely obtained from art or craft stores.

For projects that involve much repetition of masking, such as creating a rake of similarly liveried coaching stock, creating a set of templates may be worthwhile. These guides can be cut from sturdy card and followed with a blade to transfer the shape to masking film or tape. Used with care and stored safely, such templates can be reused repeatedly, maintaining a consistency of livery application.

Masking film is an excellent medium with which to create stencils and most brands can be fed through an ordinary desktop laser or inkjet printer, allowing the use of computer software to draw the desired shape. Indeed, there are also plotter and cutter machines designed specifically for transferring an image to masking film, before cutting out the shape, leaving you to simply peel away the backing and transfer the film to the subject.

Masking film is also perfect for producing masking stencils. The desired shape may be drawn out by hand or the sheet of film fed through an ordinary desktop printer (A4 or A5 sheets of film are available). Cutting requires care, although there are various plotter/cutter devices to make life easier. This machine is a Craft-Robo plotter/cutter and, once the software is mastered, some highly intricate masks can be rolled off, leaving the user only to peel away the film backing and place the stencil onto the model.

Cutting masking film requires a very sharp, pointed blade and working on a glass surface is recommended. Compass cutters will make curved or circular shapes easier to cope with, while a set of French curves can also be helpful additions to a straightedge.

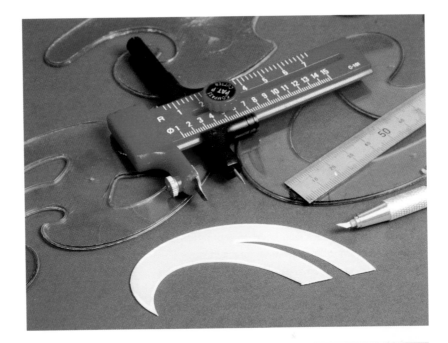

The same advice applies when cutting masking tapes. Wide tapes can be equally useful for forming into stencils or intricate shapes; indeed, tape will cope better with undulating surfaces than film.

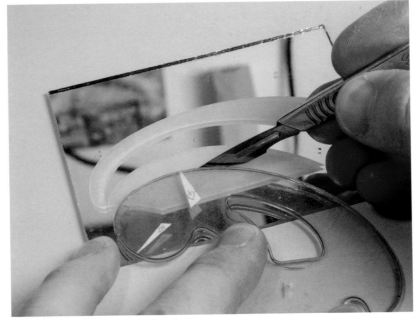

Masking tape is best cut while stuck loosely onto a sheet of glass rather than a cutting mat. Glass will not diminish the tape's adhesive, nor distort the edges while they are being cut, although the glass should be cleaned with methylated spirit and allowed to dry completely. Conversely, because films have a backing sheet, they may be better suited to cutting on a rubber mat. Either way, the importance of blade sharpness must be reiterated here as the glass will blunt a blade fairly quickly. Work on a cutting mat also requires a keen edge to avoid having to exert excessive pressure on the knife, thus distorting the film's edge.

MASKING FLUID

Fluid masking media consist of quick-drying latex solutions that can be easily brushed onto a surface and left to dry out to form a rubbery film. These are (unless stated otherwise) resistant to oil, cellulose and acrylic paints and can be peeled away once the painting process is complete. Indeed, some masking fluids can even be sprayed through an airbrush after being thinned sufficiently with methylated spirit, although this is not something that I've done on many occasions.

Fluids can produce clean lines of separation but can be almost impossible to form into a straight line unless butted against an area of moulded relief, such as a grille, boiler band or window beading. Indeed, I tend to use fluids for masking glazing or headlight lenses as it will sit happily within the moulded aperture. A small square of masking tape applied into the centre of the window before adding the fluid will assist removal later on, as is shown here. Masking

fluid is also an excellent insurance policy against seeping paint if applied over all joints or overlaps of masking tapes or film.

Apply the fluid with an old paintbrush, cleaning the bristles afterwards with methylated spirit. For smaller areas, a blunted cocktail stick will also serve as an applicator. The latter is also a perfect tool for removing the dried film, being less liable to scratch paintwork or clear plastic than, say, a pair of metal tweezers. Soaking the stick in a little meths will help to dislodge any stubborn fluid, although all surrounding paint must have hardened completely before applying the spirit and keep it away from any clear plastic glazing.

Do not leave masking fluid in place for too long as, after a few weeks, it loses its flexibility and can either be breached by further applications of paint or will be very difficult to remove. If a project is to sit unfinished for long periods, it may be worth renewing the fluid before progressing.

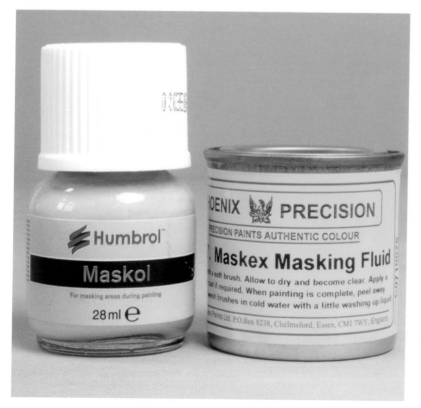

Masking fluids are available from a small number of sources, the most well known being Humbrol's Maskol. A similar formula is offered in the Phoenix Precision range and each is ideal for sealing glazing or headlight lenses, dealing with awkward raised detail or a variety of weathering techniques (see Chapter 13). Apply with an old paintbrush.

To ease the removal of masking fluid, insert a small piece of masking tape in the centre of the area to be covered, leaving part of it raised to act as a lifting tab. Then apply the fluid and, after painting, pull the tab and it should bring most of the film with it. The rest can be picked off with a cocktail stick.

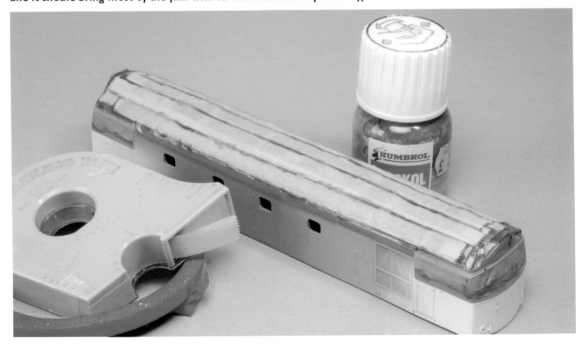

To ensure the complete integrity of film and tape, cover all joints with masking fluid. This may take an extra few minutes but it will save remedial work later. Note how the more expensive red vinyl tape has been applied to the working edge of the mask while cheaper general-purpose tape has been used as in-fill over the roof, as an effective economy measure.

Masking complex shapes such as bufferbeams is made easier with fluid. The grey primer is being preserved prior to an overall coat of black. The masking will then be reversed before the red bufferbeam is sprayed.

Masking fluids set within minutes, depending on the depth of the layer. Excess can be removed with methylated spirit and, after painting, it is simply peeled away. At times it can prove stubborn, especially when applied into tight corners. A cocktail stick will help to dislodge it, but take care not to scratch the surface underneath and never use meths in close proximity to clear glazing.

OTHER MASKING MEDIA

Some surprisingly mundane items can be utilized for a variety of masking jobs, including self-adhesive Post-it notes and Blu-Tack. Indeed, anything that's sticky and does not leave behind a permanent residue can be pressed into service, especially when using water-based or acrylic paints.

Blu-Tack, in particular, will prove very useful for situations where both tape and fluid masking is not practical. Highly uneven surfaces or areas with delicate raised details are good instances where the soft putty-like substance is suited. Although it is similar to Plasticine, Blu-Tack does not leave behind any tangible residues or colour staining. In fact, any traces that do remain can simply be mopped-up using a ball of clean Blu-Tack. Recently when building a large number of mineral wagon kits, I wanted to speed up the finishing process and began using Blu-Tack as a way of masking the body while the chassis was painted. As the majority of the wagons had uneven sides, doing this job with tape can be tedious and not wholly reliable, but the blue stuff does the job in minutes.

Other uses for Blu-Tack include masking for soft-edged paint joints. This technique is only rarely employed on railway subjects as, even on today's multicoloured network, relatively few liveries have one colour gently segueing into another, but this method of working is especially useful for patch-painting, allowing the new paint to blend seamlessly with the surrounding original finish. By rolling the Blu-Tack into sausage-shaped pieces and placing it lightly onto the model surface there is no perpendicular joint. Rather, the actual cut-off point is obscured slightly by the putty and in this way the paint only enters this recess in small amounts, creating a gentle blended finish. (For a further demonstration of this technique in a livery context see Chapter 14.)

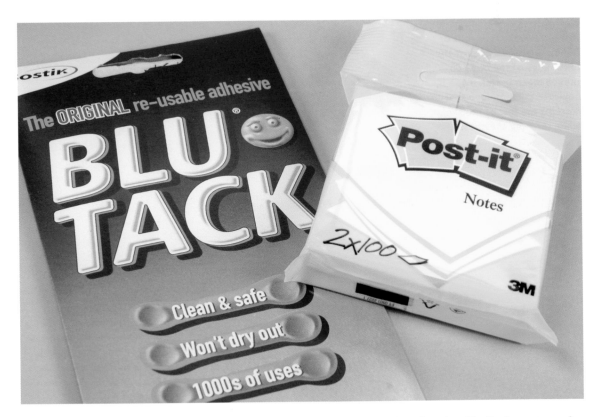

Other, less obvious materials can also prove effective masking media, such as Post-It self-adhesive notes and Blu-Tack putty. Both offer a gentle level of adhesion without leaving any harmful residues.

Post-It notes offer a quick and convenient means of masking-off areas, especially where complete accuracy is not necessary, such as weathering jobs or when introducing contrasting shades to a panelled surface. Here, this steel-bodied wagon is being sprayed in slightly different metallic shades to enhance the appearance (for more details see Chapter 11).

Blu-Tack is resistant to cellulose, oil and acrylic paints, and will prove its worth when dealing with surfaces where tape and fluid struggle. For instance, masking for wagon underframes can be difficult with tape alone, but rolls of Blu-Tack pressed against the lower edge of the body do the job much better. Tape is, however, still employed for masking the rest of the shell while spraying the chassis.

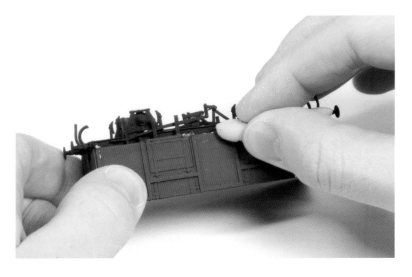

When Blu-Tack is removed it often leaves a few small traces behind. This is easily removed by taking a ball of fresh Blu-Tack and rubbing it over the remnants. Any lingering residue can finally be dissolved with a drop of white spirit on a swab, although the paint must be left to dry completely beforehand.

Another example of Blu-
Tack's usefulness is this steam
locomotive bufferbeam that
must be primed and painted.
Masking-up the rest of the
engine can be a tedious task
but, instead, Blu-Tack has
been pressed against the edge
of the beam while scrap paper
and masking tape take care
of the rest, all sealed with
masking fluid.

Blu-Tack will cling well to most
surfaces and can be formed
into any shape, even straight
lines with the help of a steel
rule. The white acrylic primer
can be applied in several light
layers until wholly opaque,
giving the red a suitable base
to achieve its full vibrancy.

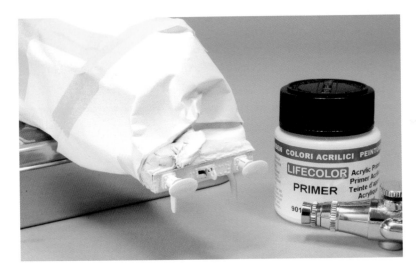

After unmasking the model
and removing any traces
of the Blu-Tack, any small
irregularities can be dealt
with by hand-brushing.
The inconsistency of sheen
between the main bodyshell
and the bufferbeam will be
disguised by a subsequent
coat of clear varnish.

APPLYING MASKS

All masking tapes or films must be secured firmly to prevent paint from creeping underneath during spraying. As we move the airbrush around and aim it in all directions to achieve even coverage, there is plenty of risk of paint reaching areas where it shouldn't. Surfaces must be spotless, with no debris or residues to hinder the adhesives, especially if the model has recently been wiped down with a chemical cleaning solvent. Ensure all such fluids have evaporated away completely and that the underlying paint is completely dry or problems will arise (see below).

It may help to draw a faint reference line with a sharp pencil when applying the mask, or even working against a straightedge to ensure a nice clean separation of colours; there's nothing worse than wonky stripes along a carriage side! As tapes are flexible by their nature, it can take some little work to get them lying dead straight, especially on an undulating surface. Once in place, use the edge of a fingernail or the side of a cocktail stick to press the edge of the mask down, working into any recesses. This is where vinyl tapes repay the user for their higher cost: they can be stretched to bed down into awkward corners or even bent around curved surfaces without losing their adhesion.

A sharp blade can be used to trim the masking in situ, if necessary, although this must be done with great care to avoid damaging any underlying paintwork. This is often the only way to cope with masking locomotive rooflines, bodyside stripes or other similar shapes and such tasks are often eased by the paint being separated by raised features of the model's bodywork. In the main, however, it will be preferential to cut most masks to shape and size away from the model, taking detailed reference measurements and transferring them to the tape or film.

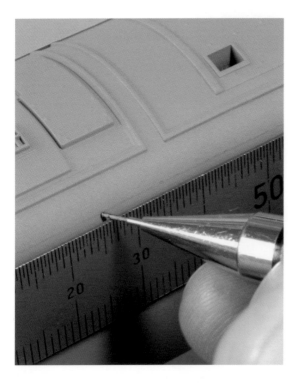

Marking reference lines in pencil eases the masking process. The marks can be removed once the mask is in place with a cotton swab slightly dampened in white spirit.

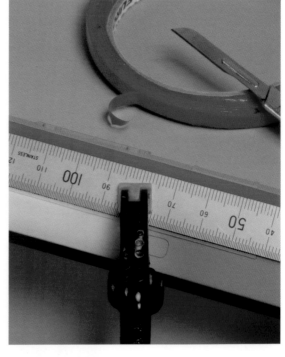

Masking dead-straight lines with flexible vinyl tapes can be a demanding task, but the process can be helped by clamping a straightedge to the model as a reference surface.

Trimming tapes and film in situ is often the most convenient way of working, but it must be done very carefully. Use a sharp blade, exerting only gentle pressure to avoid damaging the surface. The task is made easier if masking up against a moulded feature, such as raised beading or a recessed grille.

Ensure that the masking is pressed firmly into all recesses with the edge of a fingernail or cocktail stick.

With the mask finally sited and the edges pressed down, clean the working edge of any debris or adhesive residue from the tape's backing with a swab dampened slightly with white spirit. Allow the surface to dry before painting.

In times when a layer of tape or film cannot cope with a succession of raised details, the problem can be solved by cutting holes in the mask to allow the parts to protrude. A generous coating of these exposed areas with masking fluid effectively seals the mask with little fuss. A handy tip is to follow any awkward masking job with a coat of the same colour that has just been covered. This layer will seal the masked joint and prevent any of the next colour from creeping underneath. This is particularly useful when masking small yellow warning panels on diesel locomotives where various headlights, handrails and communicating doors will interfere with the seating of a mask. It's also recommended for use on corrugated sides of modern traction.

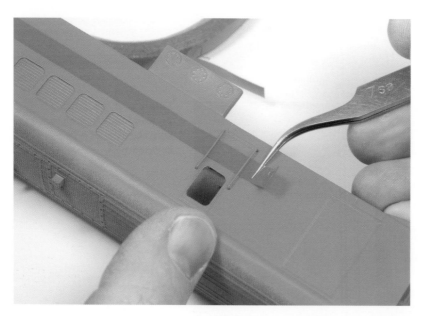

Wherever possible, intricate detail parts should be left unfitted until after the basic livery elements to ease surface preparation and the masking process. However, some features are easy to cope with, especially handrails where tape can simply be threaded beneath.

Finish the job by adding small strips of tape over the handrails and sealing with Maskol fluid.

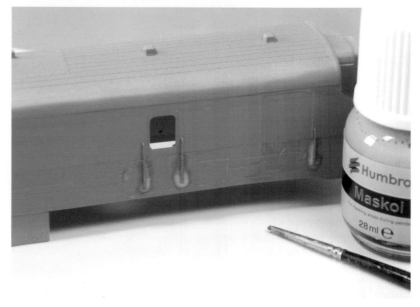

Cutting apertures in film or tape will help it to sit around raised features such as the headlight clusters on the ends of this Class 20. The openings can then be sealed with a generous blob of masking fluid.

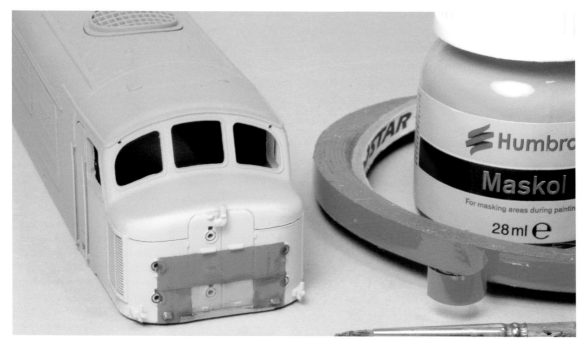

The masking of warning panels on first-generation diesels can be particularly treacherous, as illustrated by this OO gauge Bachmann Class 44. The main panel has been formed by strips of film and tape, while the round marker light recesses must also be masked somehow. Tape would never work in such a small area, so a few blobs of Maskol takes care of things, carefully applied with a fine brush.

UNMASKING

Depending on the formula of paint, masking may be removed only when the paint has dried completely. This may be anything from an hour or two after spraying to about a week later for some gloss coatings. Always peel any masking away from the new paint, lest it cause peeling. Don't forget that the paint has been applied over the mask as well and effectively we're causing a break in the paint's film when it's removed. Never rush through this stage and avoid using a sharp instrument to pick at the masking. Instead, a blunted cocktail stick will lift the edges to allow it to be peeled away.

Even low-tack tape or film can provide a test of how well the paint beneath it has adhered to the model's surface. Moreover, any deficiencies in preparation will be immediately highlighted as the mask is removed. Allowing insufficient time for previous coats to dry will also result in damage when subsequent masking is peeled away. Allow at least twenty-four hours, preferably longer for gloss enamels, before masking-up as there's nothing more disheartening than having to regress a few stages to make good damaged paint.

Illustrated here is an example of the consequences of being impatient, where an entirely avoidable occurrence ended up causing the project to take much longer than it ought to have. The Irish Rail generator van kit was being painted hurriedly for a press review and,

with the authentic livery shades only being available in enamel form, the process was taking too long; with five main paint stages (primer, orange base coat, black stripe and roof, gloss clear coat prior to decals and lining, satin clear coat to seal and finish), each needed twenty-four hours in-between, thus taking up an entire working week to achieve a fairly basic colour scheme. In an effort to speed things up, I was a bit hasty on masking over the orange and, when carefully removing the tape after spraying the black, a couple of patches were lifted, revealing the white primer beneath.

I really should have known better. If you're faced with this situation, then the only thing to do is to take a deep breath and consider your options. If it's an extensive area of destruction, you may have to strip the model back to the primer and start again. However, for isolated areas such as those on the generator van, there are remedial steps that can be taken. Firstly, however, the model should be set aside for a day or two to let everything dry out properly, lest worse damage is inflicted. Using fine abrasives, gently rub down the affected surface, levelling the paint ready for another application. Mask as necessary and spray a number of very light coats over the area, feathering out the paint over the rest of the surface to even out the coverage. When full opacity is eventually achieved, set the model aside to dry and, hopefully, when the masking is removed, the problem area should have vanished.

Removing all forms of masking must be done carefully, as the paint will have formed a film over the edge of the tape or film. Pull the tape gently away from the painted surface to ensure a clean break. The paint must be dry before unmasking, although leaving tape in place for too long may see the adhesive begin to dry out, making it difficult to remove.

Ensuring that the paint is thoroughly dry before applying further masking is crucial to avoid instances like this. A small area of the Irish Rail orange was lifted by the masking tape on this DC Kits generator van. Having rubbed down the affected area with Micromesh, the model was masked-up with tape and a little Blu-Tack, the latter to help produce a gradual blending between the new paint and the original layer.

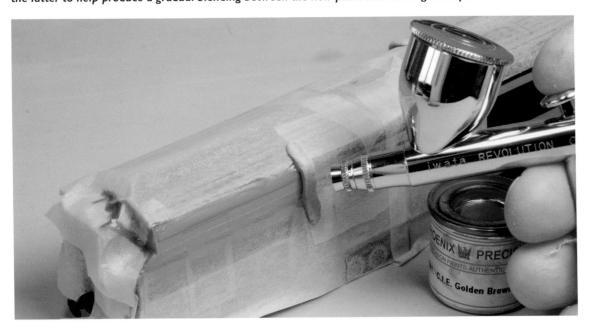

The remedial coat of orange was built up gradually and without aiming paint directly under the Blu-Tack, which was placed lightly onto the surface in a round-edged 'sausage' shape. This will leave a small recess beneath and, as only a small amount of overspray will reach into this void, a gentle transition between paint layers is achieved. This is a handy technique for effective patch-painting of new components or for achieving fading effects, as demonstrated in Chapter 14.

CREATING A UNIFIED FINISH

It's a rare thing, when all the masking has been removed, that there are no areas that need just a little tweaking. Nine times out of ten, there may be a small instance of paint seepage under the mask and this can be attended to with a sharp cocktail stick and a little white spirit. If there are other issues, such as a lack of a clean edge around raised detail, then some work with a fine paint-brush and the livery colour in question will rectify the situation. Awkward surfaces will doubtless see such things happen, small yellow warning panels being among the most troublesome. Why BR's designers couldn't be more obliging and produce only smooth-fronted diesel and electric locomotives, I shall never know.

Whenever touching-in areas by hand, it's important not to apply too thick a layer of paint or it will stand proud of the surrounding finish. Where paints are formulated to a thin consistency (Railmatch and Lifecolor especially), this can prove challenging as a number of coats will be needed to achieve full opacity. Just apply the bare minimum with each coat and patiently add further layers after each has dried properly. As will be described in Chapter 10, any minor discrepancies between the sprayed and brushed paint may be rendered invisible by applying a clear varnish coat. This will also serve to blend together each of the different livery elements into a coherent and natural-looking whole.

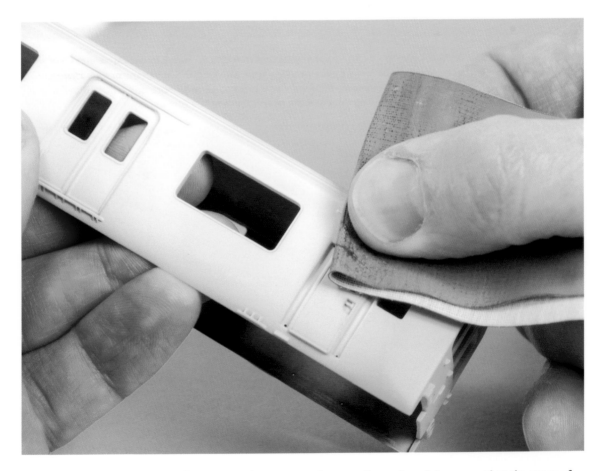

When spraying a preliminary undercoat or colour coat, such as a yellow cab end, be aware that the areas of overspray will need rubbing down gently before masking-up for subsequent layers, otherwise the surface will appear rather coarse.

There may be a need to tweak a few areas after unmasking and a cocktail stick moistened with white spirit will remove any small transgressions. Working with enamels allows such procedures to be done relatively easily up to a week or so after application, but acrylics must be dealt with within a few hours.

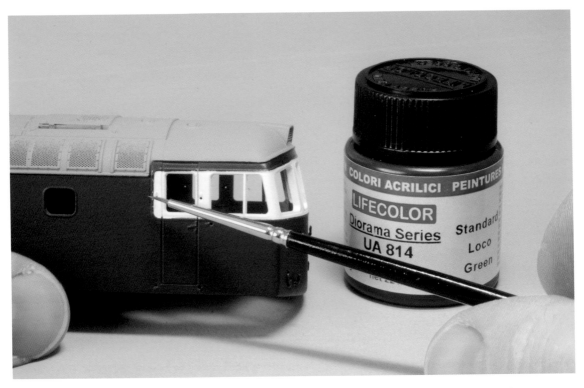

If more paint is needed in one or two small areas, touching-in by hand is the simplest way forward.

Before this can happen, however, there must be no prominent ridges between colours, giving away the former presence of masking tape or film. While this factor should ideally be avoided as much as possible during the painting process, it can be minimized after the fact with some careful abrading and polishing. Liveries made up of several contrasting stripes or bands are especially prone to such problems, including BR Network South East, Regional Railways or Intercity schemes. The masking process will invariably mean that two shades may meet beneath a subsequent layer (such as the two greys meeting beneath the red stripe on Intercity-branded vehicles) and a raised ridge will destroy the effect.

The best way of reducing paint build-up against the edge of the masking is to angle the airbrush away from it, approaching the subject from the masked side. In this way, paint is not sprayed directly into the joint. Additionally, avoid repeated passes over the edge of the tape, a succession of fine strokes just inside the border being a safer bet. As long as full opacity is achieved, the paint cover should be no worse for these precautions.

If a pronounced ridge does reveal itself upon unmasking, a gentle rub-down with Micromesh polishing cloths or other fine abrasives will flatten the surface. Excessive pressure on the abrasive must be avoided and plenty of lubricant (water) employed to avoid digging-in unnecessarily to the underlying paint. Following with a light buffing from a nail polishing stick will restore the sheen.

Pronounced ridges between colours are caused by paint building up against the edge of the mask. This is not an insurmountable problem but the effect can be minimized by avoiding heavy concentrations of paint along the edge of the masking.

Lightly abrade the surface around the ridge with fine grades of Micromesh or other abrasives, using a foam or cork backing to maintain a flat surface. Use plenty of water as a lubricant to keep the abrasives from clogging and damaging the surface.

Unless such a ridge is removed, it will show through any other paints or decals that are layered on top, such as the white stripes being here applied. Following the abrasives with a clear varnish coat will not only restore the sheen to the paints affected by the abrasives, but will also blend all of the various livery elements together.

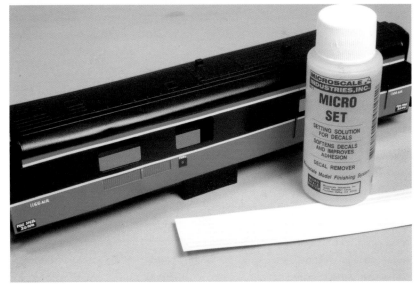

FINAL THOUGHTS ON MASKING

Masking, by its nature, is meant to help the painter to achieve quality results. Conversely, repeated masking of difficult surfaces between paint layers can also make life much more complicated and prolong a project into the realms of a modelling marathon. As always, patience and perseverance will be rewarded with a better finish.

One final recommendation is to ensure that masking is also applied with equal care on the interior of models, keeping paint away from clear glazing, electrical contacts and all working surfaces such as motors, gearboxes, coupling rod bushes, wheel bearings and so on. Paint is easy to apply, but it can sometimes be a real pain to remove.

CHAPTER NINE

COLOUR MATCHING AND BLENDING WITH FACTORY FINISHES

Detailing or modifying railway models usually involves either adding new components or altering existing ones. In some cases, this can be done without any impact on the model, especially if new parts are ready-painted before fitting. Alternatively, new metal or plastic components will need to be primed and painted in situ.

Naturally, the amount of painting is dictated by the quantity of new components and some of the projects illustrated here show how the finishing process can differ, in terms of technique and difficulty. For example, simply altering a few front-end details on a diesel locomotive presents a fairly simple refinishing task as careful masking will allow just a yellow warning panel to be replaced. Steam locomotives also have their accommodating features, such as black smokeboxes and running plates that allow new chimneys, smoke deflectors, door handles or lamp brackets to be upgraded without having any impact on the actual livery.

Touching-in or refinishing whole sections of a specific colour can be a tricky proposition although, once again, the shape of a model can help in providing clearly defined lines such as boiler bands, bodywork panels, grilles or even strips of lining or existing 'joints' between livery elements. Transitions between flat and curved surfaces, such as a steam locomotive's cab and firebox, can also be utilized as naturally occurring shadows help to disguise any minor discrepancies; having said that, any inconsistency should be avoided by careful surface preparation, masking and colour matching.

Whatever work may have been done, any affected surfaces must be rubbed absolutely smooth with fine abrasives and cleaned of all debris and greasy deposits. This crucial step will have a bearing on the quality of the final finish and, after deciding where to limit the areas of new paint, carefully apply masking tape, film or fluid (or a combination of each), ensuring that no paint will seep through any awkward corners or uneven surfaces. This is particularly important as thinned primers have a tendency to find their way into even the smallest gaps. To reduce the risk, spray the primer away from the edge of the tape or film (as described in Chapter 8) and thus avoid a heavy build-up along the 'joint' face. This is good practice anyway, but particularly so when aiming for a seamless transition between existing and new paintwork.

Once the colour has been built to full opacity over several light coats, the masking can be removed. If any seepage has occurred, some remedial work can be affected with a cocktail stick or cotton swab and white spirit. Instances such as this highlight the benefits of working with oil-based enamels, as they can be manipulated some time after application. Petroleum distillate (for example T-Cut paint restorer) is also handy in cases like this.

Blending can also be performed freehand, with little or no masking, making full use of the unique qualities of a good-quality airbrush. Gentle misting of the new paint over the modified area and surrounding paintwork should, in theory, provide a perfect finish. However, this relies on an exact match of paint shade unless a fairly generous coating of weathering is envisaged. Once again, the nature of the model can play into our hands: if we are working on an area of a locomotive roof, for example, then a little exhaust smoke or soot can be employed as a blending filter.

THE MEANING OF COLOUR

Colour, as we know it, is how our eyes and brains interpret light (natural or artificial) that is reflected from the objects around us. Humans can interpret

It's easy to blend new paint with a factory finish if the model in question offers a helping hand. This Bachmann 'Peak' has received a number of modifications to the nose ends only, so it's simply a case of treating the yellow warning panels without interfering with the blue sides or grey roof.

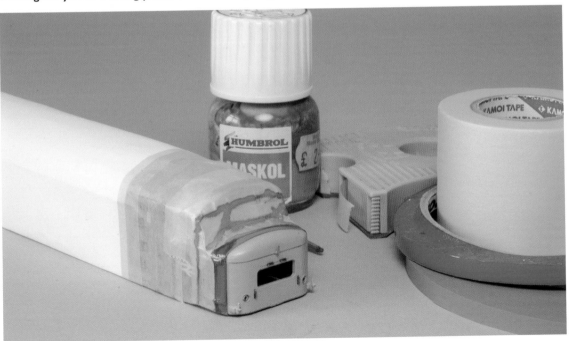

Having masked the bodyshell carefully with tape and Maskol fluid, the noses are ready for several light coats of white primer. If the top coat is to be rendered in the correct shade, the white background must be fully opaque to give the yellow full luminosity.

The warning yellow is also built up in gradual layers. Avoid creating too thick a coating of primer and topcoat as a ridge will be formed above the factory finish when the masking is removed.

With decals added and smaller details hand-painted, there are few clues to repainting having been carried out.

Steam locomotives also offer the convenience of blending in new components with minimal impact, especially if the work is confined to the smokebox or running plate areas. This GWR tank loco has received a new copper-capped chimney that has been primed and painted before fitting. Once fixed in place, a light misting of matt black, lightened a touch with a drop of grey, blended the new part with the factory finish. With practise, a steady hand and low air pressure, jobs such as this can be achieved without the need for masking, other than protecting the bright copper cap.

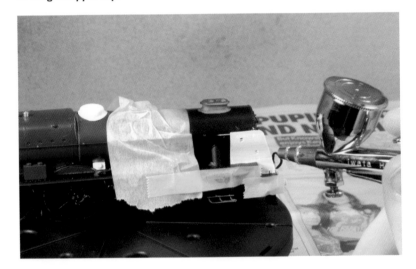

Pre-primed smoke deflectors, chimney and dome have been fitted to this Hornby 'Patriot' before the green livery was masked-up. Light layers of matt black enamel were then applied.

Full opacity was achieved after five or six coats, covering the surrounding smokebox as well as the new parts to avoid a clash of sheen with the factory finish. Note that I've worked around the smokebox numberplate and shedcode without painting them out. The new bufferbeam also has to be masked and painted red in a similar fashion to that described on page 125.

thousands of subtle shifts in colour, although we don't all perceive the same shades in exactly the same way. Our view of a single colour is also affected by its surroundings. For example, take a piece of red plastic and place it on a white background, noting how the red appears full and vibrant. However, if the same item were set on a black backing, it will look duller and slightly darker. Additionally, as any artist or photographer will know, colours appear brighter in full sunlight whereas, on a cloudy day, they will seem dull and lifeless.

Strictly speaking, no three-dimensional object ever appears in a truly uniform colour. Lighting conditions create an endless array of subtle differences in shade and perception of colour is also liable to change with distance. Atmospheric conditions tend to diffuse colours, rendering them paler to the eye the further away one is from an object. Try it for yourself by fixing a piece of coloured paper to an outside wall and considering its appearance from a foot or so away. Then step back about 20ft and notice how the shade has changed.

Landscape artists have long been familiar with this phenomenon and, accordingly, choose colours that reflect how the scene appears to them from their vantage point. The old Art School adage of 'painting what you see, not what you know' is pertinent here, since if an artist painted a village scene including a post box rendered in regulation Post Office Red, it would look truly out of place. Rather, it ought to be toned down to represent the shade as it appeared to the eye on that given day.

I've come across only a handful of fellow railway modellers who have made a policy of 'interpreting' railway colours, rather than simply opting for a tin of, say, BR Rail Blue and assuming that a locomotive must have carried a 'standard' shade. However, prototype finishes vary due to myriad reasons: differences in mixing, constituent pigments or weathering and fading.

When taking great care to represent a specific vehicle or building in terms of scale, shape and detail fittings, how many of us put the same amount of effort into discerning the exact colour? Some paint-makers go to great pains to match their output to original livery speci-

An interesting experiment to illustrate how we perceive colour and shade is to place a brightly coloured object onto a white background ...

... and then compare how the same object looks when moved onto a black backing. The colour loses much of its intensity, although the black surface does filter out contamination from reflected light.

fications but this is not always what a particular subject was wearing at a particular time. Additionally, photographic reproductions tend to distort colours, not least as film and prints fade over time. All of this might sound academic, but colour theory and scale colour does have an important role to play in model-making.

SCALE COLOUR

Model railways are, by their nature, intended to be viewed at a modest distance. On average this is around one metre and in OO gauge that equates to a scale of 76 metres. From such a distance, it follows that our perception of a maroon carriage, for example, would be different than if we were stood immediately in front of it. Although rarely mentioned in model railway circles, the idea of scaling down authentic livery shades according to the size of a model has been occupying military, aviation and nautical modellers for some time. Indeed, specifications have been drawn up by various modelling groups, providing a colour reference dependent on scale, often expressed in the percentage of white paint that

should be added to the main livery colour. All this rigid thoroughness has many drawbacks, however, especially when dealing with scales below the 1:76 ratio (OO gauge). Indeed, adopting these rules will invariably render models in N or Z gauges far too pale. Besides, working in such a regimented fashion tends to take a lot of the intuition out of the equation: surely it's more important for it to look right?

Black, in particular, is an awkward shade to render accurately in miniature. Even at full size, a black object rarely appears absolutely black. Instead, it will take on various shades of dark grey, although simply adding white or grey is not the best way to 'scale' the shade, lest it look 'washed out'. Instead, adding brown is much more effective, especially a rusty red-brown. Such shades are offered by various paint-makers as 'weathered black' and this is often best applied to scale subjects instead of a regular 'black'. Paradoxically, distance can have the effect of darkening white objects, even those that are kept sparklingly clean. A tiny amount of brown or dark grey added to the white will tone things down nicely.

Applying a livery colour straight from the tin is not always a step towards authenticity. Although this is an extreme example, 37109 carried a very faded version of EWS red and gold when captured at Bury in July 2008. Note how the shades have faded to a dusty pink and yellow.

Compared to the prototype image, this Vi-Trains Class 37 looks very different despite wearing the same livery. The model's finish is fairly accurate if tested against a swatch of the specified paint, yet the red and gold appear much richer to the eye. Weathering has toned the scheme down a little, but it still looks rather vivid in comparison to 37109.

In another view of the now-obsolete EWS livery, the dull lighting conditions and a decade of exposure to the elements have combined to render the livery elements fairly lifeless.

A good illustration of the use of scale colour is this pair of yard lamps. One has been painted with a coating of black enamel while the other has been scaled down with a dash of grey in the same black paint. Can you tell them apart? And which looks more realistic?

Customizing colours in this way is purely subjective and I know some modellers who employ these tactics in their scenic and building work, but never on locomotives and rolling stock. Others simply dismiss it completely. Personally, I've always aimed to portray my model layouts and dioramas in the fashion of a landscape painting or soft-focus photograph, hoping that each component blends together seamlessly, including the rolling stock. A model railway is, after all, just a snapshot of real life in miniature. But that's just my preference and is probably a result of my background in art and design, rather than miniature engineering.

Whether this aspect of modelling appeals to you or not, possessing a little knowledge of colour theory will prove very useful when mixing paints. Indeed, we hear lots of mention of colours, shades and hues, but what is the difference between them?

COLOUR THEORY

Firstly, let's look at the basics. All shades are derived from the three Primary Colours of red, blue and yellow. Mixing any two of these colours together produces a Secondary Colour; for example blue + yellow = green. Mixing any two of the Secondary Colours produces a Tertiary Colour (such as green +

purple = olive). Both black and white are not, strictly speaking, colours. Instead, black is more accurately classed as a shade and white as a tint. Adding black to any colour, produces a shade of the original, while adding white creates a further tint. Adding grey, on the other hand, results in a tone.

A hue is a pure pigment, free from any shades of other colours and without a hint of black, grey or white. This can also be expressed as a colour having a high chromaticity. The intensity of a colour is described in terms of its saturation, which is different to brightness, which refers to how light or dark the colour is, in comparison to pure white.

JOHANNES ITTEN'S COLOUR WHEEL

The above information – and its consequences – can be better appreciated by regarding the Itten Colour Wheel. Within the central triangle are the three Primary Colours, supplemented by three Secondary Colours of green, violet and orange. The outer circle reflects twelve different Tertiary Colours, achieved by mixing one Primary with a neighbouring Secondary.

Colours at diametrically opposed ends of the colour wheel are known as complimentary colours: for example, red and green or violet and orange. Mixing any two together results in a darker shade of each colour, depending on whether the ratio leans

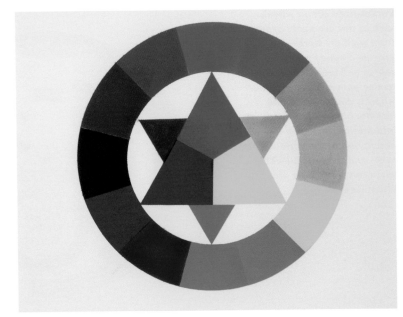

The Johannes Itten colour wheel is an invaluable reference source to keep at hand when mixing your own colours. As can be seen, the three Primary Colours of red, blue and yellow are at the heart of the diagram, with the Secondary Colours of green, violet and orange at the three points of the inverted triangle. The twelve Tertiary Colours are arranged around the circumference.

towards one or other of the ingredients. To illustrate the point, regard how red can be darkened when mixed with green, eventually being overtaken by the latter colour as the mix ratio surpasses 50 per cent of each.

Itten's colour wheel is a handy reference point when mixing specific colours that are otherwise unobtainable. Alternatively, if a replica colour does not look accurate enough to your eyes, then it can be altered to suit either your taste or to match with a factory finish. Further still, knowing how to subtly modify shades, tones and tints will help when tweaking a 'standard' livery shade to create some subtle variations, perhaps when recreating a faded or washed-out vehicle as part of a weathering project.

These three charts illustrate how the colour red can be changed by the addition of white to form a variety of tints (upper) and black to create darker shades (centre). Adding green – the complementary colour of red – produces a darker red until the mix passes 50 per cent of each. From then, the colour starts to turn into a shade of green.

Pocket-sized colour wheels such as this are freely available from good art stores and provide a handy reference source to have at hand when mixing paints. This particular wheel is double-sided and includes plenty of relevant information, including a visual description of the various tints, tones and shades achievable when certain colours are intermixed.

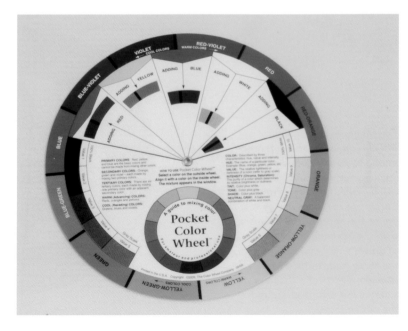

AUTHENTIC RAIL LIVERY PAINTS

Colour is a subjective matter at the best of times, but discussion of specific railway livery elements can be a thorny issue. There is, at least, plenty of choice in ready-mixed 'authentic' paints from a number of suppliers. However, they each have their own take on many popular colours. But which is right?

A truly accurate representation of an exact paint shade carried on a particular locomotive or carriage is difficult to recreate, particularly when the subject did not survive to be photographed in colour. For a time, railway staff mixed their own paints as and when they were required and, despite being provided with specifications from regional HQ, the bespoke nature of production led invariably to small but not insignificant variations. Where paint and lining have been preserved, colour-matching to these raises the problem of the samples being anything up to 150 years old and a degree of fading or discoloration of paint and varnish will affect a subtle change.

Modellers of a more modern persuasion are slightly better served as some of the real machines or vehicles are still around. Moreover, suppliers such as Railmatch obtain their paints from Manchester-based HM Guest Ltd who also supply a number of current (and some now obsolete) train operating companies. Phoenix Precision can also boast of having supplied BR and various museums and preservation centres.

As with many facets of modelling, it's what looks right that's often the benchmark and colour choice is no different. Weathering can change the look of a livery, be it by adding a filthy, dark covering or in the recreation of faded paintwork. On the pre-privatized railway, there was so much variation in livery shades, even in the corporate blue years. Age is a big factor, along with cleanliness, while the shape of the vehicle can also have an impact: the amount of grilles, doors or recessed panels on the bodyside invariably introduce both shadows and highlights and thus influence our perception of a colour.

Today, high-tech twin-pack paint formulas have removed much of this variation on full-sized prototypes, paintwork being expected to last decades with little deterioration. The new liveries that appear with regular franchise changes are often rendered by all-over vinyl transfers that offer their own challenges to the modeller in how they age and weather. A very close look at the side of a modern 'unit' will show some slight variations in shade between individual vinyl panels or repair patches.

Renderings of so-called standard schemes differ widely across ready-to-run products and paint manufacturers, as evidenced by this comparison of a number of models from different makers (from the front: Farish, Railmatch, Heljan, Bachmann). A little variety is not unwelcome, as there is usually a degree of difference between locomotives in real life.

COLOUR MATCHING

We've already mentioned the challenges of blending in new areas of paintwork by careful preparation and application, but perhaps the biggest test is to ensure that the colours being applied match the factory finish exactly. It helps to have a stock of livery paints from different makers, or at least to assemble a set of swatches with each applied over a white background (that is how paint manufacturers match their shades). Armed with these reference cards, a quick reckoning against a model will highlight which brand – and formula – offers the closest match.

In my experience, Railmatch BR locomotive green is a virtually perfect match with that employed on Heljan models, while the same maker's BR blue is also very close to the Danish firm's locomotives. The same

cannot usually be said with regards to Bachmann and Hornby products, although Lifecolor's BR blue is spot-on for many of the former manufacturer's models. There's little point in assembling a definitive colour matching reference chart, as there is much in the way of fluctuation across each range of paints and models.

If an exact match is not discerned from comparison with your swatch cards, then a colour must be mixed to suit. It's not necessary (unless you're a true purist) to start from scratch, as the closest existing paint shade can be used as a basis. But what do we add to get a closer match? That depends on the vagaries of the target shade: is it paler, greener, does it have more of a red tint, or is it darker? All of this will have to be formulated by your own eyes but, with a little practise, your mind can be taught how to identify the necessary alterations.

Modellers are spoiled by a choice of more than half a dozen versions of the same rail-themed colours, especially the popular BR Rail Blue, Locomotive Green and Coaching Stock Maroon. With this in mind, it can be helpful to assemble a set of swatches as a reference when touching-in any modifications or new parts. The various paints have been sprayed onto white-primed strips of plastic card, with each carefully labelled to avoid confusion.

Comparison of colours is best performed through a window of black card, which effectively neutralizes the shade from outside factors, helping the eyes to concentrate on the colour in question.

An example is illustrated here, taking the ubiquitous BR Rail Blue as an example. This, despite being much maligned at the time, is not a drab colour. Indeed, it incorporates a fairly complex mix with a high green content. When first applied, it can look vibrant, especially in a gloss or satin sheen. However, after a year or two in service, in all weathers and with a lax cleaning regime, the colour soon begins to take on a lifeless appearance. Perhaps this is why it became unpopular in the 1970s.

In model form, the Railmatch enamel or Lifecolor acrylic formulas are my personal recommendation as a base for mixing an exact shade, not least as they are very close to most ready-to-run models in the first place. Usually it's often just a case of lightening or darkening paint ever so slightly in order to achieve the perfect match, most commonly done by adding different shades of grey or white. At other times, however, contrasting colours need to be mixed in, such as a little green or yellow. Moreover, adding yellow ochre will darken and enrich the blue mix, while orange-red (a complementary colour to blue on the colour wheel) will do likewise, while also injecting a little extra 'green' to the shade. Practise

and experimentation is the key to mastering the theory and practice of colour theory and reference to a more thorough study of the subject is recommended (see Bibliography).

Perhaps the hardest task is to create your own authentic colour from scratch and this is confirmed by reference to the finishing of the 'Jones Goods' 4-6-0 featured here. When first built in the 1890s, the original specification of William Stroudley was for the locomotives to be turned out in his preferred scheme of 'Improved Engine Green'. Infamously, this colour is more yellow ochre than green and many have wondered whether this great engineer was colour blind! Regardless, when BR resurrected the sole surviving prototype in the late 1950s, the engine gained a coat of a very different, paler shade of yellow with a subtly revised lining style. As the only 'authentic' livery paint available is the Stroudley 'Engine Green', I was faced with having to mix my own shade. Luckily, with the aid of the colour theory mentioned above, the task was made a little easier.

Models for use outdoors pose a further problem as the effects of sunlight will cause paints of different formulas to age at varying rates. This was brought home to me after spending hours trying to match the paint on my trusty 1980s Nissan Micra, after effecting a number of bodywork repairs. As the light blue paint had faded over the years, it seemed pointless to obtain a can of the original shade, so I set to work mixing my own. After feeling proud of my handiwork, the enamel paints soon turned a much paler colour than the surrounding bodywork, giving poor Milly the look of having a heavy dose of measles!

This could have been averted (or at least minimized) by applying a protective clear coat at the end of the painting sequence. Indeed, this not only helps to blend any new paint with the old, but also affords a model some degree of protection against handling damage and exposure to the elements. Clear coats are discussed at length in the next chapter.

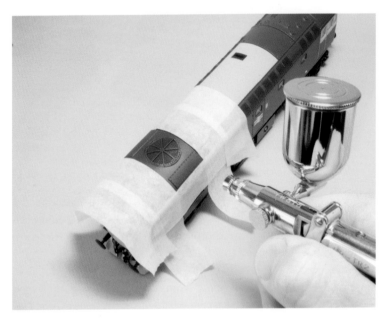

Although not a universal truth, Railmatch enamels are a close match for the paints worn by Heljan models, especially BR Loco Green. The BR Blue shade is also very similar although it needs to be blended in a little. Here, a new etched roof grille has been primed before building up the coats of blue, having made use of the model's raised panelling when masking.

With most of the masking removed (save for that protecting the yellow cab and grey roof panel), a further coat of blue is applied, using the airbrush to mist the paint over the nearby factory finish. In this way, there's no discernible 'seam' between paints, despite the two shades not being an exact match.

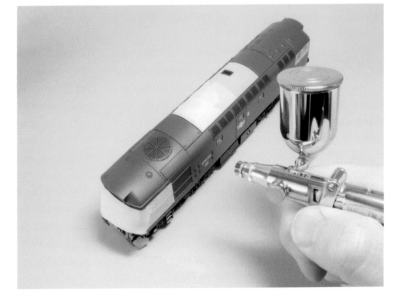

Lifecolor's versions of BR liveries are also a very close match to those applied to some ready-to-run models. To illustrate the point, the cab roof and boiler compartment of this Bachmann Class 47 has been refinished in Lifecolor BR Blue. It's almost impossible to tell the difference with the factory finish.

The BR green on this Hornby 'Patriot' was not so easy to match to a brand of paint. The new boiler-top details had been primed in white, which was probably a mistake as the model has been sprayed over a darker backing (the black plastic) without an undercoat. If a grey primer had been employed, then the Railmatch BR Green would have been more closely matched. Note how the raised boiler bands have been used as dividing lines for the masking. It took a good many fine layers to build up the colour.

When dry, the Railmatch shade of green looked just a little brighter compared to the factory finish but, happily, I'd wanted a lightly weathered finish, so a dusting of soot and dirt rendered any inconsistency in the green invisible.

Although weathering effects are covered in detail in Chapter 12, here's a quick look at how adding different shades and tints of the same colour can create some realistic effects. The Deutsche Bahn Class 103s often appeared washed out in service, being regularly exposed to mechanized washing plants, introducing broad variations of tone to the overall red livery.

Adding white, grey or black to the red livery paint introduces different tints, tones and shade, while a little green (the complementary colour of red) will darken the red in a different way, giving further tonal variation. The same process can be adapted to suit any livery.

It always pays to research your subject in depth, especially when dealing with older or more obscure colour schemes. This is not easy when there are no period colour photographs to work from, although there are numerous reference sources available. For example, Phoenix Precision offers concise livery guides, complete with swatches of livery and lining colours, detailed diagrams and prototype information.

The choice of colour to use as a basis is not always straightforward, especially if mixing a colour from scratch. For the elusive shade of yellow needed for the preserved 'Jones Goods' 4-6-0, I chose Railmatch Network Rail Sunshine Yellow for the base colour, as it's fairly neutral (without too much orange or green – the adjoining colours on the colour wheel). A little orange was added, plus a little white, to create a decent match to the colour captured in period photographs. Having deemed the original mix too near to ochre, a small amount of green and a further drop or two of white was added, to bring the colour back towards the target shade.

It took a few attempts, with some subtle changes to the mix along the way, before the overall colour was settled upon. When applied to a three-dimensional object, paint can appear very different to how it looks in a jar or on a flat test surface. The engine looks very yellow at this stage but, once the olive green and red lining is applied, it will soon look much different.

CHAPTER TEN

CLEAR COATS

A clear coat is a vital stage in the painting process, especially for projects where a high standard of finish is required. Moreover, the quality of the coating formula and the deftness of application are both determining factors in how well a completed model will appear. Regardless of how well the previous layers of paint have been applied, if they're followed by a poor clear coating then the entire job may be ruined.

This all-over covering also helps to blend together various separate paint applications and will act as a hard-wearing barrier against solvents, oils and grease, along with everyday handling. A good clear coat should also have the ability to survive temperature and humidity fluctuations. Moreover, a varnish can act as an intermediate layer between different paint formulas, while the performance of waterslide decals is also enhanced by a preliminary clear gloss coat and a sealing layer of varnish.

Choosing a good quality varnish is of paramount importance and there are plenty of high-performance formulas on the market that will provide long-lasting protection. There are also a number of lesser-quality products around that may offer certain short-term benefits, such as rapid drying times or cheapness, but they may be liable to discolouration over time. Compatibility is another issue of note, with certain types of cellulose lacquer not being suitable for application over enamels or acrylics.

PREPARATION

In line with all aspects of painting, the surface in question must be clean and any previous paint coatings completely dry. A varnish will also need a 'key' to aid adhesion to what may already be a very smooth surface. A light rub down with abrasives is the preferred option as long as the model's surface will permit it. If there are too many delicate details, then working around them will have to suffice. Ultra-fine abrasive cloths, such as in the Micromesh range, really come into their own in these instances as the finer grades can be used without damaging the underlying paint layers. Be careful of exerting excessive pressure, though, and always use the abrasive with plenty of water as a lubricant.

There's a wealth of choice among hobby varnishes, of differing formulas and performance. Railmatch and Phoenix Precision are among the best, while Humbrol's Clear Cote range offers a crystal clear finish with a short drying time. Be wary of cheap polyurethane formulas that may turn to a yellow hue over time.

Clean the model thoroughly between abrading and varnishing, as explained in earlier chapters. If applying clear coats over a fully assembled model, perhaps as part of the renumbering and renaming process, it's possible to avoid the need for dismantling with careful abrading, cleaning and masking.

CHOOSING A VARNISH

Firstly, a note of clarification: although the use of the word 'varnish' refers to a specific type of clear paint, it has entered common usage as both a descriptive term and a verb. It is in this latter form that I'll be using 'varnish', as another way of defining a clear coating, or the application of a clear paint. Secondly, and in common with 'ordinary' paints, the choice of varnish formulas and brands can be separated into three main categories: oil-based, acrylics and cellulose-based.

OIL-BASED

Enamel varnishes produce highly durable, lustrous coatings, although some brands can be prone to yellowing over time. One of their major advantages is the facility for buffing away any minor imperfections or scratches, using fine abrasives and T-Cut finish restorer, often without the need for further coatings. Depending on the formula, drying times can be anything from six hours to fourteen days.

Among the fastest-drying formulas are Humbrol's synthetic enamel Clear Cotes (Mattcote, Satincote and Glosscote), which can be handled after just a few hours if left in a warm environment. However, the dryness can be deceiving as full hardness still takes one or two days to be achieved, especially when using the gloss formula. These coatings dry to a long-lasting crystal-clear finish and find much use in my workshop. However, if I'm working on a special commission or anything else demanding of that little bit of extra finesse, then I'll forgo the temptations of Clear Cotes and opt for a higher grade formula such as Phoenix or Railmatch. I've also found that the Clear Cote finish is not as durable as other, more expensive varnishes. Humbrol also continues to produce small tinlets of 'regular' enamel varnish in matt, satin and gloss finishes (Refs. 49, 135 and 35 respectively).

Similar to the common polyurethane formula (see below), they offer a supremely tough finish but tend towards yellowing over a short period of time.

The enamel varnishes produced by both Railmatch and Phoenix Precision are highly regarded for their longevity and clear formulation. Of the two, the Phoenix brand requires much more time to cure and remains tacky for a day or two, raising the worry of dust or debris being trapped on the sticky surface. Accordingly, it's recommended to place the object in a covered, dust-free shelter to dry. If stored in a stable, temperate environment, good-quality enamels will keep for a few years without losing any of their important qualities. However, if the contents of a jar look a little past their best, then their performance may be unpredictable and it may be wise to opt for a fresh supply instead.

Polyurethane varnish is made up of plastic-based compounds that provide a tough finish with a deep lustre. Just as readily intended for use on exterior woodwork as it is for smaller-scale applications, variations on the theme are offered by a handful of model brands. Large tins of polyurethane, as found in hardware stores, can be thinned and sprayed with acceptable results, or so I'm told, although I tend to avoid these coatings, especially if applying over a light background, particularly white. Many of these varnishes are likely to develop a brown tint when dry, presumably since they are designed for use on domestic timberwork.

Besides, there are so many varnishes specifically formulated for modelling applications as to render large DIY tins redundant, especially as there is only a minimal saving in cost. Good hobby-rated brands are non-yellowing, resistant to oils, chemicals and heat (great for live steam models) and come in conveniently sized tins or jars. Phoenix Precision, incidentally, will furnish you with tins of varnish in a variety of volumes to suit projects large and small.

Putting my own personal prejudice aside, I'm sure that DIY-grade polyurethane varnishes may have some other useful applications, such as scenic tasks. Best thinned with white spirit to the usual viscosity employed for airbrushing, allow a few days for it to dry before handling.

ACRYLICS

Having the benefits of low odour and rapid drying, some water-based varnishes offer results on a par with enamels in terms of appearance. They lack the versatility of oil-based varnish, however, as well as being a little less hard-wearing. A greater number of very thin coats is likely to be required before a deep lustre is obtained and the first few layers must be applied as 'tack coats' (as described in Chapter 5) especially if spraying over enamel or cellulose paints.

Most acrylic formulas appear cloudy when in the tin – and after thinning – but will dry absolutely clear. Careful thinning and application is the key to avoiding a lumpy or runny finish. Clean water can be used, although it's far better to use a dedicated acrylic thinner, preferably from the same brand as the varnish in use.

A wide departure from hobby varnishes is the use of acrylic floor polishes, such as Klear, by Johnsons Wax. Although the original formula of this product has recently been discontinued by the manufacturer, its benefits to modellers have been well documented in the modelling press over the past ten years. Similar products remain, such as Future, and it may be worth experimenting with others as there is likely to be little to lose – you can always polish the kitchen floor with what's left.

I'm still using a 500ml bottle of Klear that I've had for more than five years and there's still plenty left, providing supremely good value for money (it cost just a few pounds) and maintaining its performance unchecked over this time. As it's designed for use on floors, Klear dries to a very hard-wearing finish and can be thinned (and cleaned) with water, although it is supplied in a suitable viscosity for spraying directly. Very few noxious fumes are emitted and, depending on how many coats are applied, either a satin or high-gloss finish can be achieved (more coats give a deeper shine). Another use for Klear is to repair scratched plastic glazing: after applying a few coats and leaving overnight to harden, the surface can be buffed with fine abrasives and a polishing compound (such as Garal polish) to leave the surface as good as new.

I can't vouch for other brands of acrylic floor polishes although the new, reformulated Klear is a distinctly brown-coloured liquid that, although going on quite clear, is not as model-friendly as its pred-

ecessor. Having said that, it can still find many a use in scenic applications. A much more viable alternative is the clear acrylic offered in Iwata's ComArt range, which is very similar to Klear in all but cost. Supplied in 4fl oz (125ml) plastic jars, the viscosity and performance is virtually identical with no need for thinning before spraying. The cost-per-millilitre is considerably higher, however, and this comparison only reflects the bargain-priced nature of Klear rather than the expense of the high-quality ComArt product, a single jar of which will last for a long time.

The pre-thinned nature of both Klear (and other floor polishes) and ComArt varnish means that it's easy to apply too much liquid at once, potentially causing runs and puddles on the surface. Build up

While many acrylic varnishes can be difficult to apply to a high standard, there are also a number of floor polishes that offer improved performance and a durable finish. Johnson's Klear is now discontinued in its original form but similar products are still on the market. Ready to spray, water can be used as a thinner and Windolene will strip the polish (wet or dry) from the surface without damaging the underlying paintwork.

Chris Wesson offers a clear lacquer in his small paint range, while automotive finishing aerosols are also a fine source (including Halfords), especially when decanted for airbrush use. Similarly, those offered in aerosol form by Just Like the Real Thing are also recommended, although they are a little expensive.

WORKING WITH CLEAR COATS

Exact drying times are hard to define as the type of thinners plays a role in determining the speed of curing. For example, white spirit takes much longer to evaporate than airbrushing thinners, although I find that a slower drying time is preferable when varnishing as the liquid can flow properly on the surface before starting to 'go off'. With fast-drying thinners, not only is the covering not as smooth, but the varnish may not dry as transparent as it should. This applies to matt, satin and gloss coats.

Due to variances in formulation, intermixing of clear coats from different brands is not to be recommended. Having said that, there are some that are compatible but, unless a mix is thoroughly tested on

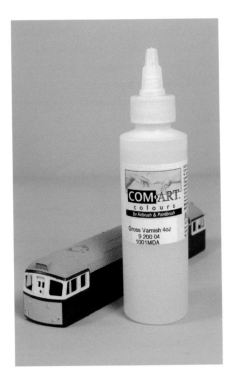

An alternative to the elusive Klear polish is this high-quality acrylic clear coat from ComArt. Superb results are obtainable, although the application takes a little time to master: build up numerous ultra-light coats, allowing each to dry in turn, until the desired sheen is achieved. The more coats are applied, the glossier the surface will be. Com-Art varnish can, however, struggle to adhere to enamel or factory-applied finishes unless they've been lightly abraded beforehand.

very light coats, leaving each to dry for an hour or two and allow twenty-four hours for the final coat to set completely before handling the model or adding decals or other paints.

LACQUER

Cellulose-based clear lacquers are the ultimate in high-quality coatings, although they are not the easiest to work with. Due to compatibility issues, they should not be used over enamel or acrylic paints and may also dissolve any freshly applied decals. However, the quality and toughness of finish is hard to beat and, with a little practice, the techniques for successful application can be mastered.

Choice of clear coat formula is important as compatibility may be an issue, not only with previous paint layers but with decals too. This Class 37 has received a set of delicate waterslide transfers from Precision Labels that are sensitive to some brands of varnish. When in doubt, opt for acrylics. Subsequent coats of enamel varnish can also follow if desired.

a scrap surface beforehand, I'd recommend keeping to one line of varnishes per application. Applying acrylics over an enamel surface – and vice versa – should not cause any problems as long as the previous layer has cured completely and, in common with opaque paints, spraying only in a warm and dry atmosphere is a necessity. Working in a cold, damp shed or garage carries the risk of condensation forming on the model's surface and turning the clear coat cloudy.

MATT, SATIN OR GLOSS

The choice between a matt, satin or gloss finish is a wholly personal choice. My own tastes veer towards the softer-looking matt or satin finishes, as I like my models to blend in with their miniature surroundings. As much of my work is for public consumption, photography is made much easier with a matt subject, avoiding the problems of light reflecting off a shiny surface. Matt coats are much easier to apply, too. Conversely, application of a gloss finish is an exacting task, requiring much more work. Many thin layers may be required to build the finish to a deep lustre and, as gloss varnishes are usually very slow to dry, so it can take days to achieve a suitable finish.

Satin is usually the most appropriate finish if the model is to be left in a pristine state as it's a welcome halfway house between the toy-like gloss and the flat, lifeless matt. Satin coatings also interfere least with the perception of the colours beneath: gloss coats introduce reflected light from the model's surroundings, while an ultra-matt sheen can give a distinctly grey appearance to a livery. Don't forget that varnishes (of the same brand and type) can be intermixed to gain a finish more to your liking. A drop or two of matt added to a satin formula will take a little of the 'glossiness' away and vice versa. Separate matting agents are also available (from Phoenix Precision in particular) to tone down gloss paints and varnishes to your own taste and this can be very helpful when trying to match the sheen of a factory finish. Test on a scrap model, allowing it to dry before comparison as the sheen will alter as the thinners evaporate.

Tailoring the sheen to match the prototype is often more important and, as this Class 57 shows, a sparklingly clean locomotive is not unheard of. When scaled down, however, too shiny a finish can simply look toy-like.

Although the shade of blue is entirely authentic, the ultra-matt finish to this DRS Class 20 makes the colour appear flat and lifeless, with a hint of grey. It may be perfect for a dusty, work-stained machine, but offers a stark contrast to the Class 57.

Again, a flat matt varnish adds a 'greying' effect to the underlying paint, evidenced by this black steam locomotive.

The combination of a high gloss preliminary clear coat, good-quality decals and a matt sealing coat produce an excellent finish, with the various legends looking like they've been painted onto the surface.

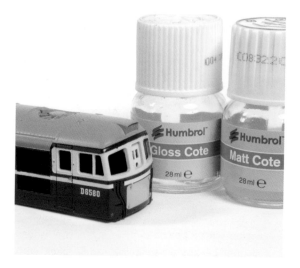

When finishing this Class 33, the Humbrol Matt Cote was deemed too flat, so a little Gloss Cote was blended into the mix to create a bespoke semi-satin sheen. Only mix varnishes of the same brand and formula to ensure compatibility.

Another bespoke sheen was created on this spotless Network Rail Class 31. Note how the repainted bodyshell perfectly matches the finish of the plastic bogies, to create as close to a factory finish as possible.

Matching the final sheen of a model to a factory-finished equivalent is not easy as these two 'Peaks' illustrate. On the left is an almost-finished conversion project, wearing a coat of Phoenix Precision satin varnish, while D67 on the right is in out-of-the-box condition. If you want uniformity among your locomotive collection, then tinkering with varnish formulas may be necessary, making use of matting agents mixed with satin or gloss coats.

A high gloss coating is of great value when lining or lettering a model by hand, as the smooth finish helps if any corrections need to be made; they can simply be wiped away before the paint or ink dries. A matt varnish should follow for freight vehicles such as this.

WHAT TO DO IF THINGS GO WRONG

It is to be hoped that this information will not be needed, but it pays to know how to handle any setbacks in the varnishing process. Perhaps the most common problem is the invasion of foreign matter into the wet coating as the model is being painted or while drying. If you see a speck of dirt appearing, it's best to leave it well alone and let the model dry, then use a fine abrasive to level the affected area before revarnishing. When working with slow-drying enamels, however, a very quick intervention with a clean cocktail stick can often extract the offending object without disturbing the surface too much. A little extra varnish applied over the area will encourage the surrounding wet coating to reflow, thus covering the small gap. It must be stressed that this is not a foolproof system and has only a modest success rate.

If for any reason the desired sheen is not achieved, allow the clear coat to harden completely (usually at least a week) before lightly rubbing down the whole model with fine abrasive cloths, starting with no coarser than 6,000grade and working to around 10,000. All that's necessary is to level the surface of the varnish and provide a 'key' for the new coating, rather than removal. Lubricate the abrasives generously to prevent clogging, then clean and dry the model thoroughly before respraying.

If a more serious problem has occurred, such as a reaction with a previous paint layer, then there is little option but to strip the model back with either coarser abrasives or a chemical stripping compound. This can certainly be a disheartening moment, but it's important that we learn from our mistakes.

Should any minor mishap arise, simply let the varnish dry completely before rubbing down with fine abrasive cloth. Here, a sheet of 6,000grit Micromesh is being used with plenty of water as a lubricant.

Changing the identity of a steam locomotive usually only involves a new smokebox numberplate and cabside numerals, meaning that only small areas need masking-up for varnishing over the new decals. Be sure to cover both the outside and inside of the glazing to guard against overspray reaching inside the cab.

Affecting a seamless transition between the modified cab sides and boiler of this renumbered Bachmann B1 proved awkward, as the sheen of the factory finish was difficult to match. Instead, the whole bodyshell (plus tender) was treated to an overall coat of satin varnish.

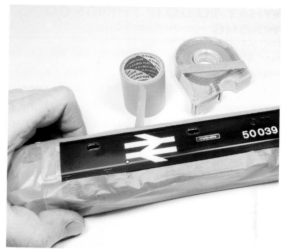

Clear coats are essential for blending in new areas of paintwork or following any other modifications. This Hornby Class 50 has received new numbers and nameplates but the model's surface now has an irregular sheen from the removal of the printed characters. Without dismantling the model, the affected areas can be treated with careful masking.

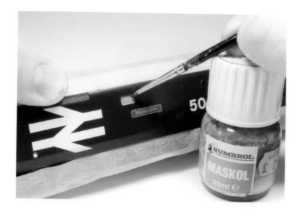

Don't forget to cover any windows with Maskol fluid.

After several light coats of Railmatch satin varnish, the model can be set aside in a covered container to keep out dust and debris. Drying times vary, but a week is not uncommon.

With the masking removed, there's little perceptible difference between the factory finish and the modified sides.

A useful tip to remember is to add a drop or two of black paint into a jar of thinned varnish prior to spraying …

… this will give a gently toned-down appearance, especially to a vivid colour such as the red framework and metallic hopper of this wagon.

OTHER APPLICATIONS

Varnish has many other uses aside from those already stated. It can be an effective and invisible bonding agent, negating the need for adhesives. For example, an overall coat onto a locomotive offers the chance of adding delicate details such as etched nameplates or shed codes while the varnish is tacky. When dry, another coat will help to fix the new parts in place. Varnish will also protect the bare metal surface of the nameplate from tarnishing.

Floating waterslide decals into a wet layer of acrylic varnish is a way of hiding translucent carrier films and achieving a 'painted-on' finish. Further light layers of varnish will then seal the icons onto the surface. Enamel and cellulose varnishes are not compatible with this method and thinner acrylics, such as Klear or Com-Art, are particularly suited, allowing the decals to be manipulated at will without drying out too quickly.

Printed card building kits greatly benefit from a light misting of matt varnish following construction, helping to combat the fading effects of sunlight upon the surface. The overall coating also unifies the appearance of the assembly, which is particularly useful for disguising shiny glue stains or areas that have been touched-in with paints, crayons or pastels. Printed signs, posters, road markings and many other scenic features should also be treated to the same attention.

Weathering powders, pigments and scatter materials can all be held in place with a delicate misting of varnish, allowing them to resist persistent handling without smudging, although a very low pressure must be employed to avoid blowing them away. Liquid fixatives for weathering powders are also suitable for spraying, usually without the need for thinning. Of note is the MIG range of powders that also offers an oil-based fixative, of a similar nature to artists' turpentine. This thin liquid is perfect for airbrush use and, when applied on the lowest possible pressure setting and from a greater distance from the subject than we would normally work, the powders will not be greatly disturbed and will be sealed in place much more effectively than by applying the liquid by brush.

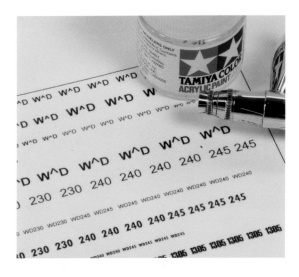

Creating your own waterslide decals is not a difficult task with suitable papers being offered for use in home computer printers. However, the printed characters must be sealed with acrylic varnish before cutting out and applying. Apply a handful of coats to ensure the surface is watertight.

Floating waterslide decals onto a base of wet acrylic varnish not only increases their adhesion but also improves their appearance. Prepare the surface with a few light coats of a thin clear coat, such as Klear or Com-Art clear coat.

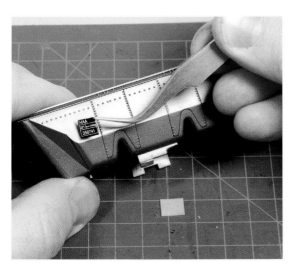

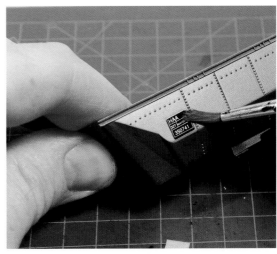

With the latest coat at the tacky stage of drying, apply the decal with the minimum of water, having lifted it from its backing paper. This is best achieved by taking the decal from the water after only around 10 seconds and then waiting for it to become loose. Then place the decal and its backing onto a sheet of blotting paper or kitchen towel, before lifting the icon away with a pair of fine tweezers.

Do not soak up any excess fluid with swabs or paper towels; instead use a clean brush to clear any moisture trapped behind the decal. Allow the surface to dry out naturally for an hour or so.

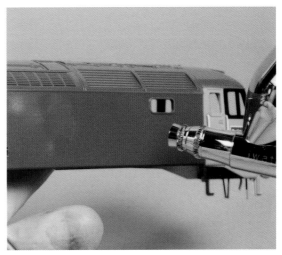

Cover with a further couple of coats of the same acrylic varnish to seal the decal in place. Any carrier film should be invisible, resulting in a painted-on appearance.

To avoid making a mess with adhesives, small etched details such as nameplates can be fixed securely with varnish. Enamels are well suited to this task. Here a loco is being coated with a layer of Humbrol Satin Cote.

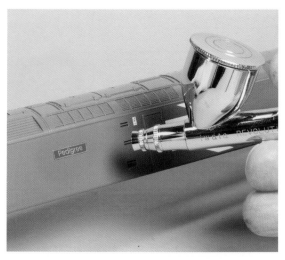

With the varnish still wet, the plates can be placed into position carefully with fine tweezers.

Make any final adjustments to the positioning and leave aside for an hour or two. A further coat or two will seal the nameplates in place and give them added protection against tarnishing.

Card and paper kits benefit from a coat of varnish, preferably matt, before being sited onto a layout. Not only does this preserve the dyes from fading, but also blends in any areas where paint or weathering has been applied.

Other printed items such as posters, signs or wagon labels will also be preserved if coated with a thin varnish coat.

When fixing loose wagon loads or other scatter materials by the use of dilute PVA glue and a syringe or eyedropper, inevitably the glue will dry to an unrealistic clear film. This is particularly noticeable on large, lightly coloured scatters such as this stone load from Geoscenics.

A light misting of matt varnish renders any glue stains invisible and creates a much more authentic effect.

Clear gloss varnish also offers many other applications such as adding damp streaks on the tank sides of this Terrier, simply sprayed in vertical strokes.

Weathering powder fixatives often come in the form of clear liquids that are easily and effectively applied by airbrush. Set the air pressure low and spray from a distance to avoid disturbing any of the powders.

CHAPTER ELEVEN

METALLIC FINISHES

Metallic paints achieve their visual effect by suspending tiny flakes of metal within a solvent solution. Produced in oil-, water- or cellulose-based formulas, such paints can be very effective in recreating bare materials such as steel, chrome, copper and brass. Each of these metals are common on both the steam- and modern-age railway and an effective rendition of copper pipes, brass fittings or steel wagon loads helps to increase a model's authenticity.

However, it should be remembered that metal particles can only be ground to a finite size and, moreover, cannot be scaled down with true accuracy. This leads to some paints giving a wholly improbable appearance, especially when employed on small scale objects. Automotive finishes or general DIY brands are the worst culprits as the metallic particles therein are fairly coarse. Good-quality metallic finishes, from specific modelling sources, are designed to produce a much softer, more appropriate appearance.

As any professional painter will tell you, applying metallic paint offers some unique challenges, whether in miniature form or on a full-size subject. Furthermore, repairing or touching-in a metallic finish is a particularly tough proposition. Perhaps not surprisingly, metallic finishes have caused a number of problems to model train manufacturers over the years, although recent advances in production methods have seen this problem consigned to history. Well, almost. Some contemporary products are still turned out in shades of flat grey rather than metallic silver, for example.

Metallic paints may have been around for a long time but it's only in the last decade or so that there's been an upturn in the quality of those aimed at modellers. Previously, paint formulas were known for a lack of adhesion or for producing uneven finishes. While there are still some poor paints on the market, the majority offer good results. Additionally, there are a select few that truly excel and the Alclad2 range is the most prominent among the latter. Cellulose-based Alclad2 paints specialize in metallic finishes and, due to their unique formulation, they can only be applied by airbrush.

Arguably, acrylic metallic paints are the least popular and are the most difficult to work with. Having said that, those offered by Tamiya and Vallejo are not too bad for small touching-in work by hand, such as locomotive cab controls and the odd pipe. Both of these brands feature a higher proportion of alcohol than the ordinary colours in the same ranges, meaning longer drying times. This permits a better flow of paint over the surface, however, and thus a higher quality of finish.

Enamels are also somewhat hit-and-miss in terms of performance, although Humbrol's small range of Metalcote paints are worthy of note, especially their capacity for creating realistic polished effects. Also boasting good credentials are the various metallic enamels offered by Railmatch, with convincing shades of copper, brass and steel in both 'polished' and 'oily' form.

It hasn't always been so, but the high quality of most of today's ready-to-run models extends to the production of superb scale renditions of metallic paint finishes, epitomized by this Bachmann JPA tank wagon.

At first glance this Pendolino and 'Thunderbird' Class 57 carry a uniform rendition of Virgin's brash livery. A closer look, however, reveals that the Bachmann 57 wears a light grey bodyside rather than the impressive silver applied to the Hornby 390.

There is a fair amount of choice in metallic paints aimed at scale modellers, with some excellent products standing out in terms of realism and performance. Enamel and cellulose paints are preferred, while metallic acrylics are more difficult to use. Virtually unbeatable for realism is the Alclad2 range of cellulose lacquers, expressly formulated for airbrush use. Various shades are available, including chrome, aluminium and stainless steel.

SURFACE PREPARATION

Metallics need just as much, if not more, care in surface preparation as ordinary paints. Their low viscosity and high lustre can be very unforgiving to a bumpy or dusty surface. However, specific paint brands require a slightly different approach to preparation, depending on the quirks and foibles of each formula. Most are suited to application over a matt background of universal primer, whereas others, such as certain shades in the Alclad2 range, benefit from application over a shiny, gloss surface. Alclad2's own formula of grey primer (see Chapter 6) is perfect for most metallic shades but Stainless Steel, Chrome and Polished Aluminium are better applied over a gloss black background. This dark backing helps to bring out the best in these particular shades, giving a greater depth to the finish. As for spraying this paint onto a shiny surface, this poses a test to the painter's skill and patience as it can be easy to cause runs and puddles if too much Alclad2 is applied too soon. Instead, apply a very light preliminary layer, in the manner of a 'tack coat' (see Chapter 6). Build the paint slowly to full opacity with several more coats applied about ten minutes apart.

The need for a coat of black does, however, raise the issue of compatibility as the cellulose Alclad2 should not, in theory, be applied over an enamel or acrylic undercoat. To be certain of a satisfactory outcome, make use of Alclad2's gloss black undercoat, sprayed in the same way as the primer, but built to a deep shine and left to cure for a day or two before proceeding. Alternatively, automotive paints will do, sprayed from an aerosol or, preferably, decanted for airbrush use. Although I hesitate to recommend this, I have managed to use a black enamel coat without problems but this must be done gingerly with an initial 'tack coat' of Alclad2 over the cured enamel (left for a week to dry out). This first layer should then be rested for a few hours to ensure all traces of thinners have evaporated before proceeding with a few more very light coats, again applied a few hours apart. Don't try this for the first time on a prized model as it may cause problems.

For smaller components, such as locomotive detailing parts, such thoroughness in preparation is neither practical nor necessary. Simply adding a good coating of primer over a clean surface will do, before the metallic paint is applied in light stages.

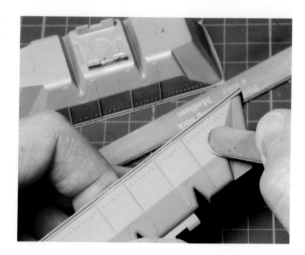

Surface preparation and priming is just as essential when applying metallic finishes as with ordinary paints. Depending on the metallic formula, either a flat matt background is required or a shinier, gloss undercoat.

Buffing up a matt primer with a fine abrasive or nail glossing pad will provide a suitably smooth and less absorbent surface on which to apply the metallic paint, thus giving better results. Alclad2 lacquers particularly benefit from application onto a shiny surface.

A gloss black undercoat is recommended for certain Alclad2 renditions of bright metals, the dark background intensifying the effect of the paint. There is a suitable black primer in the Alclad2 range, but I've used a Halfords aerosol here, applied over the same brand's grey primer.

Apply the first coat of metallic paint in a very light, translucent layer to act as a 'tack coat'. Build up the paint layers gradually, keeping the airbrush close to the surface to keep the paint going on 'wet' for a superior finish. Keep the air pressure low and the tool moving to avoid runs and spatter.

These wagon loads, fashioned from plastic section, have received coats of Alclad2 Aluminium and Steel, both of which look ultra-realistic.

Once mounted onto a suitable freight wagon and lightly weathered, the 'steel' sections look very convincing.

PAINT PREPARATION

Thinning metallic paints can be difficult, making the ready-to-spray Alclad2 formula even more tempting. Thorough mixing is the first requirement, either by shaking, stirring or a combination of both. The heavy pigments must be dispersed correctly throughout the solution if the paint is to perform and regular agitation throughout the session will prevent settlement. Alclad2 paints require only to be shaken before use, a metal mixing ball being encased in each glass jar to help break up the pigment. A good five minutes of shaking is the minimum and I find it helpful to perform this chore with a little musical accompaniment.

Enamels and acrylics also need to be shaken and stirred for a good while and this tedious chore can be alleviated by using an electric mixing tool. However, the initial agitation is best done by hand with a paint spatula, as there is likely to be much in the way of sediment at the bottom of the tin that will need breaking up gently. Stir until the paint appears a uniform colour in the container, with few streaks. Frustratingly, the mix will start to separate almost immediately, so be sure to keep disturbing it right up until it's ready for loading into the airbrush.

Judging the correct amount of thinners to add is also difficult as the paint must (in general) be reduced to a lower viscosity than regular paint, lest the airbrush struggle to atomize the mix satisfactorily. Indeed, this is one of the main indicators as to the quality of a paint formula: the finer the pigments, the easier it will be to spray. Again, keeping the mix moving will prevent settlement and also try to avoid leaving the paint in the airbrush for long periods between applications. Test spray onto a scrap surface to check for quality of paint flow: if there is any splatter then the pressure is either too low or the paint is too thick.

APPLICATION

All metallics behave in a similar way when being emitted through an airbrush and a low pressure

is vital (12–15psi). Build the paint gradually, beginning with a light misting coat to gain adhesion, followed by several equally gentle layers with the airbrush about 8–10cm from the surface and constantly moving to avoid runs, especially if working into corners or tight recesses. The paint must go on to the surface looking wet if it's to produce a good finish.

Leave enough time between coats for the thinners to evaporate (between 10 minutes and an hour depending on the formula). When full opacity is reached, set the model aside to harden completely, preferably overnight. Further masking and spraying can then proceed although, in order to avoid adhesion problems, areas where metallics are to be overcoated should be buffed with fine abrasives to provide a suitably flat surface. With this in mind, it can be easier to plan a livery application so as to have the metallic element added towards the end of the sequence. Just take care to prevent the thin metallic paints from seeping through any gaps in the masking; something that most formulas are particularly prone to do.

Even the rapid-drying formulas should be given plenty of time to cure completely before work proceeds. Some enamels need around a week to achieve their full hardness (especially Metalcote paints), while acrylics and cellulose require just a day or two. A finishing clear coat is not essential with Alclad2 paints, as they dry to a lovely sheen in their own right. However, other brands do benefit from a layer of varnish, deepening the lustre of the metallic finish and providing a more hard-wearing finish.

Regardless of the metallic paint's finish, a clear coat will always be necessary if decals are to be added and, as mentioned previously, the problem of yellowing varnishes is something to keep in mind when choosing a clear coat, as such a phenomenon will ruin the metallic effect. There's also the problem of having metallic particles over-coated in paints with high water content, leading to the risk of tarnishing beneath certain acrylic formulas.

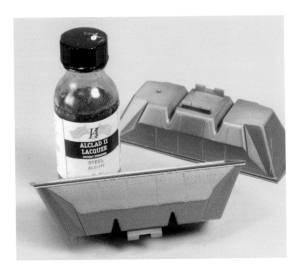

Since the 1970s the use of unpainted metal freight wagons has increased on Britain's railways, with stainless steel or galvanized coatings employed to reduce production and maintenance costs. The humble HAA coal hopper was one of the first to incorporate this feature and these Hornby HFA wagons are being backdated to represent the original pattern. A new covering of Alclad2 Steel has replaced the rather shiny factory finish.

A degree of tonal variation can be produced by masking up and spraying adjoining panels in a slightly different shade of metallic paint. In this case, Aluminium is being applied.

To create a softer effect than the harsh separating lines produced by masking the various panels, try applying the same paint freehand.

The effect of the slightly different shades of metallic paint can be appreciated by the realistic appearance of the finished wagons. The vehicle on the right was the one treated freehand, offering a smoother transition between shades than the wagon on the left. Either way, the contrast is muted further with a little weathering (see Chapter 11).

This industrial chimney stack has been given a realistic coating of Alclad2 Stainless Steel, again applied over a gloss black undercoat.

Once weathered and set into the scenic area, the superb metallic finish can still be appreciated.

Metallic finishes have a very obvious use to modellers of the steam era, with every locomotive offering at least a few exposed fittings in their natural unpainted state. Brass whistles, safety valves and injectors are just a few examples. A bulled-up engine would have these parts gleaming, while a workaday machine, like this Midland 1F, would see the metal take on more of a muted, tarnished appearance. (Photo by Nick Brodrick.)

Copper is another material used in profusion on steam motive power. This BR 9F certainly has its fair share.

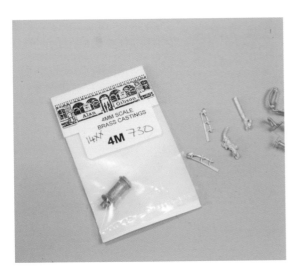

It's possible to use real brass and copper detailing components where available, especially copper wire and turned brass safety valves and whistles. However, many aftermarket details are offered in either white-metal or lost-wax brass castings.

No Great Western engine is complete without a copper-capped chimney and this casting has received a few coats of Alclad2 Copper, building the finish to an extremely lifelike rendition of the real thing, both here and on the cylinder drain pipes for a Stanier 4-6-0.

Having masked the copper cap and sprayed the base of the chimney matt black, the finished casting is ready to fit in place of the substandard unit on this little Hornby 0-4-2T.

Without doubt the new chimney is a vast improvement, but this only highlights the fact that the safety valve cover also needs replacing or repainting.

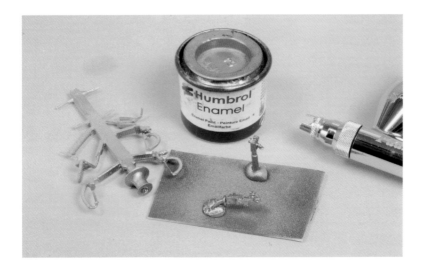

These white-metal injector and ejector valve castings have been primed and sprayed with Humbrol metallic Brass (No.54). While acceptable, the finish is a little coarser than that produced with Alclad2 paints.

To complete the injector valve, the drain pipe has been given a finish of Alclad2 Copper while the housing is masked (and mounted) with Blu-Tack.

Dipping the components into a jar of weathering wash is a quick and easy way to enhance the relief of a cast component, dabbing away the excess before the liquid dries. Traces of the dark wash are retained in the various recesses, producing an authentic appearance to this tiny part, which measures only 16mm in length.

Such is the striking visual nature of good-quality metallic paint that its use in even the smallest areas of a model can have a dramatic effect. This tipper truck is to be modelled on a layout with its payload being discharged, so the twin hydraulic rams will be clearly visible and a metallic coating is therefore essential. The whole model was masked carefully, with all tape joints sealed with masking fluid. All metallics have a tendency to seep through small gaps, especially cellulose lacquers.

A layer of black primer preceded several light coats of Alclad2 Aluminium, working up close to the subject to ensure a perfectly smooth coating.

Once the masking was removed, the rest of the model was duly weathered, keeping the polished metal surfaces clean throughout. When finished, the effect is subtle but highly effective.

SPECIAL EFFECTS

In addition to the realistic effect that good-quality metallic paints bring to a model surface, portraying either specific metals or an eye-catching livery, there are a number of ways in which these finishes can be manipulated to further enhance the level of realism. For example, buffing metallic paint with a superfine grade of Micromesh or similar abrasive (say 8,000–12,000grit) will introduce some welcome tonal variety. This is perfect for use on a vehicle or installation made up of numerous metal panels, as it creates a subtly exaggerated degree of light and shade. Humbrol enamel paints react to this procedure particularly well, although Alclad2 lacquers seem to be impervious to any abrasion. Instead, masking and spraying subtly different shades on adjoining panels will create the same effect.

One of the most endearing qualities that Humbrol's Metalcote enamels possess is the ability to be polished once completely dry. Simply rubbing a finger over a surface can be enough to burnish the paint, although a little more forceful work with a clean toothbrush will further heighten the effect. In this way, edges and raised details are enhanced and an authentic sheen given to the object. Metalcote Gunmetal and Polished Steel, in particular, respond well to this treatment and, when mixed with regular Humbrol matt enamels as part of a general weathering mix, the dry coating can be buffed in a similar way to form believable renditions of greasy or scuffed surfaces.

Humbrol's small Metalcote enamels (available in just four shades) provide a cheap and effective range of paints, perfect for producing realistic metal finishes, such as this pack of white-metal steel coils.

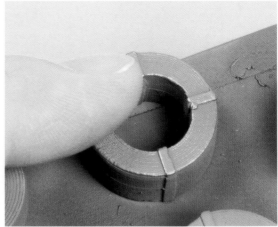

Once completely dry, the Metalcote (No.27003 Polished Steel in this case) can be polished by a finger or toothbrush to create some useful effects.

Note how well the relief in the original castings is brought to life by the polishing of the Metalcote finish.

Making any alteration to a metallic finish can be tricky, especially if trying to blend in an area of new paintwork. For enamel, cellulose and factory-applied formulas, T-Cut automotive finish restorer can help to soften the edges between the old and new paints. Applied with cotton swabs, the liquid can be buffed dry with a clean cloth.

Spraying a coat of a non-yellowing satin varnish will help to mask any difference in shade around a modified area as well as deepening the lustre of the metallic finish. But don't forget to mask any nearby glazing.

CHAPTER TWELVE

AN INTRODUCTION TO WEATHERING

Weathering forms an important part of the model-making process, although it's often overlooked by many railway hobbyists in favour of pristine locomotives, rolling stock and scenic surroundings. It's a matter of personal taste but, to my mind at least, everything in a miniature surrounding should be exposed to some degree of weathering in order for it to blend in.

'Weathering' is an all-encompassing term, referring strictly to a recreation of a real object exposed to the outside elements for anything from a matter of hours to several decades. Dirt and grime is only part of the equation and there are countless ways in which nature and the man-made world can have a visual impact on any object or material. Consider stone, for instance: it's hardly ever a uniform colour whatever its geological type. Even chalk can possess a multitude of shades, brought about by variations in the natural material and external forces such as climate and erosion. In effect, the stone has become 'weathered' and the principle applies equally to bricks, masonry, concrete, painted surfaces and vehicles. Even people can appear 'weathered', be it in the form of a faded trouser knee, the odd stain on an elbow, a swarthy face or a washed-out cardigan!

Weathering is such a vast topic that it deserves a book of its own to do it justice. Instead, the next couple of chapters will concentrate on those techniques specific to airbrushing and the unique effects that can be created with this tool. Readers are directed to the chapters on weathering contained in my previous books on locomotive detailing (see Bibliography) for a broader discussion of the subject in relation to rail traction.

The airbrush is a gift to the weathering modeller, as it not only speeds up the process but also offers the potential for ultra-realism that's unmatched by any other technique alone. That's not to say that the airbrush is the ultimate answer to creating 'lived-in' replicas of reality. Rather, it can be used as part of a combined process along with weathering powders, pigments and hand-applied paint.

The next few pages feature techniques applicable to railway locomotives and rolling stock, while the following chapter considers scenic work such as landscapes, buildings and road vehicles. Finally, Chapter 14 includes a further selection of weathering practices that demand a little more experience.

THE PURPOSE OF WEATHERING

Apart from the reasons already outlined, weathering also helps to take away the toy-like appearance of miniature objects, especially mass-produced ready-to-run model railway vehicles and buildings. The railway is seldom a clean environment, especially in Britain where inclement weather, Victorian infrastructure, urban decay and a less than fastidious approach to commercial and personal premises means that there are always patches of damp, graffiti, litter, staining and salt leaching around buildings, while the railway itself creates brake dust, exhaust staining and streaks of oil and grease in abundance.

Prototype research is important to gauge how, why and where certain objects weather the way that they do. According to your chosen modelling location and period, railway infrastructure may be meticulously manicured with pristine ballast and sparkling locomotives, yet there will still be rusty rails, greasy connecting rods, soot around chimneys and coal dust permeating through the scene. A steam locomotive shed diorama would be coated in the all-pervading dust of soot and ash, while a diesel servicing depot would feature lots of stained concrete and the odd puddle of engine oil or fuel.

Whatever your intentions may be, all of the necessary airbrushing techniques have already been covered in the preceding chapters. Indeed, it only remains to choose – and adapt slightly – the appropriate method to achieve specific effects. The misting of light layers of paint to mimic the build-up of track and brake dust along a loco-motive underframe, for example, involves the common technique of layering a delicate initial paint layer. In contrast to how we've worked before, however, it's now desirable to up the air pressure a little to purposely create a grainy, dusty finish (where appropriate). Increasing the distance between airbrush and subject also helps in cre-ating drifting effects, such as exhaust staining to locomotive or rolling stock rooftops.

The rules of mixing and thinning of paint still exist, although creating a slightly thinner fluid, along with dropping the air pressure (to around 6–8psi), allows other effects to be created. This approach suits the addition of ultra-fine streaking, especially in awkward corners or on smaller-scale subjects, although great care must be taken to keep the airbrush moving at all times. Also, paint flow should be kept to a minimum, so an airbrush with an adjustable needle stop will prove invaluable.

CHOOSING PAINTS

Provided that the subject is clean of grease and debris, enamel paints tend to adhere better to a wider selection of materials and finishes than acryl-ics. This is certainly desirable for the most intricate of work, whereas acrylics may need a light tack coat applied as a preliminary measure, after which adhe-sion will be fine. But this creates a problem when subtlety is essential and the need for several layers in confined or minuscule areas is not easy. Acrylics also need those multiple layers to achieve a degree of opacity, while weathering enamels will suffice with one light coat for most tasks.

They may take longer to dry, but enamels are also easier for the airbrush to atomize into a fine spray, thus suiting them to lower air pres-sures when thinned sufficiently. They can also be

No matter how nice a ready-to-run model may look when plucked straight from the box, it will still resemble a plastic replica rather than a believable miniature recreation of the real thing.

This Vi-Trains Class 37 looked pretty garish and 'plasticky' in its bright Railfreight colour scheme until it was toned down and improved by a realistic weathering job. Not bad for two hours' work.

A good weathering job can also make a less than perfect model more presentable, as evidenced by this very aged Mainline Collett Goods. The eye is grabbed by the extra details added and the suitably dusty and streaked black finish rather than the huge plastic tender wheels.

PROTOTYPE INSPIRATION

Looking at real life is always recommended for model-making inspiration and the art of creating realistic weathering effects is no different. Equally, an understanding of where, how and why dirt, staining, distressing and fading occurs on locomotives and rolling stock will be beneficial. The knowledge of how and when trains are cleaned is also useful as mechanized washing plants invariably create their own imprint on locomotive and carriage sides. Even manual cleaning has its impact, with streaks of roof dirt being drawn down the sides as a mop is wielded up to cantrail level (on diesels and electrics) or the burnished appearance of a steam locomotive created by an oily rag.

Looking at real trains is a great help to gain inspiration for a weathering job. This lovely little Midland Railway 1F is fairly clean, with the black livery looking nice and shiny in the winter sunshine. However, look how dusty the chassis and wheels look in comparison. Also, note how the red bufferbeam has dirt ingrained around the raised rivet heads. (Photo by Nick Brodrick.)

Also worth noting is the rusty brake blocks and streaking down the side of the boiler and smokebox. All of these features can be recreated in miniature with an airbrush and a little know-how. (Photo by Nick Brodrick.)

Diesel-age subjects gather dirt in roughly similar ways. The usually immaculate West Coast fleet of diesel traction can yet be found with a covering of track dirt after only a few days out on the network. An airbrush is the perfect tool with which to recreate such dusty deposits.

What is important to note is that dirt often builds up in layers, something that factory weathering rarely captures. Looking at this wagon reveals years of dirt and rust amassing on the side panels, with graffiti sandwiched somewhere between the livery and the muck. Meanwhile, new panels of black paint have been added so that the important classification details can be reapplied during an intermediate overhaul.

The sides and ends of this EWS-liveried Class 66 have received more attention from the cleaners than the chassis and roof, although fresh layers of dirt have since appeared as a result of operating within this Peak District quarry. Note the streaks of dark grime leaking down the bodysides from roof level and the uniform brown covering of the bogie and underframe.

PROTOTYPE INSPIRATION (CONTINUED)

A heavier concentration of dirt lies, not surprisingly, around the exhaust system. The dusty appearance of the deposits can be captured well with a matt 'weathered black' such as offered in the Railmatch enamels range.

Fuel tanks are often besmirched by spillage and other streaking patterns. Lifecolor Tensocrom acrylic paints, as described in Chapter 3, offer a very good rendition of diesel fuel.

Offering a stark contrast with his drab steed, the brightly attired driver is checking with the ground crew on his walkie-talkie. His nice new uniform may be clean but a close look at his boots reveal them to be well-weathered. Note how his feet have scuffed the bogies within the footstep frames, revealing the black paint beneath the grime.

Oil and fuel tankers offer a fascinating subject to copy in miniature, these TTAs showing telltale signs of a hard working life.

Weathering with an airbrush allows us to purposely practise bad painting techniques in order to achieve the effects we need. Setting the air pressure really low and keeping the paint fairly thick will create just the spatter effect needed for these deposits of white dirt.

The Deltics were notorious for burning oil and this preserved example is showing off the trademark stains. Note the tonal contrast in the fresher, darker streaks.

It's not only leaking oil that causes streaking but rusting bodywork does too. Corrosion at cantrail level is washed down the bodysides by rainfall, mingling with rust from other sources on the way down.

manipulated with white spirit for days afterwards, allowing tweaking of a weathering job or complete removal if necessary. Acrylics, on the other hand, are not so easy to control in the most demanding circumstances and are a devil to remove if a mistake is made. That's not to say that they have no place in the weathering process, rather their inherent strengths can be exploited for specific tasks. Scenic work, in particular, is suited to acrylic paints as working over a broad area with oil-based paints can create lots of noxious fumes. The longer drying time also leaves them open to attracting dust to the tacky surface. Acrylics will dry very quickly and thinning them to a greater extent will help to create various authentic effects such as damp patches and fluid leaks.

Enamel weathering paints offer reliable adhesion and a pleasantly dusty sheen, although a little gloss varnish can be added to give a more oily finish. The contrast in tonality and sheen combine well on this kit-built recreation of the unique Brush 10800.

According to brand, applying acrylic weathering paints can offer more of a challenge. However, their rapid drying time can be a real boon: this Terrier was painted, varnished and weathered on the same day – not something I'd normally recommend but it is possible.

In common with all previously illustrated airbrushing techniques, practise and experimentation is vital in building confidence and ability. Try some of these techniques on scrap models or other three-dimensional objects before taking the plunge with a finished kit or expensive ready-to-run model. Don't forget to mask glazing carefully with tape or Maskol fluid and consider whether a model will be easier to deal with if the body is split from the chassis. Removing wheels is also helpful in some instances as chassis components, connecting rods or bogies can act as stencils to the surfaces beneath and, once these parts move or rotate, patches of clean paintwork will be revealed. If you do dismantle a model, remember to mask the glazing on the inside too.

Mounting the model on a raised turntable will help, allowing it to be moved around without handling the model itself, which risks the introduction of fingerprints or debris into the wet paint. Ensure that you can move the airbrush around the subject freely, especially from above and below to create misting and streaking effects from track and roof level; this is why raising the model above the workbench is a welcome aid.

Above all, have fun!

Masking clear glazing and headlight lenses is important prior to applying any weathering. Maskol fluid is perfect for the job.

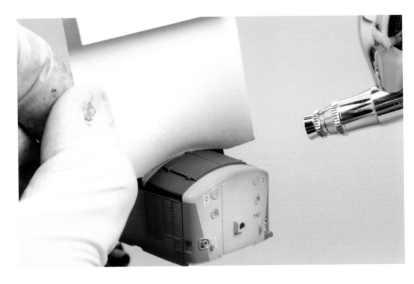

An alternative to masking the glazing with tape or fluid is to use a Post-It note or a scrap of card. Here, the latter is in use, cut to match the profile of the Class 37's nose.

Think about whether the model will be better served by dismantling certain sections that can be dealt with separately. For example, these radiator fans may appear too vivid against the dirty roof unless treated to the same weathering process.

Dismantling also removes the risk of some moving parts acting like stencils to the surfaces beneath. Spoke wheels, connecting rods and other underframe details pose particular problems.

The framing of these hopper wagons will also get in the way of airbrushed weathering, so the metal bodies have been treated separately.

To allow easy access to the model, mounting it above the work surface is recommended. Either a turntable can be used or a shoebox and strip of wood improvised for longer vehicles such as this Pendolino car.

To add a misting of track dirt to the underframe and lower edges, thin the paint as usual and spray from about 100mm (4in) with a pressure somewhere around 15–18psi. By moving the airbrush gradually in the horizontal plane, the bodysides will be left untouched as long as the paint flow (and resulting spray pattern) is kept modest. For heavier deposits, repeated passes may be necessary. Here, Railmatch enamel Frame Dirt is being applied.

As Pendolino sets are washed regularly, only the underframes and roofs retain a dirty appearance. Now working from above the model, layers of Railmatch Roof Dirt are being applied at close quarters, with the air pressure reduced to about 10–12psi. When working around the complex pantograph equipment, it's necessary to attack the model from all sides to ensure even coverage. Accordingly, each application is kept light to avoid an overly thick layer.

Introducing further tonality is possible simply by intermixing different colours into the basic weathering shade. For example, Railmatch Frame Dirt has here been applied initially, before the same paint was combined with a little Dark Rust to different ratios. Indeed, about five different shades have been applied by this point, with Roof Dirt and Weathered Black also added to the mix in varying quantities. The darker shades are concentrated in areas where shadows would be present or where the worst of the dirt was likely to be collected.

Streaks from roof level introduce still darker shades to the bodysides and this view illustrates just how close the airbrush has been working to the surface to create such fine lines without a thick, grainy finish. Pressure must be low (around 10psi) and paint diluted slightly more than usual.

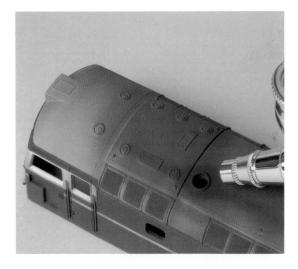

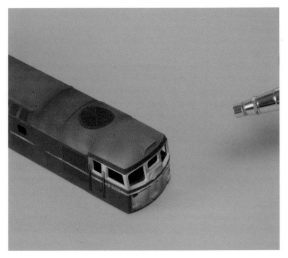

Exhaust staining differs in quantity in relation to distance from the outlet, so a concentration of paint around the port is built up in individual layers using either a 'weathered black' or general matt black, depending on how dark the staining is to be. 'Weathered black' is usually a very dark grey with hints of blue. Allow each layer to dry before adding further paint to avoid causing runs.

For a less concentrated misting of fumes, the airbrush can be drawn further away, to around 80–100mm (3–4in). Don't be tempted to go too far back or the results will be poor.

A steam locomotive will benefit from a similar misting of dark staining over the smokebox, boiler and cab, increasing in intensity nearer to the chimney. Work in a straight line from above, moving from the front end to the cab, repeating the light applications from different angles to ensure the vertical faces of the chimney dome, firebox top and safety valves are not missed.

Even an otherwise spotless steam loco needs a little soot around the exhaust.

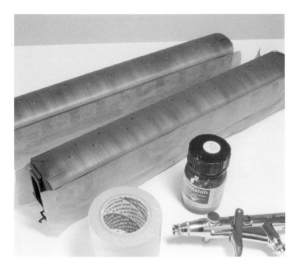

The sides and windows of coaching stock is generally kept clean of the worst deposits of dirt. My usual method of weathering is to mask up the sides and spray the roofs with a fairly generous covering of grime, especially steam-age stock. Working from side-to-side to create a look of vertical streaking, the density of colour is increased slightly at each end.

The body retains its masking while the underframes and ends are dealt with, using a variety of shades based on Frame Dirt. Minor interventions are visited upon the sides, mostly applied by hand brush to door seams and gutters. The overall effect is pleasing, with a nice contrast between the clean and dirty aspects.

Treating body and chassis separately makes handling easier. While the body is mounted on a sprung paint handle, the underframe can simply be moved around by hand using the chassis block. A basic covering in Frame Dirt is usually the starting point.

This Class 50 was commissioned to have only a very lightly weathered finish, so just the underframes and roof have been treated to various layers of enamel 'dirt'. Just a feint wisp of brown dust, however, has been misted along the very bottom edge of the bodyshell.

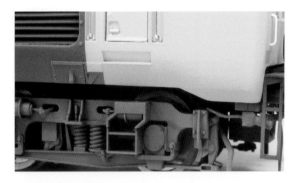

The Class 50's bogies contain a variety of weathering shades with darker patches around the axle boxes and brake dust around the shoes and linkages.

Class 50s could be pretty smoky, so the roof bears a distinctive array of exhaust staining. Very light layers begin the process, with repeated applications nearer to the ports to darken the covering.

Weathering steam traction in 2mm scale offers similar challenges, although an overall layer of grime on a workaday freight machine such as this is not so difficult. Light layers of various shades have been applied over the whole model, keeping the brown-red colours for the sides and chassis and the darker, sootier shades for the upper edges. The odd streak down the cab and tank sides also help, mixing the different paints together to gain a believable range of tones. Keep the air pressure as low as possible on small subjects and work as close as your airbrush will allow.

Diesel exhaust staining is a little more difficult to achieve in the smaller scales, although the use of an airbrush with an ultra-fine nozzle will help. This Farish Class 57 is receiving a light misting of Weathered Black around the general area of the exhausts, creating a denser stain immediately around the ports by letting the tool linger for a fraction longer, thus increasing the amount of paint landing on the same spot. This needs care to avoid runs, but on such a tiny surface it can be a more reliable method than increasing the paint flow with the trigger.

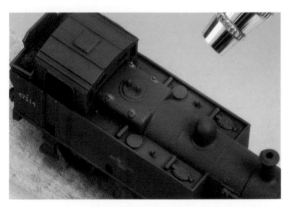

Small concentrations of contrasting colours help to bring the model to life, such as a little rust shading around the water filler hatches, smokebox saddle and chassis. Brake dust and ash staining are also welcome, although these patches should not look too garish. If they do, simply mist over another layer of the general grime to tone things down a bit.

It's a harmonious effect that we're after, so that the vehicle will look at home in a scenic setting. This Farish Jinty and its rake of wagons have all been weathered, along with much of the scenery, especially the track and tunnel mouth. Note how the mineral wagons have received layers of dirt to complement their shape and patterns of relief, rather than a random blast of dirty brown paint as some off-the-shelf models do.

Moving back up the gauges to OO, this Stanier tank has received a similar treatment to the Jinty, with many subtly different shades mingling together, offset by the odd darker streak or lighter patch of brake dust or rust. The oily deposits in and around the connecting rods were created with Humbrol enamels mixed with a little Metalcote Gunmetal (see Chapter 11).

The all-over coating of weathering paint gives the 4P a suitably neglected air for a workaday 1960s machine and the driver has had to put his rag to the forward spectacle to keep his view clear. A blob of Maskol prior to painting achieved this effect.

Tank wagons are a favourite among modellers and creating a believable weathered finish will enhance the various high-quality models currently on the market. This OO gauge Bachmann TTA has been detailed and repainted, followed by a coat of black-tinted varnish, as described in Chapter 10. Highly diluted enamel Frame Dirt is being laid onto the tank top and sides in vertical streaks, concentrating the heavier deposits around the central filler hatch.

The process is repeated over three or four stages, with the paint becoming progressively darker as more Roof Dirt and Weathered Black is mixed in.

When complete, the effect of the various layers of shade and tone create a highly realistic model.

Exactly the same processes can be applied to tank wagons of any scale. This Farish N gauge TTA is being held in place with a ball of Blu-Tack, lest the air pressure blow the little truck off its perch.

Being able to follow lines of relief, freehand, with an airbrush is a precious skill to possess as it allows some very useful effects to be created. For instance, this Parkside 7mm scale van has been enhanced with different enamel shades aimed into the various seams and recesses, introducing exaggerated shadowing and staining to an otherwise bland box-shaped object.

The Farish Class 57, with gentle streaks of rain-washed grime from the roof panels and its underframe misted with dirt and brake dust, looks much more authentic, as do the TTA wagons in its wake.

With the darkest shades judiciously applied to the upper recesses and the greasiest parts of the chassis, the humble meat van looks much more purposeful.

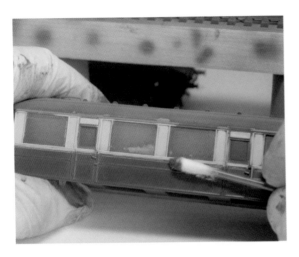

For uncared for coaching stock, especially pre-nationalization designs cascaded to lowly branch-line duties, a fairly aggressive weathering approach is needed: after masking all windows, inside and out, an overall coating of enamel Frame Dirt has been applied over one side at a time. Immediately, white spirit-soaked cotton swabs are employed to wipe most of the paint away, yet leaving deposits in the various nook and crannies. Vertical strokes only are applied as a slightly streaked appearance will result when the paint dries.

The underframe, ends and roof are left with most of the sprayed-on dirt undisturbed. Following a light misting of Frame Dirt along the bottom edge, the various elements are blended together nicely. This technique is particularly effective on surfaces with plenty of relief.

A little physical intervention after the event can produce some interesting effects. This Hornby Class 08 has been treated with various layers of Railmatch weathering acrylics, concentrating most of the 'dirt' around the footplate and the many recesses on the bodyshell. After a couple of hours, a clean toothbrush was passed over the more exposed surfaces to rub away some of the paint, leaving the satin factory finish to shine through. An extra illusion of wear and tear is instantly produced.

If wheels are left in situ while spraying weathering paints, it is a good idea to clean the treads before the vehicles enter service, regardless of whether they're power-collecting axles or not. All rolling stock wheels should be cleaned on a regular basis anyway, as it helps to maintain spotless rails and good power transmission. The Wheel Doctor from Bachrus makes the task easy: simply add a suitable cleaning solvent to the sponge and plug the unit in – the rubber roller turns the wheels against the sponge.

CHAPTER THIRTEEN

SCENIC WORK

Continuing the weathering theme from the preceding pages, this chapter is presented in a predominantly visual format in order to demonstrate how an airbrush can enhance the miniature surroundings of a model railway. After all, devoting the time to present our locomotives and rolling stock as realistically as possible is rendered pointless without extending the same treatment to the scenery.

The track and ballasted surroundings are an obvious area where an airbrush can speed up the finishing and improve the appearance, adding a layer of rust, dust, oil and grime to suit your taste. Roads and areas of hard-standing are similarly suited to an airbrush finish. Indeed, creating a believable surface on such features is difficult by hand alone. The natural landscape also benefits from some judicious use of airborne paint, either to create realistic finishes to rock formations and riverbeds or to tone down the rather garish off-the-shelf foliage products that prevail.

Painting and weathering track is a laborious chore that can be greatly accelerated using an airbrush. Begin by applying a 'rusty' shade to each side of the rails, angling the airbrush accordingly. This is best done before most of the surrounding scenery and buildings have been added, although aiming the paint carefully should prevent an excess of overspray.

Follow with a slightly darker shade to the sleepers, such as Sleeper Grime, as offered by Railmatch. My preference is for enamel paints as the level of adhesion is greater, although the fumes can be unpleasant, especially if a lot of track is being treated in the same session. Therefore, a good face mask and plenty of ventilation is a must.

Varying the shades to both rail and sleeper will create a more believable finish and areas where trains are likely to stand, such as near signals, platforms or sidings, should receive deposits of dark staining. Here Railmatch Weathered Black is being applied both between the rails and along either side, keeping the airbrush at close quarters to maintain accuracy.

It's vital to clean away all traces of paint from the contact surfaces of the rails and this task is much easier before the paint has dried. Take a track cleaning block and rub the railheads until they shine, following with a vacuum cleaner to remove the dusty debris. Take extra care around point blades and frogs, making use of fine abrasive paper where necessary.

Edges of ballast or adjoining scenery can also benefit from a light dusting of a general shade of 'dirt', softening the transition between railway and landscape. This also applies to the edges of roads and tracks where dust and dirt is often sprayed onto the bordering grass or foliage.

Rails in any scale can be treated in the same way, offering the chance to refine the aesthetics of off-the-shelf track systems, such as this stretch of standard Peco N gauge Code55 track.

The same shades and techniques can be employed on stockpiled rails and sleepers, for mounting by the lineside or in an engineer's yard. A little double-sided tape retains the piles on scraps of wood during painting and weathering. Note how the rail chairs have been picked out in Dark Rust, adding contrast to the sleepers.

Once again, the techniques involved are no different to those already described, the main variables being type and viscosity of paint, plus nozzle-to-subject distance, each creating different visual effects to suit various applications. Scenic work can be a little more forgiving of minor errors as well as offering a more suitable canvas for cheap airbrushes, especially of the external mix variety. However, more precise and subtle effects, such as smoke staining or creating shadows, are the preserve of better (but not necessarily expensive) tools.

Remember to keep air pressure low when applying paint over areas treated to a coating of scatter material and for close-up work. Consider, too, the potential of applying clear varnish coats as a means of sealing this loose material in place, helping also to limit fading of colour pigments through exposure to sunlight. Being able to reach into awkward corners of the layout is also an issue to bear in mind, especially if the airbrush will have to be used at an angle, highlighting the need for a tight-fitting lid on the paint cup. Both siphon- and gravity-fed devices should cope fairly well with use at an odd orientation, although

the former will offer the better performance for such prolonged use, especially upside down. Air lines and appendages such as triggers, handles, paint jars and air valves can cause the most inconvenience, particularly if there are delicate fixtures in place that will be at risk of damage.

Masking may be necessary to preserve certain surfaces such as the glazing of buildings or signage and Post-It notes, Blu-Tack or masking tape are especially useful in these instances. The type of surface will dictate how easy it will be to remove or lessen the amount of weathering paint added. Being of a porous nature, card or paper buildings are nigh on impossible to correct once painted, so be sure to get it right first time.

Finally, the likelihood that scenic work will involve spraying paint over a relatively large area means that the need for adequate ventilation and protection against harmful fumes gains even greater importance. Indeed, vapours will soon become concentrated over a layout and will linger there for some time unless there is a generous through-flow of air.

Roads and areas of hard-standing are much easier to create by airbrush than by hand, offering the chance of blending numerous slightly different shades together for a more authentic finish. Various greys have been employed here, each being mixed with a little brown or black.

Darker shades, sprayed in arcing movements, mimic tyre tracks emanating from the narrow entrance to this yard. Other lines here and there add to the effect. Varying the density of the tracks is achieved not only by the shade of paint but by changing the distance between the nozzle and the surface.

A quick and easy way to render areas of concrete hard-standing is to paste a sheet of plain paper or mounting card onto the layout's surface; once the adhesive has dried out, a sharp pencil can be used to rule 'joint lines' between separately cast sections. A few cracks here and there help, especially at the corners. Follow with light applications of dark grey or black, misted at a low pressure and from a very close range, following the pencil lines. Then, add the odd streak here and there, especially where vehicles are likely to traverse the site.

For installations such as this modern-image depot scene, a somewhat heavier application of dirt and grime may be desired. Where rail tracks traverse the site, heavy oil deposits are complemented by rusty shades to simulate track dirt and brake dust.

This Knightwing Models diesel fuelling stage kit includes the raised concrete pad, complete with covered drains and walkways. Some judicious shading here and there adds a further sense of relief to the otherwise flat surface.

This prototype fuelling area, at Crewe Gresty Bridge depot, illustrates the wealth of shading visible in the cast concrete grounding. Note also the staining to the walls of the adjacent building.

Regard, too, how greasy the rails are in the vicinity of the oil drainage area. Layers of dark grey, brown and black paints will mimic such deposits, especially with a little gloss varnish added to the mix.

This area of plaster has been applied in readiness for the fitting of an engine shed and the porous surface makes acrylic paints a better choice than enamels.

The initial coats seal the surface of the plaster and provide a base for other shades of grey, brown and black, concentrating the darker shades around the rails.

A hint of rust has been added in proximity to the track and the rail heads cleaned carefully. With the interior fittings in place, the odd oil spillage and damp patch have been created by spraying glossy mixes of paint at close quarters.

Meanwhile, the shed itself needs finishing. This Hornby Skaledale shed sports an unpainted interior, necessitating a primer coat, applied here by aerosol after giving the model a good wash beforehand. Note that the windows and glazing have been removed.

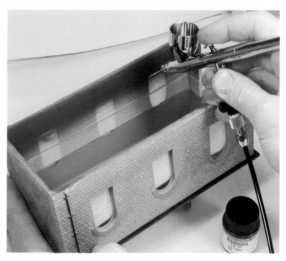

In line with prototype practice, the lower walls are painted in a darker shade than the upper reaches so, after applying the lighter paint, the interior was masked and a dull brown applied.

Other steam-era shed infrastructure also benefits from the attention of an airbrush. Both this coaling stage and water tower (Ten Commandments and Skaledale products, respectively) have been painted by hand, before dust and rust staining followed from the airbrush.

With the walls painted, vertical streaks of grime were added. The exterior was repainted by hand to a colour of stone more befitting my chosen location (and to a superior finish to the factory-applied paint) with similar weathering also applied.

Puddles and areas of dampness are easy to mimic using gloss varnish, perhaps tinted with a drop of black or green paint. Here a number of light layers were built up to give the impression of a recently created puddle at the base of this water column.

A set of scratch-built doors finish off the Skaledale shed nicely, along with the refitting of the windows and glazing. Although the outer stonework has been repainted by hand, the use of the airbrush in the weathering and interior rendering has taken this off-the-shelf model up a peg or two in the realism stakes. Smoke staining above the entrance and ash dust around the base of the walls completes the scene.

Concrete structures tend to weather in a characteristic manner, with soft horizontal and vertical lines denoting where the separate pre-cast components have been mated-up. This image of the coaling plant at Carnforth also illustrates dark streaking and staining from coal dust, as well as deposits of moss here and there adding green and brown elements to the mix. The airbrush is the perfect tool for recreating virtually all of the effects seen here.

A modern depot building, in the form of a card kit (from the Scalescenes range), is here being enhanced with streaks of rust and grime running vertically down the corrugated steel walls.

Exhaust staining above the entrance portals is a particularly important feature to recreate, blending a variety of shades. These ready-to-spray Com-Art weathering paints are perfect for such tasks, although pressure must be low, spraying distance minimal and layers built up very gradually.

I managed to get lots of excess glue on the awkward roof section whilst building this kit and, after an all-over coat of matt varnish took away the shiny streaks, judicious use of weathering paints helped to cover any other minor blemishes.

Once complete and mounted into the depot scene, the card kit looks very much at home. Indeed, it's hard to believe that it started life as a series of downloaded computer images.

For raised roof panels, the same process of applying shadows around seam lines is an effective way of introducing exaggerated relief as well as a weathered appearance.

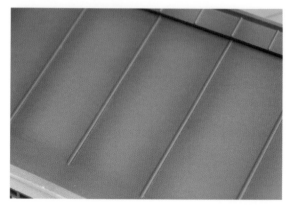

The roof has also received highlights of a lighter shade of grey, applied to the centre of each panel. This gives the model a visual lift, heightening the sense of relief further.

This area of stone paving slabs has been painted initially by hand, adding various shades of grey acrylics with a stippling action to create a lightly textured surface. The airbrush then added layers of browns and blacks around the edges of the slabs, following the mortar courses. This can be a monotonous task, especially over a large area, but the results can be worth the effort.

The lightly weathered Land Rover also sits unobtrusively in the colliery scene, having had its shiny factory finish mollified with satin varnish prior to some gentle misting of paint around the wheel arches and underframe.

The completed paving looks realistic, with the lower edges of the buildings also treated to a light misting of dark grey to avoid a hard edge between the two elements.

As industrial infrastructure gives way to nature, the grimy patina lessens, although much of the greenery has been muted with an overall spray of dark brown acrylics.

This view of Maudetown Colliery's stores depot illustrates how all parts of the layout can be subtly blended together by means of careful airbrushing: the track, buildings and infrastructure all gently segue into one another with no jarring transitions.

While painting realistic brick and stonework is best achieved by hand, applying the finishing touches by airbrush will produce a superior effect.

Areas of moss or saline streaking are easy to add with shades of green or white, while patches of dirt and grime follow previously discussed methods. Also applicable is the recreation of leaking or broken gutters, drains and downpipes by spraying layers of gloss varnish intermixed with shades of green and brown.

Rust effects can be created with paints, enhanced further by adding talcum powder to a hand-brushed mix to provide a suitably rough texture. Alternatively, real rust can be created using Scenic Rust from Deluxe Materials. When developed, the effects are good (as seen here), but some further work will offer greater rewards.

Repeated layering of a wide variety of rust and dirt shades, concentrating the darker colours at the top of this cylindrical boiler, builds up a superior finish.

Complete and set into the scene, the finished object looks nothing like the plastic moulding that it began life as.

Tunnel mouths are another area where an airbrush will excel. In common with other brick or stone structures, the initial finish should be applied by hand and mouldings such as this (from Javis Scenics) really allow the relief to stand out when painted. Treated in situ, carefully misted coats of black and dark grey mimic steam and diesel exhaust staining around the mouth, while the main handicap is getting the tool into the right place without the air line or paint cup getting in the way.

After finishing the tunnel mouth, exposed areas of cork bark set into the hillside have also been treated to various shades of paint, creating a rendition of natural stone faces. Both regular Lifecolor acrylics and Tensocrom weathering paints have been utilized to achieve the desired finish.

The odd area of clear gloss, applied in vertical streaks, mimics water seepage through the rocks and gives this cutting a suitably dank feel.

Once the layers of scatter and foliage materials have been added, the effect is complete.

The airbrush will also allow for greater realism on all manner of scenic fixtures, even trees. One look at the trunk of this impressive tree reveals a multitude of different colours and shades, something seldom captured in model form.

Woodland Scenic tree kits are a great starting point and, with the trunks bent to shape and mounted temporarily on a scrap of plywood, a coat of primer precedes layers of brown acrylics. Subsequent shading with darker and lighter mixes highlight areas of light and shadow, especially around the trunk and branch bases.

Introducing patches of green hints at areas of lichen or moss, usually found on trees in shady or damp locations. Military camouflage shades can be useful in such instances, as they are usually very subtle tones, such as the British Army Khaki being sprayed here.

Proof that just an hour or two's work is worth the effort will become apparent when the finished trees are planted into the scene.

CHAPTER FOURTEEN

ADVANCED TECHNIQUES

This final chapter is offered as a guide to a number of additional airbrushing techniques that may prove useful across a vast range of modelling projects. Adding to the experience and skills already discussed, a few of these tips should make complex livery applications or particular weathering effects much easier to achieve.

WHEN THE MASKING GETS TOUGH

Ornate liveries are likely to demand many hours' worth of work, with only a limited amount of that time actually spent applying paint. Days can turn into weeks as layer upon layer of colour is added between painstaking mask applications, proving to be something of an endurance test in many cases. It's little wonder, therefore, that many professional kit-builders subcontract the finishing process to another specialist.

However, not all schemes are so complicated and, without wanting to get bogged down in demonstrating particular examples, here is a short series of images of the refinishing of a OO gauge Hornby A4 'Pacific', showing how a seemingly unorthodox working arrangement can pay dividends in terms of duration and quality of workmanship.

Having been commissioned by an Australian modeller to produce a replica of the preserved 60007 *Sir Nigel Gresley*, the donor locomotive took some time to prepare for its new colour scheme. Not only was it awkward to remove all of the many delicate detail fittings, but achieving those wonderfully graceful but complicated curves between the blue and the black of the smokebox took some planning.

Nine times out of ten I'd have covered the dismantled bodyshell in a grey primer as a base from which to work. However, as time was of the essence, I opted to use Hornby's excellent paint job as a guide, preserving the black smokebox temporarily to help in the cutting of the masking film. After a thorough clean, degrease and rub down with fine abrasives, the masking was added and the job then progressed fairly quickly. This certainly saved many hours of work with templates and the like and the waterslide lining decals hid any minor flaws in the paint joints.

Instances such as this prove the value of experience and, by building on the knowledge already learned during your endeavours, such ideas will present themselves from time to time. Although I'd refrain from calling this approach a shortcut (the project still took about six weeks to complete), there are ways and means for making life a little easier on yourself … this is a hobby after all.

Masking may make your life easier in some respects, but it can also create extra hassle, so it pays to adapt your ways of working to suit specific tasks. This Hornby A4 project was eased along by using the factory finish as a guide for the new colour scheme. After dismantling the model and removing the handrails and other raised details, masking film was placed over the smokebox and a fine, sharp swivel-blade knife employed to follow the orange lining 'joint'.

Removing the waste masking should be done with care, ensuring that the knife has cut through the material fully to avoid tearing or snagging.

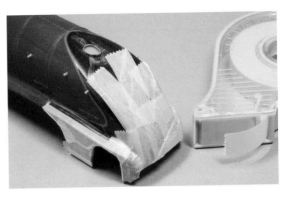

Fill in any gaps with masking tape, especially around awkward surfaces such as the running plate. Note that the inside of the chimney aperture has been masked to prevent bleeding of the new paint from within.

After a few coats of grey and white primer, the BR blue coats were gradually applied.

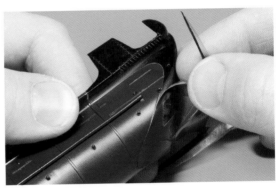

The enamel paint was allowed a week to harden before the masking was gently removed to reveal the factory-applied black and an accurate set of curves.

The masking can now be reversed, again using Hornby's orange lining as a cutting guide, before spraying the smokebox and running plate.

The finished Sir Nigel Gresley is probably one of my proudest achievements of late, crowned by a very subtle weathered finish, applied solely by airbrush using a couple of Railmatch enamels.

FADING IN AND OUT

Something not often seen among British railway subjects is the use of colour bleeding, that is the act of seamlessly blending one colour into another. Even in the multi-coloured world of the post-privatization scene, few train companies have incorporated such a device into their livery schemes, particularly in the pre-vinyl days of the late 1990s. More recently, however, a handful of operators have embraced this striking visual element and being able to recreate this effect in miniature will prove a handy skill to possess.

Similar in principle to the method demonstrated in Chapter 8, Blu-Tack comes into its own once again as a simple but reliable means of ensuring a consistent effect. Alternatively, freehand spraying can be employed to achieve much the same result. However, working without masking can lead to an inconsistent finish, especially without plenty of practice.

Bleeding, or 'fogging', one colour into another is something that is seen on a small number of contemporary liveries and it's a handy technique to be aware of. In this case, a fictional interpretation of Merseyrail's scheme was envisaged and, due to the use of metallic silver for the main livery, it was deemed preferable to apply the wrap-around yellow warning panels first. Otherwise, applying a white undercoat over the silver would make the misting process a little harder.

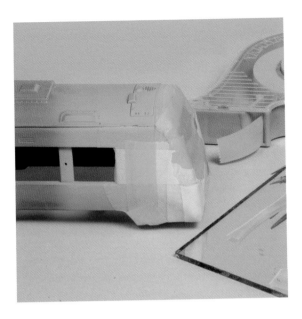

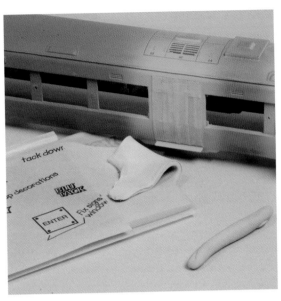

After deciding on where the misting will begin and end, the masking can be applied.

To create the bleeding effect, Blu-Tack is formed into long, thick rolls and carefully pressed into place just in advance of the hard-edged masking joint. The amount of paint that will bleed under the mask depends on the size and shape of the Blu-Tack.

Apply the following paint as normal, although the airbrush should not be aimed directly into the narrow void beneath the Blu-Tack. Instead, the natural overspray pattern will find its way into the gap.

Hopefully, when the paint is dry and the masking removed, the effect will be satisfactory. This is certainly a technique that requires plenty of practice to get right and much of the success depends on how the Blu-Tack is applied and the amount of paint managing to enter beneath it. An alternative is to create a regular paint joint that is then over-sprayed freehand to blur the edges, but this can be a tricky feat to pull off.

PAINT VS DECALS

Although it may at first appear pointless, substituting decals for careful masking and painting offers many advantages. Firstly, it negates the need for preparing a high gloss backing for the decals to adhere to and, secondly, it can save quite a few pounds when dealing with a large fleet of similarly attired vehicles. Finally it can also offer superior results when performed carefully.

When I was but a humble conservator at the National Railway Museum, the institution's esteemed painter would often amaze me with his use of hand-applied characters and logos in place of commonly available (but expensive) vinyl stickers. Even the overhead warning flashes on the BR blue Class 31 in the National Collection were painted and lettered by hand using traditional sign-writing techniques.

With this in mind, I wondered how viable a similar approach would be on a scale model – within reason, of course. Top of the list is the utilitarian BR double arrow (or 'arrows of indecision') logo that has become one of the most easily recognized visual devices in modern design history. Accurate marking out and cutting of masking film or tape will produce a splendid rendition and the size of the arrows can be tailored to absolute accuracy to suit a specific machine (they tended to vary between individual traction).

The process is made much easier by plotting and drawing the chosen symbol on a computer and transferring the image to the film via a printer. Multiple logos of varying size on the one sheet will provide a ready source for future projects. Large lettering or initials, wagon data panel backing and other contemporary devices (such as the Porterbrook 'squiggle', for example) are other possible elements to be rendered in this way.

For best results, have a few trial runs to master the art of cutting the masks and applying paint in a patient, multi-layered manner. Low pressure and ultra-thin coats that are permitted to dry in-between are vital.

The use of stencils offers a viable alternative to decals, especially for larger logotypes and livery elements such as this. The cutting stage is vital to the success of the stencilling, so take care and use a fresh blade.

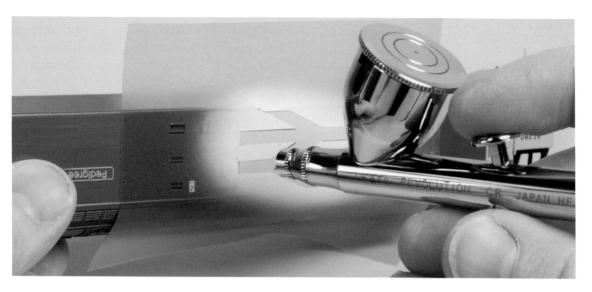

With the stencil in place, it's a good idea to apply a very light sealing coat of the underlying shade, in this case Railfreight grey. This will prevent any further paint from seeping under the mask and is a technique that can be applied to any masking situation. Build layers of colour through the stencil very gradually and avoid directing the spray up against the edge of the tape to minimize the ridging effect. Keep the airbrush perpendicular to the subject and apply paint with a low pressure.

When the stencil is carefully peeled away, the results should be something like this. Especially suited to work in larger scales (OO gauge and above), stencilling can prove a cost-effective and enjoyable solution to many livery schemes.

FREEHAND WORK

A test of proficiency in airbrushing is the use of the tool in a freehand manner. The ability to produce consistently straight lines is a skill that will open up many new possibilities, although this is not always attainable by everyone. Indeed, relatively few people are blessed with a steady hand, but aids can be devised, such as blocks of wood or adjustable 'fences' to run the wrist along in the horizontal or vertical plane. Such helping hands can go a long way to both speeding up and refining our painting technique, especially where weathering is concerned.

PRE-SHADING

A common method practised by military and aviation modellers is pre-shading. This involves running lines of black paint (or a darker shade of the intended top-coat) along recessed seam lines, cavities or grilles before the main livery colour is applied. As long as the following coats are applied fairly thin, then the darker shades will show through as exaggerated shadows.

When successfully applied, this technique can offer superb results, heightening the amount of detail and relief incorporated into even the most mediocre model. Wagons, buildings and infrastructure, in 4mm scale and above, offer the best subjects to try out this method and its use does not have to be limited to items intended for a fully weathered finish. Indeed, it can be a subtle alternative to applying 'dirt' or 'dust' at the end of the finishing process, while still providing that ever so slightly lived-in feel to an object.

Pre-shading is a handy weathering trick to have up one's sleeve. The technique involves applying black or dark grey paint into the various recesses and corners of an object prior to the main livery coats.

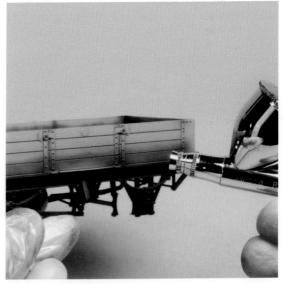

After a few light layers of the livery, avoiding laying the paint into the recesses, the darker pre-shading will show through.

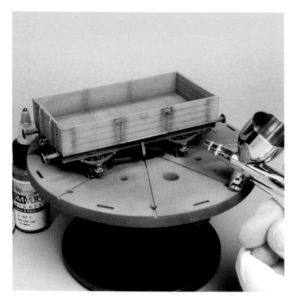

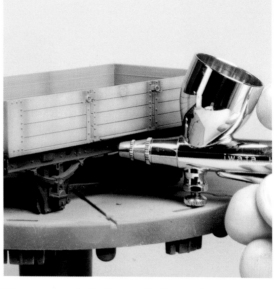

This O gauge wagon is now receiving further light coats of various weathering shades, using the pre-thinned Com-Art range of acrylics. To aid freehand work, the lower edge of the airbrush is being rested on the turntable as it passes horizontally, guiding the paint along the separate planks to introduce subtle changes in tone.

The same method of using the flat surface as a guide for the airbrush is employed to paint the underframe in a 'scale' black, with grey and a little brown mixed in. With care, this can be achieved (especially in O gauge and above) without the need for masking and any little overspray onto the planked sides will be hidden with further weathering coats.

The interior of the wooden wagon is here being sprayed in various shades, using Lifecolor's Weathered Wood diorama pack, followed by Com-Art weathering paints to add shading and dirt into the corners and edges of each plank.

After a few hours' work, the finished wagon looks realistic, with the contrast of the outer and inner timber faces looking especially pleasing. The pre-shading and subsequent weathering combine to enhance the excellent relief contained within this plastic kit (a Coopercraft product).

Pre-shading is also highly effective in OO gauge, especially on structures and freight vehicles such as this kit-based mineral wagon.

Just as the O gauge wagon demonstrated, the surface relief is heightened by a mix of pre-shading and careful weathering.

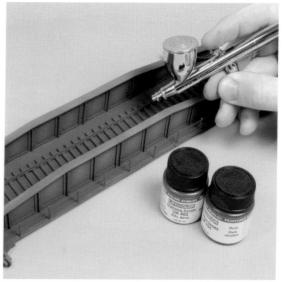

It's not just rolling stock that benefits from pre-shading. This girder-built turntable (a Dapol kit) has received some judicious shading with a mix of black and dark brown acrylics over the grey primer.

Various shades of grey were applied over the steelwork, without obliterating the darker backing. Lighter greys (plus a little dark blue to enrich the colour) have also been misted into the centre of each panel to add further variety of tone before the track and the footpath decking were highlighted with a dusting of rust shades.

This concrete well forms part of a different turntable project and the pre-shaded seams are clearly visible. Having built this Peco kit in a blind rush, my freehand work looks a little skew-whiff, but this was soon disguised by a little extra weathering once the well had been fixed into the baseboard.

The wonky shading of the well has been rectified and the entire turntable now looks well at home in its grimy surroundings.

Layering darker shades over the previous colouring mutes the rusty appearance as well as adding a more realistic covering, especially into deeper recesses such as grilles and apertures. By maintaining a narrow spray pattern (keeping the nozzle close to the surface), the previous wider coats will still be visible. With practise, such small areas can be treated evenly without the need for masking. Don't forget to maintain a constant movement with the airbrush to prevent excess paint from building up and to use the lowest air pressure possible.

Pre-shading work is not the only use for controlled freehand spraying. By following panel lines, grilles and recesses with various shades, some highly authentic effects can be produced. Having masked the glazing of this locomotive with Maskol, an initial layer of Railmatch Dark Rust and Frame Dirt is being applied.

In order to get into the tightest of corners, you can always remove the outer nozzle rim if your airbrush permits. This will eliminate the problems of blowback, but it does leave the delicate needle tip exposed to potential damage.

Weathering freehand certainly reduces the amount of time necessary for masking or dismantling. Indeed, this splendid Hattons/Heljan Class 14 was treated in just a few hours.

Vehicles and buildings with heavy seams and panels really benefit from freehand shading, such as this air-braked van with its distinctive sliding doors. The real things quickly acquired a covering of grime, especially around the door handle recesses and undulating sides.

Following a rust-tinged shade with a darker colour will complete the lived-in look and bring out the lovely detail imparted on these Bachmann vehicles. I enjoyed weathering these vans so much that I've now assembled a train of about twelve similar vehicles, even though I don't have a layout anywhere near big enough to accommodate them all!

Naturally, freehand work is easier when working on larger subjects and the nature of this O gauge Pug's surface really helps in the weathering process by providing plenty of relief to work with, especially the raised panel lines over the saddle tank.

A coat of satin varnish (with a drop or two of black paint added) prior to weathering allows the untouched areas to shine through the muck with a certain suggestion of greasiness, hinting at an oily rag being employed to keep the number and BR logo visible. Here, the deep running plates are being helped to a generous covering of rust- and dust-coloured paints. A little extra matting agent has been added to the Phoenix weathering enamels at this stage to provide a slight contrast with the dirt on the boiler and cab sides. The same mix is then applied around the underframes.

Back in OO gauge, following raised rivet detail on steam traction must be done with care if the locomotive is to be presented in a care-worn rather than neglected condition, such as this tender attached to a Great Western Castle. Light shading of dark, rusty browns and Roof Dirt draw attention to the quality of the moulded detail without it looking too obtrusive.

Welded seams also benefit from the same technique, such as on this Hornby Class 31.

Rust patches around the cylinder covers suggest the results of years of leaking and condensing steam, while the odd greasy streak (gloss varnish) portrays fresh layers of moisture. Note the brake dust adding a gentle contrast to the chassis. This Pug is still not complete, however, as there are a few more stages to get through, namely the adding of weathering powders here and there, plus some concentrated areas of grease and oil to the connecting rods and other working surfaces (applied by hand).

Generously thinned paint allows a semi-translucent finish, ensuring that the bands of dark 'dirt' do not overly jar with the surrounding paintwork.

THAT FINISHING TOUCH

Using an airbrush to impart a unique series of finishing effects is one of the fundamental reasons why these tools have become so popular among modellers. Experimentation is recommended to find more ways of adding character and realism to our models.

Something that I stumbled on accidentally was the rendition of heavy deposits of buffer grease. Using a double-action airbrush at very close proximity and a load of enamel paint mixed to a regular spraying viscosity, the air pressure must be set as low as possible (while allowing for proper atomization). Some careful feathering of the trigger will deposit a blob of paint in the middle of the buffer. Following this with a blast of clean air as the trigger is eased off (but not released completely) will form a skin on the surface of this paint. A few repeats of this process will build up the rendition of grease until the desired effect is achieved. Try it for yourself.

Spraying any paint onto clear glazing is always accompanied by the risk of irreversible damage, so it's worth gaining a good amount of confidence first. A heavily weathered locomotive should, however, have some degree of muck on at least some of its windows, even if it's just around the edges. Cutting strips of masking tape or using masking fluid is one way keeping windows protected, while these etched wiper masks (from PH Designs) make the job so much simpler. Tailored to suit individual diesel traction types, they can be fixed to the windows with a small blob of temporary adhesive such as Deluxe Tacky Wax.

When the masks and the temporary adhesive have been removed, they leave behind the characteristic pattern that would be created by the wiper blades in operation; a truly convincing touch.

The locomotive can be weathered as usual, ensuring that at least a gentle misting of dirt reaches over the masked windows.

All locomotives and rolling stock have their buffer heads daubed in a thick, tenacious grease to reduce friction between these bearing surfaces. Recreating this in miniature is important and, as an alternative to stippling the buffers by hand brush, a double-action airbrush can be used to good effect. Position the nozzle just a few millimetres from the surface and emit a short burst of paint (a mix of Humbrol enamel black, brown and Metalcote gunmetal). Immediately cut the flow of colour, while not releasing the trigger altogether so as to still be spraying clean air. Provided the paint and air are set correctly (enamel paint is best, mixed not too thinly and sprayed at around 9psi), the air will cause the paint to skin-over while also pushing it outwards, mimicking how the real buffers spread the thick lubricant while in service.

Graffiti has become an unwelcome but common sight in our towns and cities and there are numerous ways in which it can be recreated in miniature. One of the easiest methods is to employ waterslide decals such as these from Microscale. As they're of the waterslide variety, the finished model must be given a gloss coating before the decals are applied. In an effort to gain maximum realism, this Irish generator van has been finished and weathered before the 'tags' are applied, followed by a further clear coat to seal the images in place. Setting solutions help the decals to sit onto the uneven surfaces, applied by hand.

Once the decals and clear coat had dried, further weathering was added to take away the garishness of the graffiti and give the impression that they were applied some time ago.

At the time when I built this model, the prototype van had been withdrawn and was sitting in a Dublin yard awaiting its fate, gaining a few defacements along the way. It was in this state that I decided to portray it. Although these decals are designed for the US market, the modern style of vandalism is pretty ubiquitous (showing a lack of imagination, perhaps?).

AFTERWORD

I sincerely hope that this book has informed readers as to how an airbrush works and how to use it, perhaps demystifying a few facets of the subject along the way. Additionally it is to be hoped that I've adequately conveyed the many positive attributes that such a device can bring to the railway modelling hobby.

My profession brings me into contact with countless fellow modellers of the active, prospective and armchair varieties, and I've lost count of how many times I've heard stories of how an airbrush has been tried but quickly discarded, due mostly to a lack of comprehension of how to get the best results from it. Indeed, the dearth of adequate information on this subject has been a personal source of frustration. It is to be hoped that this volume has addressed that situation. Furthermore, it has been my intention to inspire people to simply have a go, whether for the first time or to enhance one's existing technique with a little extra knowledge and experience.

The range of theoretical and practical methods covered in these pages do not necessarily have to be committed to memory or mastered immediately, but can be assimilated over time by repetition and practise. With this book kept close at hand as a reference source, it should readily prove its worth. Confidence and familiarity with your tools and equipment can only be built over time, however, with perseverance through the odd mishap and a patient mastering of the basic facets: mixing, thinning, setting air pressure and handling of the airbrush. In other words, one must learn to walk before running.

Never be afraid to experiment or to find your own way of working, as long as the results are to your satisfaction. Improvements in your modelling output can be expected as a reward for persistence and the greater efficiency enjoyed by airbrushing potentially frees up valuable time for other modelling tasks.

Finally, I hope that you enjoy learning and developing your airbrushing technique, not least as a happy modeller makes for a more productive one.

Airbrushing can genuinely change your life! The added convenience and heightened quality of finish can take your modelling to another level. It can also be great fun.

USEFUL CONTACTS

USEFUL ADDRESSES

The Airbrush Company Ltd
Unit 7, Marlborough Road
Lancing Business Park
Lancing
West Sussex
BN15 8UF
Tel: 01903 767800
www.airbrushes.com
Airbrushes (including own-brand Premi-Air),
compressors, paints (including Lifecolor and
Com-Art), extraction booths, tools, equipment,
airbrushing tuition

Axminster Power Tool Centre Ltd
Unit 10, Weycroft Avenue
Axminster
Devon
EX13 5PH
www.axminster.co.uk
Craft and hobby tools including airbrushes and
compressors

Chris Wesson Models
11 Hestia Close
Romsey
Hampshire
SO51 8PA
Tel: 01794 511535
Email: chris.wesson@tiscali.co.uk
A small but high-quality range of steam-era cel-
lulose paints and clear lacquers

The Color Wheel Company
PO Box 130
Philomath
Oregon 97370
USA
www.colorwheelco.com
Handy colour mixing reference sources

Crafty Computer Paper
Woodhall
Barrasford
Hexham
Northumberland
NE48 4DB
Tel: 01434 689 153
www.craftycomputerpaper.co.uk
Materials for DIY waterslide transfers and other
craft resources

C-Rail Intermodal
Morven
Roome Bay Avenue
Crail
Fife
KY10 3TR
www.c-rail-intermodal.co.uk
Transfers, paints and kits for modern ISO con-
tainer traffic

Deluxe Materials
Unit 13, Cufaude Business Park
Bramley
Hampshire
RG26 5DL
Tel: 01529 455 034
www.deluxematerials.com
Adhesives, fillers and applicators

Expo Tools
PO Box 66
Pembroke
SA72 6AJ
Tel: 01646 672440
www.expotools.com
Badger airbrushes and parts, plus own-brand range of airbrushes and accessories

Finishing Touches
4 Manor Court
Blaby
Leicestershire
LE8 4FW
Tel: 0116 2785134
Model paints and paint stripper

Fox Transfers
4 Hill Lane Close
Markfield Industrial Estate
Markfield
Leicestershire
LE67 9PN
Tel: 01530 242801
www.fox-transfers.co.uk
Transfers and Railmatch paints

Graphic Air Supplies
Unit 1, Levens Hall Park
Lund Lane
Killinghall
Harrogate
North Yorkshire
HG3 2BG
Tel: 01423 522836
www.graphicair.co.uk
Extraction booths, filters and accessories

Howes Models Ltd
Unit 2C/D Station Field Industrial Estate
Rowles Way
Kidlington
Oxfordshire
OX5 1LA
Tel: 01865 848000
www.howesmodels.co.uk
Railmatch paints, modelling components and transfers

Just Like the Real Thing
26 Whittle Place
South Newmoor Industrial Estate
Irvine
Ayrshire
KA11 4HR
Tel: 01294 222988
www.justliketherealthing.co.uk
High-quality rail-themed paints (aerosols) and solvent cleaner/degreasing agents

Luthiers Supplies
The Hall
Horebeech Lane
Horam
East Sussex
TN21 0HR
Tel: 01435 812315
www.luthierssupplies.co.uk
Suppliers of Lubrasil and other fine-grade abrasives plus water-based Garal polish

Model Hobbies
Unit 2, Bank Works
Warren Street
Stoke on Trent
ST3 1QB
Tel: 0845 643 1304
www.modelhobbies.co.uk
Suppliers of Alclad2 paints, glues, tools, accessories and kits

Phoenix Precision Paints
PO Box 8238
Chelmsford
Essex
CM1 7WY
Tel: 01268 730549
www.phoenix-paints.co.uk
Enamel paints, primers, varnishes, thinners, masking fluid and painting accessories

PH Designs
www.phd-design.co.uk
Etched brass windscreen masks for modern traction

Relish Models
9 Ferry Close
Selby
North Yorkshire
YO8 6YX
Tel: 01757 638660
www.relishmodels.co.uk
Vallejo paints, finishing materials and modelling supplies

Scalescenes
www.scalescenes.com
A large and growing range of downloadable card building kits in various scales

Ten Commandments
20 Struan Drive
Inverkeithing
Fife
KY11 1AR
www.cast-in-stone.co.uk
Scenic accessories

USEFUL WEBSITES

George Dent Model Maker: A Model Maker's Diary
http://georgedentmodelmaker.blogspot.com

Badger Airbrushes
www.badgerairbrush.com

De Vilbiss Airbrushes
www.devilbisseu.com

Humbrol Paints
www.humbrol.com

Model Rail Magazine
www.model-rail.com

Iwata Medea Inc.
www.iwata-medea.com

Paasche Airbrushes
www.paascheairbrush.com

Railway Modeller's Web
www.rmweb.co.uk

Revell Models and Paints
www.revell.de/en

The Testor Corporation (Aztek Airbrushes)
www.testors.com

Vallejo Paints
www.acrylicosvallejo.com

BIBLIOGRAPHY

BOOKS

Boocock, C., *Railway Liveries: BR Traction 1948–1995* (Ian Allan, 2000)

Boocock, C., *Railway Liveries: Privatisation 1995–2000* (Ian Allan, 2001)

Carter, E.F., *Britain's Railway Liveries 1825–1948* (Harold Starke Ltd, 1963)

Dent, G., *Detailing and Modifying Ready-to-Run Locomotives in OO Gauge, Volume 1: British Diesel & Electric Locomotives, 1955–2008* (The Crowood Press, 2009)

Dent, G., *Detailing and Modifying Ready-to-Run Locomotives in OO Gauge, Volume 2: British Steam Locomotives, 1948–1968* (The Crowood Press, 2009)

Dresser, C., *Principles of Decorative Design* (Cassell, Petter, Galpin & Co., 1873)

Gorman, T., *Finishing Scale Ship Models* (Chatham Publishing, 2006)

Green, B., *Airbrushing and Finishing Scale Models* (Osprey Publishing, 2008)

Haresnape, B., *Railway Liveries: London, Midland & Scottish Railway* (Ian Allan, 1983)

Haresnape, B., *Railway Liveries: London & North Eastern Railway* (Ian Allan, 1984)

Haresnape, B., *Railway Liveries: Southern Railway* (Ian Allan, 1982)

Hornung, D., *Colour: a Workshop for Artists and Designers* (Laurence King, 2005)

Huntley, I., *Painting and Lining Scale Models* (Argus Books Ltd, 1976)

Jackson, A., and D. Day, *The Modelmaker's Handbook* (Pelham Books, 1987)

Lessard, M., *Airbrush Painting Techniques* (Osprey Publishing, 1999)

McIllmurray, J., *Advanced Aviation Modelling* (The Crowood Press, 2005)

Peacock, I., *Airbrushing and Spray Painting Manual* (Special Interest Model Books, 1997)

Rathbone, I., *A Modeller's Handbook of Painting & Lining* (Wild Swan, 2008)

Shephard, R., *The Finishing Touch* (R.G. Shephard, 2006)

Welch, M., *The Art of Weathering* (Wild Swan, 1993)

ARTICLES

Cabus, T., 'Des Trucs et des ficelles pour debutants', *Train Miniature* (October 2007), pp.30–31

Dent, G., 'Airbrush Supertest', *Model Rail* (October 2009), pp.46–51

Dent, G., 'Paint Supertest', *Model Rail* (February 2010), pp.74–81

Dent, G., 'Varnish Supertest', *Model Rail* (March 2010), pp.74–80

Huntley, I., 'A Question of Colour', *Model Trains* (July 1980), pp.386–388

Huntley, I., 'A Question of Colour', *Model Trains* (August 1980), pp.430–432

Lavery, J., 'Beginner's Guide to Airbrushing', *Hornby Magazine* (August 2010), pp.48–53

INDEX